The Copper Scroll Project

THE COPPER SCROLL PROJECT

AN ANCIENT SECRET FUELS THE BATTLE FOR THE TEMPLE MOUNT

SHELLEY NEESE

NEW YORK

LONDON • NASHVILLE • MELBOURNE • VANCOUVER

THE COPPER SCROLL PROJECT

AN ANCIENT SECRET FUELS THE BATTLE FOR THE TEMPLE MOUNT

Published in New York, New York, by Morgan James Publishing. Morgan James is a trademark of Morgan James, LLC. www.MorganJamesPublishing.com

The Morgan James Speakers Group can bring authors to your live event. For more information or to book an event visit The Morgan James Speakers Group at www.TheMorganJamesSpeakersGroup.com.

ISBN 9781683509158 paperback
ISBN 9781683509165 eBook
Library of Congress Control Number: 2017919473

Cover & Interior Design by:
Christopher Kirk
http://www.GFSstudio.com

All Scripture quotations, unless otherwise indicated, are taken from the Holy Bible, New International Version®, NIV®. Copyright ©1973, 1978, 1984, 2011 by Biblica, Inc.™ Used by permission of Zondervan. All rights reserved worldwide. http://www.zondervan.com The "NIV" and "New International Version" are trademarks registered in the United States Patent and Trademark Office by Biblica, Inc.™

In an effort to support local communities, raise awareness and funds, Morgan James Publishing donates a percentage of all book sales for the life of each book to Habitat for Humanity Peninsula and Greater Williamsburg.

Get involved today! Visit
www.MorganJamesBuilds.com

In memory of my grandmother, Mildred Ford, a light to my path.

ACKNOWLEDGMENTS

I am grateful to my editor, Joan Tapper, whose expertise refined a manuscript in need of refining. I am grateful to Jen Dean and Christina Ankeney; every writer should be so lucky to have creative friends with an eye for edits. I want to thank Dr. Kenneth Hanson for letting me borrow your Dead Sea Scrolls knowledge and keeping this manuscript abreast of the latest scholarly debates. Thanks to Angel Melvin and your help with the website, photography, and all things design. I am indebted to my agent, Dan Balow. Thank you for taking a risk on a first-time writer and your patient belief in the book's potential. Thanks to the support of my colleagues at *The Jerusalem Connection*, Marilyn Henretty and Marilyn Levar. Thanks to my boss, Jim Hutchens, for letting me pour so much time into what most would have considered a tangent, but you honored as a life mission. Thank you to my parents and in-laws and your practical show of support every time I needed childcare so I could go to Israel. And most significantly, I want to thank my husband, Brian, who has been my cheerleader from the start. You sacrificed our most precious asset, time, in pursuit of this decade-long endeavor. And of course, I want to thank Jim Barfield and his wife Laurie. Thank you for letting me be your shadow and share your story. And thank you for being the kind of people who never let a dream die or a goal flounder. As I hope the following pages prove, your tenacity is infectious.

CONTENTS

FOREWORD

Seventy years ago, the desert of central Israel was filled with expeditions to unearth ancient documents known as the Dead Sea Scrolls. A French explorer happened upon two brittle copper rolls on a shelf in a cave that together came to be known as the Copper Scroll. An ancient treasure map, the Copper Scroll has mystified scholars and delighted Dead Sea Scroll enthusiasts since it was first opened.

An arson investigator from Oklahoma, I am an unlikely candidate to decipher the Copper Scroll. As the principal subject of the book in your hands, I understand the hazards here all too well: navigating the quagmire of scrutiny from academics and religious factions, on the one hand, and dodging the political trip wires surrounding the Copper Scroll's connections to the Temple Mount, on the other. My quest exposes the underworld of actors who try and stop archaeological progress for fear of igniting political disputes and land claims. The story profiles the colliding interests of Arab versus Israeli, Christian versus Jew, and secular versus religious. I have found myself, at one time or another, in the crosshairs of every one of these flashpoints. The task of chronicling the madness required a seasoned author with thick skin.

Yet Shelley Neese exceeds all expectations for such an undertaking. Her strong journalistic background, her linguistic skills, and her Israel-based advanced education make her uniquely qualified for this exposé. A massive dose of patience has also been required as she embedded herself in our team for a decade. *The Copper Scroll Project* is an experience shared by myself and an army of devoted supporters. Relaying our goals, mission, and purpose sets our boundaries, and no one could have knitted those objectives into an intriguing story better than Shelley.

Our team is not made up of treasure hunters. We are dedicated to returning the ancient artifacts and treasures listed on the Copper Scroll to the people of Israel. That obstacle-laden journey, however, has forced us to maneuver the complicated world of Israel antiquities. In the book, Shelley enlightens and guides the reader through the difficulties and oppressive atmosphere created by what I believe is a fear of conflicting religious and academic revelations knowing that any revelation from a Copper Scroll discovery could upend long held beliefs. Shelley explains these roadblocks that have prevented a conclusive excavation at the site my research has identified. Should the project's research produce a discovery of biblical artifacts, it will also produce a fear of the fulfillment of established biblical warnings. Shelley details our efforts to reveal to Israel—indeed, the world—the meaning of the Copper Scroll, which promises far more than treasures, and she does so masterfully.

My skills as an award-winning investigator prepared me for the task of compiling the hard-hitting evidence to convince a litany of authorities in Israel. Equally, Shelley's academic style and investigative documentation contained in *The Copper Scroll Project* is invaluable for those wanting more than a mere story of trials and successes. The frustration and elation that Shelley records paint a vivid picture of the cliff-hugging path we have all shared since the initial discovery in December 2006. What you read in these pages will often strike you as impossible, but I assure you that every word of it is true (although, of course, some of the names have been changed).

Now we wait. Is there a scholar, a rabbi, an antiquities authority, or an interested reader with the influence strong enough to loosen the stranglehold that prevents this project from completing our excavation? We hope for that missing link between God's timing and the fulfillment of the mission of *The Copper Scroll Project*.

In 2017, the Israeli Antiquities Authority launched Operation Scroll, a renewed endeavor to systematically explore every cave in the Dead Sea region. If I am correct, the wilderness area of the Judean Desert will one day be the focal point of a massive recovery operation to secure holy ritual vessels and perhaps even more sacred scrolls. I feel confident that those hidden manuscripts lie waiting in a dark protective cave filled with messages, instructions and valuable wisdom from the heart of Israel's past leading to a much deeper understanding of the Bible and an unrevealed history.

CHARACTERS

John Allegro: Member of the Dead Sea Scroll publication team who orchestrated the opening of the Copper Scroll and conducted the first expedition based on his reading

Michael Arbuthnot: Host of the television series "Secret Worlds"

Rabbi Naphtali Hertz Bacharach: Seventeenth-century Kabbalist in Amsterdam who included the Treatise of the Temple Vessels in his manuscript *Emeq HaMelekh* ("Valley of the King")

Henry Wright Baker: Engineering professor at the Manchester College of Science and Technology who opened the Copper Scroll

Laurie Barfield: Jim's wife

Michael Barfield: Jim's son

Shawn Barfield: Jim's son and videographer

Gabriel Barkay: Israeli archaeologist in charge of the Temple Mount sifting project

Flynn Bloom: Owner of the Arad home that served as the *Copper Scroll Project* headquarters

Eitan Campbell: Longtime director of Masada

Robert Cargill: Assistant professor of religious studies at the University of Iowa and biblioblogger

Henri de Contenson: French scholar who led the expedition to Cave 3 and discovered the Copper Scroll

Yaakov Dahan: Director of Qumran

Roland de Vaux: Chief editor of an international and interconfessional Dead Sea Scroll publication team and the first to professionally excavate Qumran

Shuka Dorfman: Head of the Israeli Antiquities Authority

Barney Eaton: Self-proclaimed philanthropist who took Jim and his family on a disastrous trip to Israel

Moshe Feiglin: Israeli legislator and founder of the Manhigut Yehudit ("Jewish Leadership") political faction

Blake Foster: Con-man who claimed to be a philanthropic professional consultant

Yehuda Glick: Founder of the umbrella group, Temple Mount Heritage Foundation, and victim of a targeted assassination attempt

Oren Gutfeld: Israeli field archaeologist who cleared the tunnels at the base of Hyrcania over a period of six years

Kenneth Hanson: Judaica scholar at the University of Central Florida

Hananya Hizmi: Successor to Yitzhak Magen as the Staff Officer in Israel's Archaeology Department of the Civil Administration

Vendyl Jones: Former Baptist preacher turned veteran explorer who pursued the treasures of the Copper Scroll for almost forty years

Mack Kizer: A successful cattle-rancher and the *Copper Scroll Project*'s primary benefactor

Chris Knight: Jim's Aide-de-camp

Yitzhak Magen: Staff Officer in Israel's Archaeology Department of the Civil Administration for 25 years

Florentino García Martínez: Professor at the University of Groningen in the Netherlands who is responsible for the popular English translation of the Dead Sea Scrolls

Józef Milik: The official Copper Scroll translator who promoted the antiquity as a work of fiction

Bob Morgan: Continental Airlines pilot who conducted a decade-long clandestine tunneling operation at Hyrcania to finish what John Allegro started

Juanita Pahdopony: Dean of Academic Affairs at the Comanche Nation College where Jim taught a course on investigative report writing

Yuval Peleg: Deputy Staff Officer in Israel's Archaeology Department of the Civil Administration

Shmuel Sackett: Cofounder of Manhigut Yehudit with Moshe Feiglin

Faidi Salahi: Antiquities dealer in Bethlehem who sold three scrolls to Professor Eleazer Sukenik

Mar Samuel: Archbishop at the Syrian Orthodox Monastery of St. Mark who posted an ad for Dead Sea Scrolls in the *Wall Street Journal*

Avi Sandler: An Israeli tour guide who claimed to be a retired IDF general with connections

Khalil Eskander Shahin (Kando): Christian cobbler in Bethlehem and central figure in the black market of Dead Sea Scrolls

Gershon Solomon: Founder of the Temple Mount Faithful and Jim's first contact in the Temple Mount movement

Asher Levy: Active member of the Temple Mount pressure groups

Jean Starcky: Member of the Dead Sea Scroll publication team who took the pictures of the marble tiles in Beirut with the text from *Treatise of the Temple Vessels*

Eleazer Sukenik: The first academic to recognize the importance of the Dead Sea Scroll manuscripts and procure three of the initial seven scrolls for the state of Israel

Hillel Weiss: Spokesperson for the Sanhedrin

Mike Winger: Owner of a successful dent-repair business and long-time friend of Jim

Tamar Yonah: Host for Israel's most popular English-speaking radio show

"The credit belongs to the man who is actually in the arena, whose face is marred by dust and sweat and blood; who strives valiantly; who errs, who comes short again and again, because there is no effort without error and shortcoming; but who does actually strive to do the deeds; who knows great enthusiasms, the great devotions; who spends himself in a worthy cause; who at the best knows in the end the triumph of high achievement, and who at the worst, if he fails, at least fails while daring greatly, so that his place shall never be with those cold and timid souls who neither know victory nor defeat."

—President Theodore Roosevelt, 1910

CHAPTER 1
PROMISE

Driving down Highway 90, the smell of sulfur wafted through the rental car's windows. As the odor grew more putrid, Jim Barfield knew that he was nearing the Dead Sea. The milky blue waters had a way of brining everything they touched. Pillars of salt appeared a few miles ahead, lining the tepid lake like lumpy ice sculptures, each taking on definitive shapes of their own. The Negev desert had become as familiar to Jim as the flat plains of his native Oklahoma.

Jim rolled up the windows and fiddled with the air conditioner, double-checking that it was blowing at maximum capacity. No amount of Freon could overcome these soaring summer temperatures. It was June 11, 2014. Still, Jim's sweaty palms had as much to do with his nerves as the heat. For the entirety of the trip, Jim oscillated between a sense of doom and exhilaration. In vain, he tried to suppress the emotional extremes and summon only quiet confidence.

Now that the plateau-perched ancient ruins of Qumran were within site, his stomach felt like it had twisted into a Boy Scout's square knot. He stared straight ahead, focusing on the wavy heat mirage hovering over the pavement. His wife Laurie sat in the passenger's seat. His friends and co-conspirators Mack and Chris looked out the back windows, as did his son Michael. All were silent, partly from anticipation and partly because the drastic change in altitude made their ears feel like they were stuffed with cotton balls. The alarm on Jim's watch started beeping, breaking through the silence. He had set it for a phone conference two weeks ago, and it beeped every day at the same time.

Jim—a retired firefighter and arson investigator—was on his thirteenth trip to Israel. Eight years had passed since his first declaration that he had cracked the code to the Copper Scroll. The Copper Scroll is a 2,000-year-old metal document listing over sixty locations for vast amounts of buried gold, silver, coins, and utensils from the Jerusalem Temple. According to Jim's research, the hideaways described in the Copper Scroll had exact architectural matches within Qumran. If he was right, the ancient desert monastery cradled a secret even bigger than the Dead Sea Scrolls.

Rumors of Jim's Copper Scroll quest had reached Moshe Feiglin, an Israeli legislator. Feiglin made headlines in Israel for his amplified denouncement of the lack of religious freedom on the Temple Mount (*Har Habayit* in Hebrew). Feiglin, an Orthodox Jew, visited the Temple Mount on a regular basis and was routinely arrested for "provocation," meaning prayer. Feiglin's form of protest was passive, on the surface. What is more peace-loving than prayer? However, in Jerusalem, Feiglin's enemies viewed his visits as an act of war. And in this war, Feiglin was a frontline soldier, waging battle in the Knesset, Israel's parliament, for the world's most sacred religious territory.

At the hallowed Temple Mount, Muslim authorities disallowed Jews from any forms of public worship. A contingent of religious Jews like Feiglin, undersized in numbers but thorough in strategy, believed the time had come for Israel to actualize its sovereignty over the Temple Mount. They preached that the Temple Mount was the heart of the nation, embodying the Jewish people's identity and future. Until the embattled Jewish state fully reclaimed its sacred heart, it was in danger of losing its spiritual pulse.

Feiglin told his supporters, "It is not existence that makes destiny possible. Just the opposite: It is destiny that makes existence possible. And our destiny is completely tied up with the Temple Mount. The farther we stray from our destiny, the weaker we become."

After hearing about Jim Barfield's Copper Scroll research, Feiglin recognized how their pursuits dovetailed. No physical evidence from the interior of the Jewish First or Second Temples had ever been unearthed. If the Copper Scroll launched a rescue operation of sacred artifacts, Feiglin anticipated a national religious awakening in Israel. For that, the Knesset member was prepared to take big risks and even expand the battlefield to Israel's Dead Sea region.

In Jim's first face-to-face meeting with Feiglin, he explained how the archaeological authorities in charge of Qumran were hesitant to conduct an excavation that threatened the ruins. To convince them of the validity of his research, Jim needed proof that caches of precious metals were hidden at deep depths throughout the site. Jim, working with an established Israeli archaeologist, applied for a permit to do an electronic scan of Qumran with a high-quality metal detector. The permit request was denied without explanation. Without the permit, Jim was out of options.

Feiglin lacked patience for bureaucratic quicksand. He also had something Jim lacked: parliamentary immunity, which in Israel is quite broad. The Knesset member asked Jim to meet him at Qumran with the metal detector. Feiglin was keen to forgo the permit process and scan the site himself. They had no intention other than to collect data in a noninvasive manner. However, if their actions were mistaken for looting or damaging the antiquities site, their efforts were technically punishable with five years of jailtime.

On the morning of their covert operation, Feiglin arrived at Qumran minutes after Jim. Feiglin's driver parked beside four tour buses. Beyond the gate, a large group of Asian tourists with headsets shuffled from the ruins to the indoor museum. They wore scarf head coverings and umbrellas. Even from a distance, they smelled like a herd of sunscreen, a common trait among modern pilgrims. Jim knew he wouldn't be there long enough to necessitate sun protection.

"Shalom. Welcome to Israel," Feiglin greeted Jim and his four travel companions in good English.

Feiglin scanned the horizon around him. As the bird flies, Qumran is about eighteen miles southeast of Jerusalem, but it feels like a faraway place. The craggy terrain and ancient olive trees of Jerusalem disappear. Barren limestone cliffs take their place.

"So, where is the metal detector?" Feiglin asked. "I've actually never held one before."

Jim pointed to an inconspicuous canvas carrying case at his side. Jim cautioned that once the equipment was taken out and unfolded, all hopes of discretion were lost. The Lorenz Deepmax Z1 was a portable metal detector with a six-foot coil and required four people to operate. It was arguably the most sensitive, stable, and deep-penetrating detector on the market. Chris and Mack held the corners of the coil to maintain its cube shape. Laurie and Michael kept their distance and stood guard beside idling buses.

"Are you sure you want to do this?" Jim asked.

"Yep," Feiglin replied.

"Do you have a plan for when the security guard or site director confronts us?" Jim asked.

"Nope," Feiglin lowered his chin. "But when they do, leave the talking to me."

"And if you are arrested, do you have a good lawyer?" Jim asked.

"Yep," Feiglin smirked.

"Will that lawyer be helpful to me?" Jim croaked. He itched his eyes, stinging from the tinge of salt in the air.

"Probably not," Feiglin replied, giving Jim a firm pat on the shoulder.

Looking to Jim for approval, Chris added with an earnest air, "Looks like we are going-for-broke."

Feiglin paid the entrance fee for everyone. The young woman behind the desk smiled when she noticed the name on the credit card; the spectacled face in front of her belonged to the notorious politician making waves throughout Israel. The men ambled over to Qumran's most prominent structure, the watchtower. With thick slanting walls like a decaying pyramid, the building is Qumran's most prominent two-story structure.

Before today, Feiglin's focus was Jerusalem; he had given little thought to Qumran since an elementary school field trip. Feiglin was not the first to overlook the unimpressive ruins. Various adventurers passing through the Negev in the nineteenth and early twentieth centuries mistakenly labeled the piles of field stones as either a Byzantine monastery, the biblical city of Gomorrah, or a Roman fort. The rubble mostly blended into the landscape. Qumran was made famous only after the history-shaping discovery of the Dead Sea Scrolls in nearby caves. Excavations of the site indicated that it had been occupied intermittently since the seventh century BCE. No one knew the initial purpose of the settlement. Its last phase of occupation lasted around 220 years, right up until the Romans bombarded Jerusalem in 70 CE.

According to Jim's theory, the perimeter of the watchtower was a critical hiding spot referenced in the Copper Scroll. Jim was anxious to scan the area even though they would be in full view of Qumran's armed security guard. He unpacked the equipment and quickly demonstrated how to get the best reading. The four men needed to walk at the same pace, in a back and forth pattern, and drag the coil between them. Feiglin's job was to hold the control box and push the red button to start and stop the scans. Jim strolled alongside them, his hands clasped behind his back.

After they completed their scan of the watchtower, a security guard approached the men and asked what they were doing. Jim's heartbeat pounded in his throat. Feiglin gave the guard a vague explanation in Hebrew which Jim did not understand. The guard turned and walked away. The groundskeeper for the site stood off to the side with his arms folded, staring curiously at the group and the boxy metal detector.

"Let's do the rest quickly," Feiglin suggested. "I told him we were doing a little scientific research." He pushed up on the duffel bag straps holding the control box and battery pack, trying to ease their pull on a hot day.

"These guys seem fine with us for now," Jim said, "but we don't know if they are actually calling the police or the archaeological authorities and telling them to get out here."

Feiglin and Jim's crew hurried to scan three more sites, all areas that Jim identified as potential hiding spots for Copper Scroll treasure. While they scanned the sites, they had no idea if they were getting a positive read, no immediate gratification. The Lorenz detector made a constant high-pitch humming noise. A bar graph jumped around on the flat-panel display. The detector's logger stored away the information until they could download the data onto a computer and process it with specialized software.

The team walked out to the parking lot. Jim thanked Feiglin for his collaboration.

"I'm not one to sit around waiting for things to happen," Feiglin said.

"I like that," Jim responded. The Israeli politician and the American firefighter shook hands in mutual respect, promising to keep in close contact.

Feiglin returned to Jerusalem for a vote at the Knesset. Jim drove straight to the Ein Gedi Nature Reserve, an oasis of palm trees twenty miles south. Jim wanted to put a little distance between he and Qumran.

Ein Gedi was packed with Israeli teenagers in their swimsuits, scrambling up the cliff in pursuit of spring-fed pools. Some of the same tour buses that had been at Qumran drove up to Ein Gedi as the next stopover on their strict agenda. Popular among biblical tours, Ein Gedi is the famous location where King Saul and his army tried to hunt David down "upon the craggiest rocks, which are accessible only to wild goats." (I Samuel 24:3, *New International Version*)[1]

Jim sat down at a sticky wooden table under a cluster of date palms. The others sat down beside him, adjusting positions to follow the shade. He pulled out a small computer to transfer the files from the memory stick. As the software transformed the data into colored images and contoured maps, they held their breath. Laurie looked away from the computer screen. Nearly breathless, she said, "I want to see it, and at the same time I just can't look at it."

Jim's son agreed. "After years of work, and much of your savings, what if the scans turn up blank?"

The computer beeped to indicate all the files had finished downloading. A sluggish breeze moved through the palms above, but Jim didn't feel it. The beam of all his expectations narrowed into tight focus. Jim clicked on the first icon to pull up the data. Each display was color coded to indicate what type of metal, if any, the detector located. Hovering over each other, the group gasped. Jim strained to make sure he was seeing correctly. The images showed that at all four of the sites, large amounts of precious metal objects were buried deep underground.

Jim let out a loud sigh, a sigh of relief that he felt like he had been suppressing for eight years. "Now we know one thing for sure," Jim said. "The Dead Sea Scrolls are the tip of an ancient archaeological iceberg."

THE DEAD SEA SCROLLS

In 1946 or 1947—no one knows for certain—a Bedouin goatherd nicknamed Muhammad the Wolf led his flock around the cliffs lining the northwest edge of the Dead Sea. As the livestock grazed on sparse vegetation, Muhammad wandered around the boulders. According to one of several variants of the account, he hurled a stone into a cave to startle a stray goat and heard pottery shatter. Too frightened to lower himself into the cave alone, he returned several days later with at least two relatives from his Ta'amireh tribe. Though they fantasized about finding gold and silver, instead they stumbled upon a cache of oddly shaped clay vessels with bowl shaped lids. Inside one jar, they discovered three ancient leather scrolls, intact and wrapped in linen.

The Bedouin carted their scrolls back to their camp. The tribesmen stored the bundle in a goat skin bag and hung it from a tent pole. Unfamiliar with the aged script, they debated whether they should repurpose the old strips of leather. Fortuitously, Muhammad's uncle thought to take the scrolls to Bethlehem on market day. Their first foray into the black-market antiquities trade aroused more suspicion than success. One trader sent them on to the next. In the end, they arranged for a Syrian Orthodox merchant, Khalil Eskander Shahin, known as Kando, to sell the scrolls for a commission. Kando owned a general store and cobbler shop near the Church of the Nativity. Archbishop Mar Samuel, head of the Syrian Orthodox Monastery of St. Mark, made the purchase soon after he saw the scrolls in Kando's possession. As the former librarian at St. Catherine's Monastery at Mt. Sinai, the Archbishop had experience with ancient scripts. Once Kando took out his commission, the Bedouin returned to the desert the equivalent of sixty dollars richer.

Hoping for an even greater return on his investment, Muhammad the Wolf's relative returned to the cave and retrieved four additional scrolls. Again, one of the scrolls found its way to Kando. The other three scrolls were sold to an antiquities dealer in Bethlehem, Faidi Salahi. Salahi intended to put the scrolls in front of a Hebrew scholar capable of realizing their full worth.

On November 24, 1947, with the British Mandate approaching expiration, the nascent Jewish nation was caught up in a bloody civil war with Palestinian nationalists. Jerusalem was divided by barbed wire, booby traps, and makeshift walls as British troops strained to quell the violence. Professor Eleazar Lipa Sukenik, from Hebrew University, received a call from an Armenian friend, acting as a middle man for Salahi. He promised to reveal an antiquity of interest to Sukenik.

They met at the gateway to Military Zone B, separated by a barbed-wire fence. The Armenian held up a sample fragment of leather. Though Sukenik heard tales of inscriptional materials floating around the black market, it was only once the Jewish scholar laid eyes on the ancient lettering that he comprehended the importance of the desert find. Even through barbed wire, Sukenik recognized the writing style as similar to first-century ossuaries (bone coffins) in Jerusalem.

Five days later, Sukenik acquired a proper pass and traveled to Salahi's home in Bethlehem, ignoring travel warnings and the wishes of his wife and his son. Salahi permitted Sukenik to take the scrolls and study them before negotiating a price. On a bus full of Arabs, the Jewish scholar carried the Hebrew scrolls under his arm, wrapped like an ordinary parcel. Once Sukenik was in the privacy of his home, he unrolled a fragile scroll with trembling fingers. He logged the intensity of emotion in his diary: "I suddenly had the feeling that I was privileged by destiny to gaze upon a Hebrew scroll which had not been read for more than 2,000 years."[2] As he poured over the text, he heard the radio announce that the United Nations General Assembly voted in favor of the establishment of a Jewish state. Spontaneous celebrations broke out in the streets.

On behalf of Hebrew University, Sukenik purchased Salahi's three manuscripts: The *War Scroll*, the *Thanksgiving Psalms*, and a second copy of the *Isaiah Scroll*. Sukenik got word that the rest of the scroll archive was in the hands of Mar Samuel. However, the Archbishop proved a more reluctant negotiator than Salahi. He didn't like dealing directly with Israelis, representatives of the enemy nation. He scoffed at Sukenik's offer of 2,400 dollars—all the paleographer could afford during a time of war. Thinking he could demand half of a million dollars for the ancient parchments in America, Mar Samuel smuggled the scrolls out of Jerusalem to a Syrian Orthodox Church in New Jersey. Sukenik died believing all hope of acquiring the scrolls for the Jewish nation was gone.

Despite the intense interest surrounding the now famous scrolls, Mar Samuel failed to secure a western buyer. Frustrated and out of options, Mar Samuel published an advertisement on page fourteen of the *Wall Street Journal*: "Biblical manuscripts dating back to at least 200 B.C. are for sale. This would be an ideal gift to an educational or religious institution by an individual or group." As fate would have it, the Israeli archaeologist and army General Yigal Yadin was in New York giving a lecture the day the ad appeared. Yadin was the son of Sukenik.

Combining his experience as an intelligence operator and utilizing his connections in the world of academia, Yadin arranged for a Jewish American professor to assume a fake (gentile) identity, meet with Mar Samuel to authenticate the scrolls, and then surreptitiously purchase the scrolls—collectively known as the Dead Sea Scrolls—on behalf of Israel for 250,000 dollars.

As an extra precaution, they were flown back to the Jewish nation on three separate airplanes.

The Dead Sea Scrolls made for a symbolic birthday gift for the state still struggling to survive out of utero. The texts are celebrated icons of Israel's heritage—a people long recognized for the literary gifts which they bequeathed to the world. The Egyptians have their pyramids, the Chinese have their wall, the Greeks have their marble temple, and the Incas had their mountain ridge citadel. The Jews have their scrolls, monuments built from words rather than mortar.

Predating the oldest known copies of the Hebrew Bible by a thousand years, the Dead Sea Scrolls, a spiritual time capsule, launched a new era in religious scholarship. Even the most rigid skeptics of the Bible's authenticity were silenced as the biblical scrolls matched the traditional text that formed the basis of modern Bibles in an astonishingly close way. Every biblical book, apart from Esther, found representation in the Dead Sea Scroll collection.[3]

THE COPPER SCROLL

As the fame of the Dead Sea Scrolls exploded, the rates paid per scroll rose exponentially. The Bedouin hobby of cave hunting suddenly had lucrative potential. Between 1948 and 1956, archaeologists and Bedouin raced against each other, exploring every cave opening they spotted in the high cliffs overlooking the western shore of the Dead Sea. Being the Sons of the Desert, Bedouin had a clear advantage. Eleven caves, in total, contained nearly 900 scrolls, the majority of which the Bedouin found.

The state of preservation ranged from long, complete manuscripts to penny-sized fragments. Only a third of the Dead Sea Scroll manuscripts were biblical texts. Thirty-five percent were extra-biblical texts, un-canonized but popular religious writings from the Second Temple period, including biblical commentaries, or *peshers,* and reworked biblical texts. The manuscripts provide historians a wide-ranging look into a critical—although previously misunderstood—period when Judaism was redefining itself under tyrannical Roman rule. Another third were sectarian manuscripts, particular to the mysterious Jewish group that penned them, presumably the Essenes.

In the instance of Cave 3 (all the caves were given official numbers), the archaeologists were the ones to get lucky. On March 20, 1952, Henri de Contenson, a young French scholar with Jerusalem's École Biblique, mounted a scroll-hunting expedition to scout desert terraces and cliffs which the Bedouin might have overlooked. The expedition was sponsored by the Jordan Department of Antiquities who controlled the environs at that time. The archaeologists, working with two dozen hired Bedouin, were nearly a mile and a half north of the Qumran compound when they came across a large natural cave. The cave's entrance was narrow and rock-covered, barely perceptible to the scanning eye. A collection of pottery sherds in a ground slope tipped the archaeologists off to the cave's opening. They broke through the barred entry. For eleven days, they carefully cleared the mountain of debris. The cave contained forty scroll jars, shattered from the crushing weight of the collapsed ceiling. After two thousand years of exposure, all that was left from the once robust library were five intact jars housing disintegrated scrolls. Blackened leather fragments from fourteen precious manuscripts—like Ezekiel, Lamentations, and Psalms—rested inside ancient rat nests.

On the last day of the excavation, the team noticed that a large limestone rock from the ceiling collapsed in front of what appeared to be a lesser side cave. Like a false wall for a castle's secret chamber, the rock camouflaged the nook and barred it from intruders. Curious, workers carefully chipped through the chalky barricade. Resting alone on a low shelf were two stacked copper rolls, coated with the same sea green patina as the Statue of Liberty. The scroll's strategic position allowed it to narrowly escape the collapsed ceiling. Nature had created the perfect hiding place for the most intriguing manuscript in the Dead Sea Scroll collection: The Copper Scroll.

The Copper Scroll was the last of fifteen manuscripts to be found in Cave 3. According to the Dead Sea Scroll cataloguing system, the Copper Scroll's scientific reference is 3Q15. Rather than papyrus or leather, the Copper Scroll is inscribed on thin sheets of almost a hundred percent pure copper. Copper was particularly valuable in ancient times and much more strenuous to inscribe. Each letter had to be hammered out with chisels. The choice of copper indicated that the contents of the scroll were of such importance that the scribe wanted to be sure it could withstand the ravages of time. As the copper oxidized, the green patina behaved as a natural preservative. For the most part, it worked. The Copper Scroll was left almost entirely intact, a small number of words and numbers missing. Originally measuring over seven feet long and a foot wide, the scroll is one of the largest ancient metal documents ever found.

When the ancients rolled the copper sheet, a difficult task considering it was created as a wall plaque, they snapped it in two, breaking it at the rivets. As de Contenson retrieved them, one roll was twice the width of the other. Archaeologists immediately understood that the Copper Scroll was a monumental find because of its material composition and careful preservation. After 2,000 years, the copper coils were green and brittle. The scrolls crumbled at the slightest touch. What no one yet knew was the significance of its contents.

CHAPTER 2

CRAZY

⌒

I am an editor and columnist for *The Jerusalem Connection*, a nonprofit organization that covers all things Israel for a mostly Christian audience in the United States. In August 2008, I attended a conference for Christian Zionists in Fort Worth, Texas. Branded the *Days of Elijah,* the two-day event was designed to educate Christians and activate their support for the Jewish state.

I arrived late, squeezing into a parking spot between oversized vans with church names emblazoned on the sides. Crowded round tables with welcoming groups of Baptists, Pentecostals, and Evangelical Christians filled the room. The conference décor denoted a theme of Texan cowboy meets Israeli *kibbutznik*. Metallic Stars of David mixed with paper Lone Stars adorned the stage and tables.

In between speakers, a Christian praise and worship band took the stage. At this moment, a man named Blake Foster, hearing I was a journalist, worked his way over to my seat. Despite the loud shofar blasts echoing off the walls, Blake struck up a conversation with me about the U.S. monetary system. He believed it was headed for collapse, and he would be among the few prepared for it.

"Gold is the answer," Blake said. He poked his finger at the air. "Gold has an intrinsic value created by God." With that, Blake handed me a business card for a bank based solely on the gold standard. He thought I should write an article on gold. I was still appraising why Blake was hocking his conspiracy theories at *Days of Elijah* when a man in cowboy boots strode by us. Blake grabbed him by the arm and pulled him over.

"Shelley, meet the guy who cracked the code on the Copper Scroll," Blake said.

I shook hands with a man with ramrod straight posture. He sported a pure grey mane that went well past his shoulders and a goatee.

"My name is Jim Barfield. It's a pleasure to meet you, ma'am." As the conference paused for a lunch break, Blake spotted a popular author and walked off without an adieu. Jim and I went to the coffee area stationed among a hive of busy kiosks. All around us tables were piled high with Judaica and Israeli souvenirs.

"Congratulations on your discovery," I replied to Jim. "But what's the Copper Scroll?"

At similar events, I had already met several self-proclaimed experts in a range of specialties: biblical feasts, Hebrew language, U.S. foreign policy, counter-terrorism, and now gold. The Copper Scroll was new to me.

"A treasure map from the prophet Jeremiah," Jim answered. "Actually, I don't like to call it a treasure map. These items are holy. Essentially, it's a map listing hidden vessels from the Temple sanctums."

I gave Jim a quick once-over, searching his face to determine whether he was the well-intentioned kind of crazy or scary crazy. His complexion was swarthy. His drawl was Southern. I had no idea how to place him, mostly because of his wildly long grey hair. Was he a Vietnam War vet? A cowboy hippie? An Apache Indian?

"Did you find this scroll, this catalogue of Temple items, that you are talking about?" I asked.

"Gosh, no!" Jim chuckled in a disarming way. "The Copper Scroll was discovered sixty years ago in a cave near the ruins of an old sectarian settlement named Qumran. It's part of the Dead Sea Scroll archive."

I lived and studied for several years in Israel and had visited the scrolls housed in the iconic wing of the Israel Museum, the Shrine of the Book. The Shrine of the Book was a state-of-the-art, climate-controlled facility built to house the first Dead Sea Scrolls purchased by the state of Israel. The structure was designed with security in mind as much as aesthetics. If war broke out with Israel's neighbors, always a likely scenario, the grotto with the scrolls is constructed to sink further underground, locking under a protective metal cage. The shrine is most recognizable for its white dome which represents the unique bowl-shaped lids of the pottery jars that preserved the manuscripts for two thousand years. At one point in my graduate studies at Israel's Ben Gurion University, I attended a lecture series on how the scrolls provided valuable insight into a dramatic episode in Jewish history. But I had still never heard of a scroll made of copper.

"Most people didn't know what to do with the Copper Scroll," Jim explained. "Compared to the other Dead Sea Scrolls, the Copper Scroll is boring—a short list of places that no one has any reference for," Jim explained. "I never had use for it either, until one unforgettable day when I gave it a closer look."

"Are you an archaeologist?" I asked.

"I'm not an archaeologist. I'm a retired fire marshal. But, by applying a little arson investigation skill to the Copper Scroll, I figured out something that has eluded the experts for fifty years."

By this point I was wishing I had a more informed background on the subject instead of taking Jim's word for it, but research would come later. Right now, I had someone standing in front of me making a striking declaration.

"Can you tell me where these Temple items are buried?" I asked.

"I can't do that," Jim cautioned with a grin. "But I will tell you that I have shown my research to the Israel Antiquities Authority, and one of their archaeologists is interested in checking my theory. I'm going back to Israel next month to work out the details of a possible dig."

When he name-dropped the Israel Antiquities Authority (IAA), my skepticism melted into intrigue. The IAA confronted crazy phone calls from treasure hunters and gold diggers on a daily basis. Assuming he was telling the truth, I wondered how this hippie-cowboy got a meeting with the IAA. The organization was cloaked in secrecy. They held archaeological discoveries sometimes for months before allowing press releases. Their staff often declined interviews.

Jim scribbled his email and phone number for me on the back of a glossy pamphlet he snatched from a merchandise table. Though I still wasn't sure what to make of Jim, I tucked the pamphlet safely away and went back to my table.

When I sat down, a colleague of mine from Washington DC leaned in close. "Be careful, Shelley," he mumbled quietly. "Everyone has a story."

I left the conference a little early to meet a writing deadline. Back home, I sat staring at a half-finished article. I couldn't shake the conversation with Jim Barfield. His assertions about the Copper Scroll lingered in my mind.

I Wikipediaed *Copper Scroll* and I Netflixed a mediocre documentary, *Lost Biblical Treasures*. Unassuaged by the surface details, I hit the library circuit and checked out the seminal work of John Allegro, *The Treasure of the Copper Scroll*. I blazed through the doomsday thriller, *The Copper Scroll*, by Joel Rosenberg; and made a clandestine Kinko's copy of the expensive but thorough *Copper Scroll Studies*, edited by George J. Brooke and Philip R. Davies. From an online academic journal archive, I got all the most up-to-date information on the Copper Scroll from academic all-stars like Jodi Magness and Judah Lefkovits.

I sifted through the mounds of internet myth-making about the Copper Scroll to find recently published field findings from a decade-long excavation at the Qumran ruins, written by Israeli archaeologists Yitzhak Magen and Yuval Peleg. Although none had yet to penetrate the Copper Scroll code, the subject had already caused much ink to flow.

OPENING THE COPPER ROLLS

For over three years after its discovery, the Copper Scroll sat untouched in a museum in Amman, Jordan. Scholars deliberated the best way to pry the metal coils open. Experts at Johns Hopkins University, specialists in reconstituting corroded metal material, determined the copper's flexibility was impossible to restore enough to unroll the metal. Instead, they suggested cutting the coils into thin strips. But, no scientist in Baltimore wanted to accept the liability.

While the Copper Scroll awaited a heroic opening, Professor George Kuhn from Germany studied the coiled metal through its glass casing in Jordan. Conservators cleaned the antiquity with a crude brush and coated it with preservative. Forbidden from handling the delicate copper, in 1953, Kuhn utilized mirrors and captured photographs of the letters protruding from the outer layer of the rolls. Despite his limited visibility, he made out fifty words, a few of which were used repeatedly: *dig*, *cubits*, and *gold*. Kuhn was the first to speculate that the artifact was a treasure map.

After learning of Kuhn's suspicions of treasure, one member of the Dead Sea Scroll publication team, John Allegro, strongly pushed to execute the

Copper Scroll's opening. Made up of seven international scholars, the rarefied group was charged by the Jordan Department of Antiquities with releasing the contents of the entire Dead Sea Scroll collection.

The most famous Dead Sea Scrolls, such as the book of Isaiah, were beautifully preserved on long sheets of parchment. Much of the Dead Sea Scroll corpus, however, was discovered in pieces, scattered across cave floors. Surviving rodents and weather for twenty centuries took a toll on these texts.

With thousands of snippets, many in poor condition, the Dead Sea Scroll publication team had the prodigious task of cleaning and piecing the inscriptional material together like jigsaw puzzles. They spent their days squinting and smoking over glass encased fragments spread across long tables. They separated fragments to match handwriting styles, parchment shades, thickness of the leather, and damage patterns. For most of the scholars—overwhelmed with their heavy workloads—opening the Copper Scroll was a lower priority than their writing deadlines. For Allegro, however, the copper rolls weighed heavily on his mind.

By order of the Jordanian government—which viewed Israel, the newfound Jewish state, as their prime menace—no Jews could be part of the publication team. The political ruling hindered progress on the publication of the Dead Sea Scrolls. Jordan kept at bay those responsible for the most advanced scholarship in the field of Hebrew script. In their place, Jordan actively recruited international (read: non-Jewish) paleographers—analysts of pre-modern writing forms.

Roland de Vaux, a Dominican priest from France, was selected as the chief editor of an international and interconfessional scroll team. De Vaux was a natural choice since he lived in Jerusalem and had worked as the head of the École Biblique, the renowned French archaeology school. The rest of the editors came from America, France, Germany, and England. Three were Protestant: F.M. Cross, John Strugnell, and Claus-Hunno Hunzinger. Three were Catholic: Jean Starcky, Patrick Skehan, and Józef Milik. John Allegro, an expert in Semitic studies from Britain, was agnostic.

Allegro was considered the maverick of the group, or as his colleague Strugnell titled him, "the stone in the soup."[1] Most of the editors had a conservative approach to their scroll work: slow, methodical, and private. Allegro, however, hastily translated the scrolls assigned to him and quickly made con-troversial conjectures about their contents. He enjoyed the limelight of press conferences and knew how to angle his conclusions to attract the media. The other editors resented his love for publicity. They judged his actions as reck-less, and his editorial work, sloppy.

In Allegro's defense, he was instrumental in presenting the value of the Qumran library to the public. While his colleagues seemed to write with only the betterment of academia in mind, Allegro wrote almost exclusively for the lay press. He refused "to let important questions be hidden away on bookshelves." By bringing the scrolls to the "thinking public," they too could partake in the spirited debates over the translations and interpretations.[2] His colleagues preferred to keep their monopoly over scroll scholarship.

Allegro returned the enmity of his colleagues. He begrudged their pro-tracted work speed—quietly kindling misgivings that the Roman Catholic clique of editors had sinister reasons for suppressing the release of the scroll translations. Though no such motives were ever proven, Allegro spread a conspiracy theory that the scrolls undermined Christianity. Allegro posited that some of the sectarian Dead Sea Scrolls cast doubts on the originality of the gospel accounts of Jesus. Only once the full Qumran library was finally released for scholarly research in 1991 (after forty years of delays!), did rumors of a cover-up fizzle out.

When it came to the Copper Scroll, Allegro's persistence paid off. Allegro goaded the Jordan Department of Antiquities to bring one of the copper rolls to his hometown in Manchester, England. He hoped to find an engineer who could cut the roll into strips. If successful, he could get permission to bring the second roll to England. Allegro first approached Manchester University, his alma mater, but when the head of their metallurgy department dithered, Alle-gro searched for a more fervent expert. He found one in Henry Wright Baker. Baker was a professor of mechanical engineering at the Manchester College of Science and Technology. An expert in metal cutting and machine tool design, his technical skills—combined with a good dose of religious faith, courage, cheerfulness, and curiosity—perfectly suited him for the task.

Baker constructed an elaborate, although crude-looking, device out of retired British army materials and other tools he borrowed from the school of dentistry. The machine had a circular high-speed saw, spindle, cradle, vacuum and attached fan. If it worked, the copper roll would rotate on its own while Baker made precise cuts with the saw. As the fan blew away dust, the vacuum removed it. The cradle protected the fragile artifact from applied pressure. Still, according to Allegro, the whole contraption "jumped on its stand every time the knot on the string, connecting the motor to the saw, ran over its pulley wheel."[3]

One night in the summer of 1955, after making the finishing touches on the spindle and stiffening the oxidized copper with adhesive paste, Allegro and Baker agreed to meet at the lab early the next morning. They were ready to make the first test cut. Allegro felt apprehensive, but he hoped Baker had the courage to go through with it. He did. Late that same night, Baker rang Allegro to announce that the machine worked. He made the first lengthwise cut and was staring at a strip of the preserved scroll. Baker confessed that he had experimented without Allegro, so he could be alone in his misery if the artifact shattered into tiny pieces.

Baker worked nonstop. Within a week, the first coil was completely opened. Allegro, hardly able to contain his excitement, sent a letter to his friend G. Lankester Harding, the director of the Jordan Department of Antiquities. "For goodness sake send, or much better, bring that other scroll!" Allegro wrote. "We can hardly wait till it arrives, and it will be cut within a week of its appearing."[4]

Meanwhile, Harding was navigating the governmental changes and growing anti-British sentiment in Jordan which would eventually lead to his ouster. Despite the rough timing, he secured the second copper roll and spirited it to Manchester a month later. Baker cut the second scroll in the same manner. What remained were 23 curved metal strips, neatly contained in plaster molds, which Baker customized onsite.

Allegro made a preliminary translation of the mysterious text exposed on the concave side of each strip. From the very first reading, Kuhn's notion that the copper rolls were referring to hidden treasure proved correct. Before Allegro had sent the first facsimile of the Copper Scroll to his colleagues at the scrollery, he fired off a congratulatory letter to Harding. "These copper scrolls are red hot," Allegro declared. "I hereby make my reservation on the treasure-hunting party for next spring."[5] Allegro never doubted the scroll's historicity; it was an eyewitness record of a momentous clandestine event.

Allegro's excitement was tempered by concern that the news of the Copper Scroll's contents would set off a country-wide treasure hunt. Bedouin were already skilled and enthusiastic locators of antiquities. If they heard of underground gold and silver, it was possible they might raze entire archaeological sites. Accordingly, the scholars diminished the manuscript's importance. Six months after first interpreting the text, a press release issued from Jerusalem characterized the Copper Scroll as a "collection of traditions," not to be believed based on the fantastic size of the hoard. When *The New York Times* ran a front-page story on the Copper Scroll, they mocked its authenticity, writing that the manuscript was "something that might have been written in blood in the dark of the moon by a character in *Treasure Island*."[6]

The Copper Scroll strips were soon carried back from England to the National Archaeological Museum in Amman, Jordan where they remain to this day, separated from the rest of the Dead Sea Scroll collection.

READING THE SCROLL

After the scroll was initially opened, studying the enigmatic script was a privilege bestowed on a select few. Now various transcriptions, translations, and Copper Scroll replicas abound. No one authoritative translation of the Copper Scroll exists. For their own convincing reasons, every translation has significant variations.

The competing translations of Allegro and his colleague, Józef Milik, are the most commonly cited since they set the groundwork for Copper Scroll research. Allegro, the first to comprehend the copper strips, made a provisional translation of the text on the spot. Though he immediately sent it to the editors in Israel, as a professional courtesy, he withheld his translation from further dissemination. According to the rules of the scrollery, Milik was designated as the official Copper Scroll translator—a privilege apparently given since Milik was at Cave 3 when the scroll was found. Milik had to be the first to formally release its contents.

Though Milik was the most talented of the editors, he worked at a snail's pace. Allegro's patience lasted three years at which point he broke down and finally published his own provisional translation of the Copper Scroll before the release of Milik's definitive translation. This act won him no favor among his peers, even after Allegro admitted that Milik's translation was the superior of the two. Ultimately, however, it was Allegro's translation that first captured the public's imagination.

The Copper Scroll is a difficult text to read and understand, composed in a form of Hebrew unlike the rest of the Dead Sea Scrolls. The method of spelling and word choice is categorized as early Mishnaic, a type of Hebrew that is post-biblical, but barely. Though the scroll was given a first-century period of production (25–68 CE), some of the scroll's writing style seems to imitate biblical Hebrew, including its square-form script. A handful of biblicized words date as far back as 500 BCE. At the same time, the overall dialect strikes scholars for its use of everyday Hebrew and Greek loanwords. The author deploys many technical words and architectural terms that could only date to the Herodian period. At least eighty of the words used in the Copper Scroll were previously unknown to scholars; they don't appear in any other ancient Hebrew texts.

Scribbled in the margins, next to seven of the locations listed on the scroll, are two or three letter Greek ciphers. The ciphers confound most scholars; even Jim saw them as indecipherable.[7] One scholarly proposal is that the letters represent the initials or abbreviations of the eyewitness involved in the operation.[8] Another possibility is that the ciphers are part of an inventory code, pointing to the existence of a document which once coupled with the Copper Scroll.

Translation problems are also rooted in the Copper Scroll's etching. The handwriting is unskilled, often crowded—making it difficult to know where one word begins, and the other ends. The scroll has thirty scribal mistakes. Several letters are incomplete or backwards. In several places, text was lost to deterioration. The scribe mistakenly puts the Hebrew letters meant for the end of words in the middle of words. On occasion, he writes in cursive, instead of the formal Hebrew block letters. In the last several columns (there are twelve in total), the writing gets progressively garbled. Letters look unfinished or hurried.

As a way of explaining the shoddy work on the scroll, some experts hypothesize that the task of chiseling the letters was given to an illiterate person, as a measure of caution. If a hired embosser didn't understand the meaning of the words, he wouldn't know how to go back and loot the treasure. Judging from the adjustments in penmanship, however, many Copper Scroll experts believe the metal document was inscribed by several different amateurs. The alternating scribes were simply unfamiliar with the tricky task of hammering backward letters. Embossing, as opposed to engraving, was a design scheme rarely recorded in other ancient texts. While mistakes are expected, some authors made them more than others.

TREASURE

Despite the difficulty deciphering the scroll's language, the text screams buried treasure, listing out around 4,500 talents of precious metal. A talent in first century Israel converts to approximately 75 pounds, bringing the total weight of Copper Scroll treasure upwards of 168 tons! Judah Lefkovits, author of *The Copper Scroll: A Re-evaluation*, argues that the abbreviation used in the Copper Scroll which is assumed to refer to a talent, is in fact a symbol for *karsh*, an ancient Persian weight unit worth a fraction of a talent. If that was verified, the total weight of Copper Scroll bullion would still be quite significant, but more in line with reason, based on the amount of precious metal in circulation at the time. Whether the Copper Scroll is referring to 168 tons or 60 tons,[9] the quantities beg the question: Where did the treasure come from? There were few places in the ancient Middle East that had access to such a fantastic stash. The treasuries of the Tabernacle, Solomonic Temple, the Second Temple, and Herod's Temple are the only buildings in Israel's history famous for abundant wealth.

According to the Bible, during Moses' tenure on Mount Sinai, God gave specific directions for constructing a portable tent for communal worship.[10] The Tabernacle, known in Hebrew as *Mishkan*, was meant to be an earthly microcosm of God's celestial sanctuary. To imitate heaven, artisans required a good deal of gold and silver. The people held a collection. The response was so generous that Moses had to send word throughout the camp to stop the donations.

How did nomadic and newly freed slaves own abundant valuables? The Exodus story briefly mentions that, before their dramatic delivery from Egypt, the Israelites asked their Egyptian neighbors to help finance their exodus. After witnessing the terrifying signs and wonders of the God of Abraham, the Egyptians provided for the Hebrew slaves whatever they asked. And so, the Bible laconically states that they "plundered the Egyptians."[11]

Inside a curtained courtyard, the Tabernacle furniture included a large copper altar, accessible by ramp, for animal sacrifices. Next to it was a bronze laver for the priests to wash their hands and feet. Gold-plated beams and poles bolstered the holy place's tapestries and overhangs. Composed of two sections, the Tabernacle's first room contained a gold-plated menorah, table of showbread, and altar for incense. Behind the inner veil, they kept the Holy of Holies, or *Kodesh Kodashim*. The cubic sanctuary housed the Ark of the Covenant—a material object most exceptional in an otherwise aniconic religion for its connection to the immaterial God: His throne and footstool. The Ark was fashioned by the artist Bezalel from acacia wood, gilded with gold, and topped with two winged cherubs. The angel's gold wings stretched out over the Ark's pure gold cover. Inside the Ark, only four feet long and two and half feet deep, Moses placed the tablets of stone with the Ten Commandments.[12]

Solomon, the third king of ancient Israel, was the architectural visionary behind the First Temple, providing a permanent home for the Ark of the Covenant in Judah's eternal capital, Jerusalem. According to the Bible, Solomon was the richest and wisest king in all the earth.[13] Likewise, the Temple he built was known across the land for its ornate beauty—a symbol of national unity. In the Holy of Holies, the cedar floors, walls and ceiling were overlaid with plates of gold. The Ark was tucked behind a screen of golden chains. Precious metals and gems were extensively used to create the hundreds of implements necessary for conducting ritual sacrifices. I Kings records that, under Solomon, the Temple treasury brought in 666 talents of gold each year. The treasury was supplied by the dedicated tithes of the faithful and the spoils of King David's military victories.[14] And silver, the most common metal listed in the Copper Scroll, was in the age of Solomon "as common in Jerusalem as stones."[15] Nevertheless, on probably eight different occasions during the first two centuries of the Temple's existence, the coffers were looted by Israel's neighboring enemies.

In 537 BCE, fifty years after the Babylonians decimated Solomon's Temple, Jewish exiles were permitted to return to Jerusalem. They returned in four waves over a hundred-year period. Under the leadership of Nehemiah and later

Ezra, the returnees restored their capital city. Despite immense opposition, they built up Jerusalem's walls, repopulated the city, cut taxes, and consecrated a new Temple. They also imported a more mature and refined form of the Jewish faith where sacred texts dictated their law codes, worldview, and sacrificial system. Biblical accounts reveal that the Babylonian exiles were not depleted of resources upon their return. King Cyrus of Persia not only funded the rebuilding of the Jewish Temple, he returned 5,400 of the Temple's gold and silver relics—the same vessels Nebuchadnezzar had used in his pagan shrines.[16] The Second Temple, however, was no match to the former's glory and splendor. When the Second Temple was consecrated in 516 BCE, those who survived the exile wept from disappointment.

Five centuries after the time of Ezra, during Judaea's years of Roman occupation, King Herod made major renovations to the Temple. Despite Herod's cruelty as a ruler, he was an excellent builder. He added retaining walls and doubled the size of the Temple's surrounding plaza. The expanded Temple—with its spacious outer courts, gilded edifice and stately columns—became known as the most breathtaking building in the Roman Empire. Josephus Flavius, the renowned first-century Jewish historian, maintained that the Temple's gold and silver furnishings numbered in the tens of thousands.

Naturally, Herod's Temple had a well-stocked coffer. Jews in the land of Israel, and in the growingly affluent Diaspora, brought substantial tithes to the Temple through regular free-will offerings. By the dawn of the Common Era, every dutiful Jewish household gave an annual half-shekel tax to the Temple to sustain the caste of priests and provide for the costly business of carrying out sacrifices, vows, and rites. The treasury—consecrated for Temple use—likely accumulated until 70 CE when General Titus and the four Roman legions eliminated the Jewish sentries, breached the city walls with battering rams, slaughtered the Old City's defenders, set fire to the Temple, and plundered the coffer. To add insult to trauma, Roman coins were specially minted with inscriptions flaunting the capitulation of Judaea.

Josephus, in the eighth chapter of his *Wars of the Jews*, documents an otherwise unknown story of a Temple priest, Jesus the son of Thebuthus, and Temple treasurer, Phineas, who relinquished hidden vessels to the Romans in exchange for their lives. The list of Temple vessels they handed over is extensive, including priestly garments and solid gold vessels.[17] Upon returning to Rome, the legionnaires paraded their Jewish prisoners and spoils through the streets. The still-standing Arch of Titus in the Roman Forum commemorates the victory and the victor. In the marble relief, the soldiers hold up the stolen Temple lampstand, table of showbread, and silver trumpets. (In solidarity with my Jewish friends, I refused to walk under the Arch of Titus when I visited Rome.)

Despite the Tabernacle and Temples' legendary abundance of fortune, no trace of it remains today. Archaeology has yet to produce a single artifact from the Temple sanctums. Historians can only guess that what wasn't stolen from the First or Second Temples was burned, obliterated, or lost by Jerusalem's many invading armies. That is, unless certain items were successfully secreted away, in anticipation of the Temple's destruction. The Copper Scroll's very existence hints at a dynamic salvage campaign. A few items from the Temple inventory are named outright in the Copper Scroll.

According to the translation of P. Kyle McCarter, a professor at Johns Hopkins University, the Copper Scroll's fourth location points to Temple ritual vessels: *On the mound of Kokhlit: vessels of contribution with a lagin and ephods. All the contribution and the seventh (-year) hoard and the second tithe is disqualified. Its entrance is at the end of the aqueduct on the north, six cubits toward the frigidarium.*[18] Benedictine archaeologist Bargil Pixner believed that the Greek word *lagin* could more specifically be translated as *breastplate*, the jeweled garment worn by the high priest.[19] Ephod was the fine linen apron worn under the breastplate.

Column three in the Copper Scroll contains a reference to garments, probably priestly. Paleographer Al Wolters theorized that a slight scratch after garments was the Hebrew letter *yud*, transforming the word into the first person singular possessive: *my garments*. The intriguing implication could be that a Temple priest was one of the compilers of the Copper Scroll, hiding his own vestments with the rest of the ritual objects.[20] The priestly garments were consecrated. Like all ritual objects bearing the name of God, they were not allowed to be thrown away, only stored.

Though translations differ, the Copper Scroll does not directly reference the holiest Temple furniture: the menorah, table of showbread, or altar for incense. Nevertheless, the Copper Scroll's language points to other sacred furniture, including a possible cryptic reference to the Ark of the Covenant. Wolters reads the final hiding place, *In the cavern of the Presence [Shekinah] on the north of Kokhlit—its opening is north and tombs are at its mouth.*[21] Shekinah, when used in the Bible, designates the divine radiance as it dwells in the Holy of Holies, both in the Tabernacle and the Temple in Jerusalem.[22] The Shekinah is the spirit or presence of God. At least to me, the *cavern of the Presence* sounds like a cleverly worded reference to a cave hiding the Ark.

POSSIBILITIES

A month after the Fort Worth conference, I pulled out the pamphlet with Jim's scribbled contact information. After a crash course on Copper Scroll studies, I felt better equipped with questions than I had been at our first introduction. I rang Jim for an official interview.

"It couldn't have gone better!" he exclaimed, before recounting his recent trip to Israel. After seeing his research for a second time, a successful archaeologist with the Israel Antiquities Authority agreed to take the lead on an excavation to test Jim's research. The dig was tentatively scheduled for December 2008.

Though the IAA normally shunned rookie explorers, Jim's ideas roused their curiosity. Jim was the style of freethinker that the late Kuhn once prescribed for the Copper Scroll. When Kuhn predicted that the Copper Scroll was in fact a verbal treasure map, he cautioned the doubters to approach the unique scroll with an open mind. In 1954, Kuhn warned Dead Sea Scroll scholars: "We must have the courage to draw surprising first conclusions and consider them as possibilities, provided that we also have the courage to correct these deductions should new points of view arise. In short, we must leave ourselves completely open to all possibilities."[23] Kuhn understood that the Copper Scroll was like nothing ever unearthed before. To come at it with scholarly preconceptions was like wearing intellectual handcuffs.

Jim Barfield had no preconceptions. Why would he? He was a firefighter from Oklahoma, with no formal training in any archaeological or linguistic science. "The others applied so much knowledge that they couldn't see clearly," Jim said with a simplicity befitting his humble academic background. No doubt, Jim was well known among investigators for his raw talent in solving arson cases—analyzing evidence, eliminating fringe data, uncovering clues, and connecting forensic dots. It was yet to be proven if his skills transferred successfully to the decoding of the most enigmatic of the Dead Sea Scrolls.

CHAPTER 3

SOURCE

It was November 2008. Most of the retired men in Oklahoma were either anxiously awaiting the launch of deer hunting season or crossing their fingers for the Oklahoma Sooners to make it to the national championship game. Jim, on the other hand, was conducting speaking engagements, spreading the word about his upcoming excavation with the IAA.

One weekend, Jim and Laurie were driving to Dallas to speak at *Etz Chayim*—a Sabbath-keeping, law-observant Messianic congregation. Since Dallas was a good halfway point between my home in San Antonio and Jim's home in Lawton, Jim suggested that I meet up with them. If I could make it, Jim guaranteed we could sit down, and he would show me his entire 296-page investigative report. I bounded into my minivan and headed for Dallas.

As I waited in the lobby of *Etz Chayim*'s small building, a man with silver hair, black Levi's, cowboy boots, and a belt buckle with the letter *B* sauntered through the door. Even by his proud gait, Jim was impossible to mistake, to say nothing of his platinum locks.

As I found out that weekend, Jim's long hair was not by virtue of his Vietnam War veteran status or Native American ethnicity. In April 2006, shortly before he made the Copper Scroll revelation, he took the Nazarite vow. He did it as a symbol of setting himself apart for an interval of time—an act of thanksgiving or dedication. For the duration of the vow—according to Numbers 6—a Nazarite must avoid cutting his hair, taking any fruit of the vine, or going near a dead body. Before the vow, Jim kept his hair cropped short, as required by the army and fire department. Becoming a Nazarite was the first item on his retirement bucket list. "My fire marshal days weren't that long ago. My hair grows really fast," Jim explained.

Laurie wore gold-framed glasses, a blue silk blouse, and trendier jeans than her husband. A petite woman, she has high cheekbones and a delicate nose. Laurie gave me a quick hug by way of introduction. She held Jim's arm, and we all walked into the meeting hall together.

PUZZLE PIECES

Jim speaks at Messianic congregations and Christian churches. He loves both, although his spiritual journey more closely aligns with the Messianic movement.

In the United States, the Messianic movement gained traction in 1970s charismatic churches. Messianics usually have two stories of conversion: when they first came to Jesus and when they later came to Judaism. Though most Messianics do not believe they are obligated to observe all 613 of the biblical commandments, they are drawn to Jewish law to imitate Jesus, identify with the nation of Israel, and/or adapt a faith like early Jewish believers in Jesus. They almost never falter in referring to Jesus by his Hebrew name *Yeshua* and God as *Elohim*. Most Messianic congregants are non-Jews, and totally new to Jewish practices. How intensely they delve into those practices varies widely by congregation and individual.

When Jim began his talk at *Etz Chayim*, he knew the audience was curious how to peg him. Jim wasn't wearing a *kippah* (skullcap). He didn't have obvious *tzitzit,* tassels that hang from Jewish prayer shawls. Laurie wore pants, and high-lighted, rather than covered her strawberry-blonde hair. The Messianics were waiting to hear if he said Jesus or *Yeshua*; that would tell them all they needed to know. From the podium, he addressed their probing glances right away.

"My name is Jim Don Barfield. My friends call me Jimmy D. I follow Torah as best as I can, and I believe *Yeshua* is the Messiah." Several attentive audience members gave little whoops of approval. Jim responded, "But I was saved on my knees in a Pentecostal church, crying like a baby out to *Jesus.* And that was real too." Jim had their attention now.

From there, Jim introduced the audience to Laurie. Sitting by me, under the chill of a swamp cooler, she stood up, waved quickly, and sat back down.

"I met her at a hamburger drive-in over thirty years ago," Jim said. "She was a beautiful carhop on roller skates. We've had some good times and tough times." He paused and smiled at her. "And they were all her fault." Laurie chuckled along with the audience. It was one of Jim's few stock lines but Laurie didn't mind one bit.

"Now, who here knows about the Copper Scroll?" Jim asked. He put his thumbs in his belt loops.

Judging from the hand raises and murmured responses, most everyone in the room had at least heard of the scroll. Messianics often exhibit an unusual depth of biblical knowledge.

One stated reason why many leave conventional Christian churches is because they are tired of studying the same thirty percent of the Bible repeatedly. The majority of Messianics read the rabbinical commentaries. They memorize Hebrew prayers. They study the history of ancient Israel and the early apostolic community. And many possess a strong foundational knowledge of the Dead Sea Scrolls. Knowing this, Jim has two very different prepared talks: one for Messianic congregations and one for Christian churches. At moments, the biblical knowledge in the room was so presumed that it came off as an insider joke. Since the group was already familiar with the essence of the Copper Scroll, Jim launched right into his interpretation on the source of the metal document.

"We have to lead with II Maccabees for the history," Jim began. Despite the PowerPoint slides projected on the white wall behind him, Jim had no need for a script. He strode across the stage, occasionally clapping to make points as the facts and history flowed out of him.

From the outset of his presentation, Jim credited his Copper Scroll education to his contemporary, Vendyl Jones, the Baptist minister who turned into a Copper Scroll fanatic and a maverick archaeologist. "Vendyl Jones was the first to promote the integration of II Maccabees with other textual artifacts that described a First Temple rescue operation," Jim said.

Though Vendyl was a colorful and controversial figure, Jim felt allegiance to him. Vendyl's excavations and theories went largely unrecognized in scholarly circles, but among lay religious people—both Christians and Jews—he held popular appeal. His search for the Ark of the Covenant was closely followed.

The assertions of Jim and Vendyl punch a hole in conventional Copper Scroll scholarship, which almost universally attests to the Copper Scroll's Second Temple origins. Epigraphers—experts in the distinctions of ancient inscriptions—date the Copper Scroll to around 70 CE, the time period when the Jewish Temple in Jerusalem was destroyed by the Romans. Some of the technical language in the scroll is specific to the late Second Temple period. Carbon-14 tests on the parchment Dead Sea Scrolls indicate they were copied sometime between 250 BCE and 115 CE. Carbon dating the Copper Scroll, however, is impossible because solid copper has no organic material components.[1]

One congregation member, well-read on Dead Sea Scroll scholarship, openly challenged Jim's unorthodox dating of the Copper Scroll. Jim replied with a sardonic smile, "None of the Dead Sea Scrolls had copyright." He meant that even though the Copper Scroll language and style dated to the first century, it still could be a reworked version of an older tradition, either oral or written. The Copper Scroll may use Second Temple period language to describe a First Temple period event. To be sure, many of the scrolls retrieved from the caves were, in fact, reproductions of texts penned hundreds of years earlier.

"Vendyl did wonderful research on the circumstances leading up to the scroll," Jim added. "We don't see eye to eye on the locations of the treasure. I still agree with him on the history and the importance of II Maccabees to the Copper Scroll story. I also agree with him on the relevance of a mysterious book from the Netherlands."[2]

II MACCABEES

II Maccabees is a late edition apocryphal work—included in the Catholic canon but not in Jewish or Protestant Bibles. Maccabees concentrates on the Jewish revolt against the oppression of the Seleucid dynasty in the second century BCE. The book begins with two letters written by Jews in Jerusalem to Jews living in Egypt. In the second chapter, the author relates a lost account of the prophet Jeremiah overseeing a Temple rescue operation. The Jeremiah reference seems anachronist and out of context since the remainder of the book is devoted to the heroic efforts of the Maccabees, events that occurred five centuries after the famous prophet. However, given the central theme of purifying the Temple, the Jeremiah account was likely meant to give hope to the Egyptian diaspora that the reclaimed Temple will one day again be stocked with its holiest vessels.

Much of the prophet Jeremiah's biography is known from his exceptionally long biblical book. At a young age, Jeremiah, a Levite, received a divine warning about the rising Babylonian empire. Jeremiah foretold an invasion which would ultimately devastate Jerusalem and leave the Temple smoldering. In the Temple courtyards, Jeremiah renounced the moral decay of his people. For forty years, he warned that the only way the coming collapse could be halted was if the people of Judah truly repented and peacefully submitted to God and his sacred laws. Jeremiah lived through five different Kings of Judah; almost all of them cringed at the prophet's gloomy oracles. To them, he reeked of defeatism. At different points, he was accused of treason, beaten, and thrown in a dungeon. Even though Jeremiah regretted his very existence, he was not silenced.

For a short period, Jeremiah and his scribe Baruch went into hiding. However, Jeremiah "received an oracle," as prophets are liable to do. According to II Maccabees, Jeremiah and his band of followers capitalized on the chaos enveloping Jerusalem and managed to slip vessels out of the Temple. The author writes, "Jeremiah came and found a cave-dwelling, and he brought there the tent and the ark and the altar of incense; then he sealed up the entrance."[3]

Disciples of Jeremiah followed him, intending to mark out a path to the hiding spot—like Hansel and Gretel's breadcrumb trail. Jeremiah's men grumbled when they couldn't locate the sealed cave. Jeremiah retorted, "The place is to remain unknown until God gathers his people together again and shows them mercy. Then the Lord will disclose these things, and the glory of the Lord will be seen in the cloud, just as it appeared in the time of Moses and when Solomon prayed that the place might be gloriously sanctified."[4]

The weeping prophet's predictions about Jerusalem's fate proved true. In 587 BCE, after a year and a half of ravaging every other rebellious city in Judah, the Babylonians saved Jerusalem's full destruction for last.[5] Nebuchadnezzar's army set up camp, encircling the city walls for eighteen months. In raw, almost documentary-style language, Jeremiah itemizes the horrors of the siege in Lamentations. Famine struck beleaguered Jerusalem, as the Babylonians allowed no food or supplies into the city. Families chose between starvation and cannibalism. Corpses piled high in the streets. The whole city smelled of death.

Judah's archers were quickly overwhelmed by giant battering rams and flaming arrows. The starving Israelites hardly had the strength to resist when the Babylonians finally breached the walls and splintered open the city gates.

The foreign army tore through the city, sacking the royal palace and the beloved Temple. Jeremiah sat in prison while fires raged all around him. Along with looting thousands of Temple vessels and stripping Temple furniture of its gold and gems, the foreign invaders carted off in chains the elect of Jerusalem's citizens—the royal family, soldiers, artists, and skilled workers. Only the poorest people of the land were left. Mass displacement of refugees was Nebuchadnezzar's custom upon defeating nations. Though Jeremiah at first stayed in Israel—among the remnant left in the ashes—he eventually and reluctantly immigrated across the border into Egypt. After that, the prophet vanished from the biblical record.

TREATISE OF THE TEMPLE VESSELS

Emeq HaMelekh, a technical Kabbalistic manuscript on the workings of Jewish mysticism, was published in Amsterdam in 1648. Rarely circulated, *Emeq HaMelekh* ("Valley of the King") was authored by Rabbi Naphtali Hertz Bacharach. By way of introduction, Bacharach inserted a story of a covert plot to hide Solomonic Temple treasure, seven years before the Babylonians breached Jerusalem's walls. Bacharach titled the seemingly ill-fitting prologue *Treatise of the Temple Vessels*, or in Hebrew *Massechet Kelim*.

In Bacharach's story of the *Treatise*, there are five primary characters, righteous men with access to the Temple: Shimmur the Levite, Hezekiah, Zedekiah, Haggai, and Zechariah son of Iddo the prophet. Though Shimmur directed the mission, he is a previously anonymous actor on the Temple stage, unknown from any biblical or rabbinic texts. The other conspirators include two of the prophets still known to us today: Haggai for his singular focus on reconstructing a Second Temple; Zechariah for his colorful prophecies of a coming kingdom.

Jeremiah's name is absent from the *Treatise*. While Jim admits that it might seem illogical to connect the *Treatise* to II Maccabees, he wonders if Shimmur and his men were commissioned by the biblical prophet. Perhaps Jeremiah was the anonymous puppet master. One hint of Jeremiah's anonymous cooperation with Shimmur is that the *Treatise* names Jeremiah's scribe, Baruch, as a co-conspirator. According to the *Treatise*, Baruch assisted Zedekiah in hiding treasures. (Bible readers remember that Baruch had prior experience hiding away artifacts important for Israel's future.[6])

Shimmur the Levite and his four leaders enlisted the help of a hundred priests, the "fittest men of Israel." Transporting the great wealth of the First Temple was no feeble task, requiring the help of terrestrial and celestial recruits. The *Treatise* states that the angels Shamshiel, Gabriel, and Michael safeguarded the valuable instruments from the Babylonians. To be sure, what the Copper Scroll lacked in its sober verb-less catalogue, the *Treatise* made up for with sumptuous prose and embellishment. According to an English translation that Jim received from Vendyl, the *Treatise* opens with a catalogue of the Temple's most sacred vessels:

These are the vessels dedicated and concealed when the Temple was destroyed: The Tabernacle, the curtain, the holy menorah, the ark of testimony, the golden forehead nameplate, the golden crown of Aaron the priest, the breastplate of judgment, the silver trumpets, the cherubim, and the altar of burnt offerings, the curtain of the communion tent, the forks and the bread molds, the table [of showbread], the curtain of the gate, the copper altar, the sacred garments of Aaron which were worn by the high priest on the Day of Atonement, bells and pomegranates on the hem of the robe of the high priest, the holy vessels that Moses made on Mount Sinai by the command of the Holy One, the staff, and the jar of manna.[7]

For ten sections, the *Treatise* goes into detail as to the fabulous wealth secreted away from the Temple: thousands of musical instruments, millions of talents of gold and silver, piles of gems and precious vessels. The treasures are described in the most imaginative ways, and on a scale far larger than the Copper Scroll. For instance, the Temple's golden tables originated in the Garden of Eden, and they radiated like the sun and moon. Precious stones, dropped from heaven, also make up the inventory.

In 2013, the first English translation of the *Treatise* was published by the Old Testament Pseudepigrapha Project. James Davila, the translator, defined the *Treatise* as "an entertaining piece of rabbinic fiction." He added that the authors of the *Treatise* "worked with relatively few constraints on their imagination."[8] Davila believed the *Treatise* tried to merge inconsistent traditions about Temple hiding operations.

While the Copper Scroll made a few coded allusions to Temple items, the *Treatise*'s long deposition spelled out every item that ever existed for ritual Temple use. Yet the *Treatise* lacked concrete descriptions of the bullion's hiding places. Instead, the *Treatise* whimsically pointed to vague geographic locations known from the Bible: in the Tower of Babel, under the great willow in Babylon where they hung their lyres, and in the spring of Zedekiah. Unlike the Copper Scroll, the *Treatise* made no effort to encourage the reader to look for the hidden wealth. Instead, the text insists that sanctified vessels are not meant to be revealed until the coming of the Messiah.

Like Davila, I was first inclined to dismiss the *Treatise* as a medieval work of fiction by a mystical rabbi with a flair for hyperbole. I did not accept that it illuminated the Copper Scroll. However, an electrifying shock ran through my spine when I read through the *Treatise* for the first time. Bacharach's third paragraph states, "These are the holy vessels and the vessels of the Temple that were in Jerusalem and in every place. They were inscribed by Shimmur the Levite and his companions, on a *luach nechoshet*." With my expanding Copper Scroll vocabulary, I knew that *luach nechoshet* meant copper tablet.[9] Israeli archaeologists have uncovered precisely one *luach nechoshet*.

MARBLE TILES

For Milik, a scholar who refused to entertain tales of Temple booty, the *Treatise*'s reference to a copper tablet proved the Copper Scroll's fictional status, not vice versa. Even though the Copper Scroll gave a dry inventory rather than a dramatic narrative, Milik guessed they were parallel accounts. He supposed that the Copper Scroll existed as a prop for ancient folklore. The prop concept was validated, in Milik's own mind, when an additional, ostensibly older, copy of the *Treatise* surfaced in Beirut.

Jean Starcky, a member of the scrollery, was in Beirut around 1955 when a Lebanese Christian woman showed him two solid marble tiles with a truncated version of the same text as Bacharach's *Treatise of the Temple Vessels*. Starcky immediately called to mind Milik's belief that Bacharach's *Treatise* was connected to the Copper Scroll. A dutiful colleague, he took a picture of one of the tiles and sent the grainy black and white photograph to Milik.[10]

Despite Milik's already exhaustive workload with the Dead Sea Scroll fragments, he designated time to translate the text from the photographed tiles, considering them an important part of his Copper Scroll research. The tiles have a different introduction than Bacharach's *Treatise*; they declare that the caches are hidden "west of the high mountain." They also give an abbreviated version of the *Treatise*, probably owing to the difficulty of etching letters on marble. Still, to Milik, the tiles proved the *Treatise* tradition was perhaps older and more widespread than Bacharach's medieval *Treatise*. Although neither version of the *Treatise* text was as ancient as the Copper Scroll, Milik used the legend to downgrade the Copper Scroll to Jewish mythology, what he termed the "work of a crank."

The *Treatise* explains its creation: "These five [men] inscribed these verses in Babylon together with the other prophets that were with them, including Ezra the Kohan, the scribe." Taking the *Treatise* literally is a difficult task because of its whimsical motif. What the text appears to be saying is that after Shimmur and his men hid the treasure and documented the hiding spots on a copper sheet, they were exiled to Babylon. Only once they were in exile could Ezra catch his breath and write down the chain of events, for the sake of history. The marble tablets are too modern to be the exact product of this effort. Still, could they be a copy or reproduction of the verses inscribed in Babylon? From there, it's possible that the tradition was passed on orally, long enough for this curious text to be preserved and duplicated, once by a scribe in Lebanon and later by a Jewish mystic in Amsterdam.

It took Jim two hours to reach the finale of his tapestried history lesson. The smell of coffee and lure of pastries filled the back of the room, where a few women with headscarves and floor-length skirts arranged refreshments. Out of goldfish crackers and coloring pages, bored toddlers turned backward in their seats to stare at the desserts. A dozen adults scooted to the end of their chairs, their hands poised to shoot up as soon as Jim invited questions. Jim reiterated to the audience that the source of the Copper Scroll could only be understood when aligned with the three texts. "They were all pieces to an ancient puzzle with magnificent consequences," Jim said, "even if scholars think they are total malarkey." II Maccabees, Bacharach's *Treatise,* and the marble tiles attest to each other and the validity of the Copper Scroll.

Jim concluded, "The Copper Scroll is authentic. I have no doubt. I believe it is pointing to First Temple vessels. If my research is correct, I know exactly where the Copper Scroll caches are hidden." Bodies leaned forward, hoping for at least a hint of the hiding spots. Kicking up a leg and mimicking an exaggerated country accent, Jim cried, "The Father has blessed my socks off." Jim ended the talk as a cliffhanger. For large audiences, he never divulged the exact hideaways of the deposits.

After he finished the Copper Scroll lecture, Jim mingled with the congregants. Several women chatted with Laurie and me. One woman asked her if Jim ever got nervous to speak in front of people. "In thirty years, I don't think Jim has ever been nervous for anything," she answered. Then she added, "Anxious? All the time. But nervous? Almost never."

As a fire marshal, one of Jim's three main responsibilities—in addition to investigations and checking for fire code compliance—was public education. Going to elementary schools and explaining fire safety was a highlight of the job, allowing him to refine his oratory skills with young audiences who were easily bored, but forgiving.

Jim sat across the room, nodding politely as four men with open Bibles debated scripture with each other. Two of the men believed the Ark was never meant to be found again, and the other two argued that finding the Ark would signal the end of times. One young man, righting his tilted kippah, approached Jim. He slightly misquoted the apostle Paul in I Corinthians and told Jim: "God hath chosen the foolish to confound the wise."

Jim let out his characteristic pealing laugh and fake pouted. "People remind me of that verse so often that it kind of hurts my feelings."

A woman with waist length hair and an embroidered poncho interrupted the gaggle. She grabbed Jim's forearms tightly and prophesied, "When you open the cave, look up. In the top right rock shelf, you will find a video camera. The footage on that camera is of Ron Wyatt finding the Ark. Angels made that video." Jim gingerly avoided endorsing Wyatt—a Seventh Day Adventist explorer, who among many other things professed to have found the remnants of Noah's ark in Turkey; Egyptian chariot wheels in the Red Sea; and the Ark of the Covenant in Jerusalem. During his lifetime, Wyatt never produced a shred of evidence. Jim sputtered out a joke about angels hopefully operating cameras better than Laurie.

NONDISCLOSURE

After the address at *Etz Chayim*, Jim, Laurie, and I grabbed takeout Indian food. Jim's eyes were bloodshot from adrenaline surge. His voice was hoarse. Still, Laurie and he invited me back to their hotel room. I was ready to hear for the first time where he believed the caches of Temple items were located.

Jim's bound and printed investigative report laid on the undersized hotel room desk between Jim and me. It was no different in style than anything he would have done for an arson case in Oklahoma except, of course, for the ancient Hebrew and Israeli maps. This was his *magnum opus*, never leaving his sight, much less his possession. Jim joked, "Now should you be caught or killed, disavow any knowledge of what I am about to show you." Taking a bite of his samosa, Jim turned to the first page. The fluorescent lighting in the hotel room cast a glare over the glossy maps. He held the report at an angle and read his introduction to me:

In the following pages, you will be guided through what appears to be an enigmatic maze from ancient history. In fact, the Copper Scroll is no more difficult than following written directions needed to guide you through a neighborhood, *if* you know which neighborhood.

With that, Jim handed me the report to read the first pages which describe his methodology for establishing a starting point for the Copper Scroll's locations. Seeing his eyes grow sleepy, I feverishly skimmed the portions about his supporting evidence and his translation work until I got to the first of the locations. He had me at the first map for the first line: "under the ruins." I was more intrigued than ever.

While Jim made self-deprecating jokes about his Hebrew and his lack of formal education, he still seemed unduly certain about his conclusions. Where did this sense of certainty come from, and was it a healthy dose or dangerously extreme? I couldn't decide.

On the one hand, he was so likable and well-spoken that it made anyone want to root for the guy. He had a genius for connecting with people. There have been many sensationalist Bible explorers, like Ron Wyatt and Vendyl

Jones, who in hindsight seem either wistfully delusional or intentionally decep-
tive. They built entire followings based off of their cult of personality, polished
biblical knowledge, and infectious ambitions. Was Jim Barfield any different?

"Jim," I asked. "Why should an Oklahoma firefighter under a Nazarite vow
be the one to crack a 2,600-year-old mystery of biblical proportions?"

Taking a sip of his complimentary hotel room coffee, he looked sideways
at Laurie, whose eyelids were getting heavy. He slid his ponytail holder out
and let his hair fall straight. Combing through it with his ink-stained fingers, he
replied, "We will have to save that conversation for another trip."

CHAPTER 4
DISCOVERY

As a firefighter in the 1990s, Jim had time to read during long shifts at the firehouse. In the process of his informal biblical studies, which included the Dead Sea Scrolls, he jotted down notes in his journal about numerous dates and prophecies that caught his attention.

"I can't tell you why or exactly when I started digging into the Dead Sea Scrolls. But studying them became a compulsion," Jim recalls. "I would read going down the road on the back of the fire truck, after lunch, and on breaks from training. After work, I stayed up late into the night, sitting in my recliner, cross referencing the Bible and the scrolls."

Jim's journal evolved into a *Messiah Timeline* depicting biblical chronology from the creation of Adam and Eve. At the outset, the purpose of the timeline was to assist Jim, and his historian's mind, in processing the events and prophecies of the Bible in sequential order. Extracting dates from prophetic books helped him understand Israelite history from a broad scope. Jim counted forward and indexed prophecies like Ezekiel's 390 days, Jeremiah's seventy years, and Daniel's seventy weeks. Highlighted on his *Messiah Timeline* were the lives and reigns of the patriarchs, kings, and prophets.

What differentiated Jim's chronological digest from something you might find on the desk of an earnest seminary student were the additional oracles Jim pulled from the Dead Sea Scrolls. He plugged in dates from the unique *Melchizedek Scroll*, a fragmentary extra-biblical manuscript with eschatological (end times) teachings. Jim believed the *Melchizedek Scroll* pointed to the year of Jesus' crucifixion: "And the Day of Atonement is the end of the tenth jubilee in which atonement shall be made for all the Sons of Light and for the men of the order of Melchizedek [a mysterious priestly sect]." Unlike other self-educated scroll enthusiasts who use the scrolls to promote New Testament-based readings, Jim did not typically see hidden Christian associations in the ancient writings. The *Melchizedek Scroll* was his exception.

With a yellow highlighter, Jim underlined on his timeline every fiftieth year since the point of creation, also known as years of Jubilee—a Jewish observance occurring at the end of seven cycles of Sabbatical years. He modeled this approach off the Dead Sea Scroll *Jubilees. Jubilees* was a popular read during Second Temple times, as evidenced by the fifteen copies found in the Qumran library. The book was eventually rooted out by rabbinical authorities in the canonization process. *Jubilees* paraphrases and redacts portions of the Torah to map out the chronology of biblical events from the time of creation to the battle of Joshua at Jericho. The author, supposedly Moses, bases the sequence of events off the Jubilee cycles.

For twelve years, well before Jim ever touched the Copper Scroll, he built on his *Messiah Timeline* as his spiritual hobby—a unique cathartic exercise. Initially written on a sheet of high-quality butcher paper, the timeline stretched out thirty feet and had 6,000 notations on it. "I had to start wearing glasses 'cause of all the hours I spent stooped over it, penciling in events," Jim confessed to me.

Friends in Jim's Bible study used to roll their eyes when he needed to reference something on the timeline and had to go through the process of rolling it out across the floor. Once Jim mastered Microsoft Excel, he made a digital version of the timeline. He distributed copies of it on discs to anyone who asked.

When Jim first met the veteran explorer Vendyl Jones, the intention of the meeting was to discuss their mutual passion for biblical chronology. Jim had read Vendyl's publications and understood him to have encyclopedic knowledge about the Dead Sea Scrolls. He'd also heard one of Vendyl's many public lectures about his thirty years of archaeological excavation in the Judean wilderness, searching for the Ark of the Covenant. Jim hoped for an occasion to meet Vendyl in person. Indeed, an unusual sequence of events brought him to Vendyl's doorstep.

VENDYL JONES

As an aid for his timeline studies, Jim signed up for an online Hebrew class through Israel National Radio. His teacher, Miriam Ben Yaakov, was an American Jewish woman who had been spending time living and working in Israel. While he waited in a chat room for the class to commence, Jim small talked with the teacher about her home state. As it turned out, she was originally from Oklahoma, and her house was two miles down the road from Jim and Laurie. When Miriam finished her stint in Israel and returned to Oklahoma, the Barfields and Miriam began sharing Sabbath dinners together. Miriam became a cherished family friend.

One evening, in May of 2006, during a lively conversation about dating events in the Bible, Jim rolled out the *Messiah Timeline* to show Miriam his prized possession. Though, as a Jewish woman, she had little use for the New Testament portions of it, Miriam was impressed with Jim's attention to detail and the countless hours of preparation that went into the timeline. Staring at the marked-up butcher paper, with her temple propped up on three fingers, Miriam said, "You know who would really love the scriptural puzzle you've cobbled together: Vendyl."

"Vendyl? Do you mean Vendyl Jones, the explorer?" Jim asked.

"Yes, oh, well, I was Vendyl's secretary for years. He and his wife Anita are longtime friends of mine." As Miriam explained, she pulled out her cellphone and made a call to Anita as if to prove her point right away.

Jim gave Laurie an animated look. He pointed to Miriam and pantomimed his mind being blown away.

"Hi, Anita," she spoke into her phone. "Yes, it's Miriam. I have a remarkable couple you must meet. How do you feel about a weekend visit?"

The next Friday, Miriam, Jim, and Laurie drove to Vendyl and Anita's home in Grandview, Texas. Vendyl answered the door wearing a leather vest, holding an unlit ivory pipe. He gave a hearty "Shalom" and shook hands with his guests. While Anita gave Laurie a tour of the house, Vendyl asked Jim to walk with him out to the patio to check on dinner. A charred turkey breast sat on the grill.

In an article for *Texas Monthly*, a journalist aptly contrasted the Hollywood Ark hunter, Indiana Jones, to the real-life Ark hunter, Vendyl Jones: "While

Indy is the strong, silent type, Vendyl could talk a zillion vipers into sub-mission."[1] In addition, the bald and droopy-eared Vendyl was no heartthrob. Vendyl had a pretentious edge, sharp intellect, an even sharper temper—and despite his Baptist background—enjoyed a strong drink.

As they stood by the grill, Vendyl pulled out a cigar and began telling Jim his life story. He explained that since he was a child, his Christian mother always read to him from the Bible, every book from Genesis through the Apocrypha. Even in utero, she preached the scriptures to her belly through a paper megaphone. Naturally, as an adult he went into full-time ministry. While serving as pastor for a Baptist church, Vendyl began to question parts of the New Testament, even from the podium. Ultimately, he was asked to step down from his preaching position. He dissented from the faith of his youth to organize a following of Noahides in America.

Noahides make up a tiny society of gentiles who study the Torah and follow the seven laws of Noah. After the world was devastated by flood, Jewish tradition teaches that God established new moral standards for the "sons of Noah" to prevent a relapse into wickedness. The laws, which should be enforced by courts of law, include prohibitions against idolatry, theft, sexual immorality, murder, blasphemy, and eating the flesh of a living animal. Jews believe that gentiles who observe the seven laws are guaranteed a place in the world to come; the remaining 613 laws are binding specifically for Jews.

In 1967, for Vendyl to study Hebrew, he moved his family to Jerusalem. Shortly after his arrival, Israel's Six Day War broke out. Vendyl volunteered to fight with the Israel Defense Forces (IDF). His unusual color-blindness gave him a tremendous advantage against the Jordanian army. The camouflage used by the Jordanians to hide their anti-tank positions shone like the glint of metal to Vendyl, easily identifiable in the thick undergrowth of the valley. The IDF used him as a forward spotter. His role in the war won him a bit of notoriety among Israelis, a mention in TIME Magazine,[2] and a permanent visa.

After the war, Vendyl returned to his university studies and volunteered for excavations happening at Qumran. Vendyl was gripped by the Dead Sea Scrolls, particularly by the Copper Scroll. When the contents of the Copper Scroll were first published in 1962, Vendyl studied the details of the scroll meticulously. He was convinced that the Copper Scroll was connected to the story of Jeremiah and the Ark of the Covenant from II Maccabees—a favorite story from his childhood. He anxiously waited for Israeli archaeologists to mount an expedition in search of the Copper Scroll fortune. They did not.

Vendyl rejected the Copper Scroll translations of Allegro and Milik. Instead, his second wife, an Israeli and amateur linguist, Zahava Cohen, rendered her own unusual reading. Vendyl never published her full translation, but he based all of his conclusions off her work. According to Vendyl, the key landmarks in the scroll were locations 26 and 27, translated: *In the River of the Dome [Wadi Kippah]* and *In the Cave of the Column with two entrances.* Using his contrived translation, Vendyl focused his search on the *qalal*, the urn which held the ashes of the red heifer. The word *qalal,* as it is listed in the Copper Scroll, could refer to any type of vessel, but Vendyl insisted it was specifically the urn which held the ashes of the red heifer. Vendyl believed finding the *qalal* was an essential first step before reinstituting Temple worship. Vendyl's passion was fueled by a fifteenth-century prophecy, etched on a piece of wood, which predicted a God-fearing gentile was destined to locate the ashes. One of the Torah's regulations for Temple access required the faithful to be sprinkled by the ashes of a red heifer. Orthodox rabbis believed that only at the end of the messianic process could a new red heifer be found and prepared for sacrifice.

Vendyl imagined the Temple inventory was secreted through subterranean tunnels that started from under the Holy of Holies in Jerusalem and stretched eastward for eighteen miles toward the Valley of Achor. Vendyl based his theory on the tradition that King Zedekiah and his court tried to escape Jerusalem through an underground tunnel. Though modern Jerusalem still hosts a subterranean hive of unexplored caves and pathways, a miles-long tunnel heading out of Jerusalem to Jericho has never been located.

Walking the stark hills around Qumran with a topographical map, Vendyl looked for clues that matched the Copper Scroll's text with the facts on the ground. He scaled the desert gulch, poked around caves, and commissioned aerial photographs. One cave, half a mile up the road from Qumran, appeared to have two natural rock columns on its façade and twin entrances that led to separate cavities. He believed he had found the *Cave of the Column.* Close by, he also found a dome-shaped rock formation sitting on a dry riverbed: The *River of the Dome.* Vendyl was convinced that he had correctly identified the two primary reference points given in his wife's translation of the Copper Scroll. The *River of the Dome* had no cache of its own but was simply a pointer to the *Cave of the Column*.

Unlike most Copper Scroll experts, Vendyl claimed the document wasn't listing dozens of different locations. To him, all the scroll's descriptions of hiding spots were clues that applied to a single cave complex. If he could excavate the *Cave of the Column*, he believed he would uncover a labyrinth of rooms, piled with all the Copper Scroll's wealth. Vendyl, however, was not an archaeologist. Without a license, he had no way to apply for a dig permit on his own. The lone wolf needed a partner.

CAVE OF THE COLUMN

Pessach Bar-Adon was well known in Israel for his distinguished career. In 1961, he led a dangerous scroll hunting expedition and stumbled upon the Cave of Treasures—a gigantic trove of pre-historic ritual metal objects. When Vendyl Jones family happened to move into an apartment near the famed desert archaeologist, Bar-Adon was advancing in years and widowed. Vendyl's family showed Bar-Adon hospitality. In turn, Bar-Adon—moved by Vendyl's ambition—applied for a permit to excavate the *Cave of the Column*.

From 1977 to 1982, Bar-Adon and Vendyl conducted several seasons of excavations at the *Cave of the Column*. It didn't matter to Vendyl that the area had thoroughly been excavated by three different archaeologists down to bedrock, or that the aging Bar-Adon often napped at the dig site. They found nothing more than trifling bits of pottery.

Vendyl remained undeterred. In 1988, several years after Bar-Adon died of a stroke, Vendyl managed to partner with another professional archaeologist, Hebrew University Professor Joseph Patrich. Per their agreement, Vendyl would provide Patrich with the money and manpower to reexamine four scroll caves. He was looking for signs of habitation. Under Patrich's excavation license, Vendyl would operate with a fair amount of autonomy at the nearby *Cave of the Column*. Both Vendyl and Patrich's crews planned to work simultaneously throughout the season.

Weary of the slow progress made in previous dig seasons, Vendyl organized his largest excavation to date. Because the Copper Scroll demanded digging to great depths, Vendyl ramped up his efforts by using a conveyor system with a high capacity to move rock and debris out from the cave. At this point in his career, Vendyl had accumulated over a hundred thousand dollars' worth of equipment.

One morning, while Patrich was off-site to teach at Hebrew University, Patrich's excavation supervisor unearthed a first-century oil juglet wrapped in palm leaves. The crew beckoned Vendyl over to their cave. When they held the clay vessel in the sunlight, a dark liquid residue oozed out. Vendyl paid for the substance to be tested at Hebrew University Pharmaceutical Department. The chemical analysis indicated that the liquid was balsam oil. Although olive oil is the traditional oil used to crown biblical kings, Vendyl alleged the oil was the *shemen afarsimon,* the anointing oil described in Psalms 133. According to Vendyl's interpretation, the juglet was from Solomon's Temple and the first artifact found from the Copper Scroll.[3]

The impressive find was celebrated on the cover of the *New York Times,* featured in *National Geographic,* and later displayed in the Israel Museum. Patrich and Vendyl squabbled over who deserved credit. The juglet was found at one of Patrich's caves, not the *Cave of the Column.* However, Patrich was off site the day of the find, and Vendyl paid for the oil analysis. They each tried to usurp the other in press releases. In the end, a unique find—the alleged goal of their endeavor—severed their working relationship.

In 1992, Vendyl launched a new expedition on his own. His wife made a revision to her Copper Scroll translation which suggested that Vendyl should concentrate his excavation at the northern entrance to the *Cave of the Column.* There, his volunteers uncovered almost 600 pounds of a reddish debris which looked to be stored in a manufactured pit. Vendyl believed the pit was in fact a storage silo, and the red powder was incense used in the Temple. He had the substance chemically tested by Dr. Marvin Antelman, a consultant for the Weitzman Institute. Acting as a private consultant, Dr. Antelman agreed with Vendyl that the material was completely organic. He said the dirt contained nine out of the eleven highly refined spices used by priests to purify Temple worshipers at the altar of incense.

At a press conference held in the desert, Vendyl ignited a sample of the spices to exhibit that the incense, after thousands of years of storage, still produced a pleasing aroma. To be sure, his incense claim sparked even more controversy than the juglet. Antelman's professional validation, which Vendyl actively courted, was subject to serious doubt. Vendyl's critics maintained that the "incense" was in fact dirt with a red hue. A follow-up analysis conducted by chemist Kenneth McMurtrey inferred that the red dirt was consistent with the geology of the area and showed "no evidence that it may once have been processed by humans, intended for any particular use by humans."[4]

Soon after his press conference, Vendyl's already shaky relationship with the Israel Antiquities Authority corroded. The IAA ordered Vendyl to shut the dig down. It was an illegal excavation since the self-styled archaeologist no longer had academic coverage from Patrich. Plus, his methods were too destructive. Completely unauthorized, he had used a bulldozer to clear a road to his excavation site. Vendyl refused to quit. Instead, he declared war on the IAA. He hired a lawyer and went to the Israeli press saying that he would only leave if he was given a court order.

Vendyl firmly believed he was on the right track despite his few finds and despite the significant roadblocks from the Israeli authorities. The next excavation season, Vendyl spent tens of thousands of dollars, all donated from his network of benefactors, to have the *Cave of the Column* scanned using a molecular frequency generator. According to Vendyl, the high frequency radio emissions confirmed that a massive concealed chamber existed in the wall between the two cavities at the *Cave of the Column*.

Never one to follow the rules, Vendyl found every possible way around the IAA. Since, technically, the *Cave of the Column* was outside of Qumran, and therefore in a nature preserve, he got geological, rather than archaeological, excavation permits. To evade watchful monitoring, Vendyl dug with his volunteers in the dead of night. They tunneled their way through the wall that supposedly had a concealed chamber. According to his wife's translation, the *passage between the two caves* hid the caches. A passage in the wall never surfaced. Instead, the crew kept hitting bedrock.

For his final expedition, Vendyl intended to drill a borehole through the bedrock and fish a pin-camera into the hollow. Israel Nature and Parks Authority gave him the geological permit for drilling, though the permit came along with strict instructions to access the drilling site via helicopter to avoid any further ecological damage. He had already stripped the interior of the *Cave of the Column* and expanded its twin entrances. The Parks Authority forbade him from moving any more earth. Employing a full-time helicopter cost Vendyl two thousand dollars a day. Vendyl felt confident that despite his restraints, he was destined to reach a glorious end to his long journey.

Making a quasi-announcement on Israel National Radio, Vendyl said he intended to discover the lost Temple vessels on August 14, 2005, *Tisha B'Av*—a day of mourning for the loss of both Temples and other calamities in Jewish history. A prominent unnamed Kabbalist blessed his mission. When the anticipated day arrived, the borehole did not lead to a cavity. Vendyl's crew packed their bags. The whole expensive operation left Vendyl in serious debt and living back in Texas in a downsized house.

At the time of Jim's meeting with Vendyl, the pioneer was pushing 77 years of age and coming to grips with the closing of his career and a failing memory. Nevertheless, Vendyl's knowledge of the Bible and the Dead Sea Scrolls invigorated Jim. Over kosher wine and challah bread, they talked for hours about Jim's timeline and Vendyl's life experiences. Each time Jim thought Vendyl was closing out the conversation, the old explorer reached for more wine and launched a fresh story. Staring contemplatively at the wine clinging to the sides of the glass, Vendyl twice repeated his catch phrase; "Archaeology is like reading a book backwards: one page at a time, one layer of history at a time."

Jim's intention for the meeting was to pick Vendyl's brain about the Dead Sea Scrolls and have Vendyl critique his *Messiah Timeline* based on his deep biblical knowledge. But after decades of walking and breathing the Copper Scroll, every conversation wound its way back to Vendyl's theories on the ancient metal document. Vendyl's mind dwelled in a world where the Temple still stood, Israel's tormentors were knocking on the gates, and somehow a group could spirit away sanctified ritual objects.

FIRST FIVE

The Copper Scroll was not always of particular interest to Jim—a surprising fact since the rest of the Dead Sea Scroll collection occupied a prominent place in his Bible study. Jim read through the Copper Scroll once and it struck him as a boring inventory. He felt no affinity for the one Dead Sea Scroll that offered zero historical narrative or spiritual insight.

Before Vendyl, Jim understood that even if archaeologists had set their minds to intentionally dig for Copper Scroll treasure, the ancient directions were mostly meaningless to them. Granted, a few place names from initial translations—like Jericho, Valley of Achor, and Mount Gerizim—were still identifiable in modern times. But most of the descriptive addresses in the Copper Scroll appeared too narrow in their specificity to be known outside of their era. Standard translations of the scroll speak of tombs, dry wells, caves, and pools belonging to people and places unknown to us today. For example, according to a popular English translation of the Copper Scroll by Florentino García Martínez location eight reads, *in the cellar which is in Matia's courtyard.*[5] But, who was Matia? And where was her courtyard? Other burial places are too generic to narrow down. Martínez translates location 37 as *in the burial-mound which is at the entrance to the narrow pass of the potter.* Who was the potter? The treasure map's clues give the impression that they are reminders for the conspirators involved, who anticipated a near-term recovery of the vessels.

One morning in December 2006, Jim woke up mulling over a conversation with Vendyl. According to Vendyl, the Copper Scroll had more prophecy in the first line than all the other non-Biblical texts put together. In between books at the time and still adjusting to the leisure of retirement, Jim decided the Copper Scroll was worth briefly re-reading with his first cup of morning coffee and a jelly-filled Hanukkah donut. In his small study, which doubles as a guest bedroom, he leaned over his copy of Martínez's translation of the Copper Scroll. On his desk there happened to be a diagram of Qumran. Jim didn't remember placing it there, but given his affinity for eccentric Bible study, it was not entirely surprising. Rabbinical commentaries and copies of non-canonical books spilled onto the floor.

Jim wrapped a blanket around his shoulders and read the first line of the scroll: *In the ruin which is in the Valley of Achor.*[6] Most Copper Scroll experts feel that the opening line applies only to the first cache of treasures. Jim, on the other hand, interpreted the initial phrase to be a dry preamble, an introduction to the place where all sixty plus of the caches were secreted. In the scroll's plethora of directions that followed, the scribe never told the finder to change sites. For Jim, the key to understanding any map, whether graphic or verbal, is determining the point of origin.

No valley in Israel is named Achor today. Though there are several different contenders for the location, biblical scholars most commonly associate the Valley of Achor with the rugged gorge which sweeps through the northeastern edge of the Judean Desert for over five miles. Going with the popular identification of Achor, Jim's first undertaking was to identify a ruin in those sloping confines. The valley has no shortage of archaeological remains, but one ruin at the southern edge stood out among all the rest: Qumran.

Jim followed his inkling and continued to read the scroll; his eyes jumped back and forth from the verbal clues in the scroll to the physical depictions on his diagram of Qumran. Jim was curious if some of the descriptions of wells, cisterns, and pools in the Copper Scroll matched up with Qumran's architecture. If not, he was prepared to check the next closest ruins in the valley. In a process of elimination, Qumran was Jim's first trial site.

Harkening back to his investigator training, Jim used what he termed a fingerprint methodology. First, he needed to find a match in the Qumran ruins for the following line in the text: *Pass under the steps leading to the east forty cubits: a chest of money and its total: the weight of seventeen talents.*[7] Jim oriented a Qumran map to the cardinal directions of a compass. He looked for steps heading east and, sure enough, there were steps near the center of the Qumran complex headed east. But were the eastward-facing stairs forty cubits long?

When Jim first showed me his report, he explained, "As an investigator, I was as meticulous as heck. Tracking down Qumran's stair measurements felt pretty natural." Searching around online, Jim lucked upon the exact measurement of the eastward facing steps in an IAA official document.[8] The IAA's report—output from ten years of excavation—was made public mere months before. At that point, Jim had never been to Qumran, but he was happy to take the IAA's word for it. According to Yitzhak Magen and Yuval Peleg—the most recent excavators at Qumran—the steps leading east measured 19.5 meters, 64 feet. By taking the most commonly accepted measurement of a cubit (48.76 centimeters), Jim ran a standard conversion calculation. He couldn't believe the answer. The steps measured 39.98 cubits long! Jim threw off the blanket and kept going.

Encouraged by the three-fingerprint matchup for the forty-cubit stairs, Jim tried to stay subjective. "I had to assume it was a coincidence," he said, "and keep studying the evidence until it all was overwhelmingly pointing at Qumran."

The third location in the scroll, according to Martínez, reads: *In the great cistern of the courtyard of the peristyle, in a hollow in the floor covered with sediment, in front of the upper opening: 900 talents.*[9] Peristyle is a Greek loan-word to describe an enclosed courtyard or colonnaded walkway. The Copper Scroll transliterates the Greek word "peristyle."

Qumran did in fact have a large courtyard encased by a wall, transforming it into a peristyle. The peristyle stood on the north end of the compound. In its heyday, the peristyle was surrounded by protective rock walls; today the walls are reduced to a mere outline. Adjacent to the peristyle is a prominent cistern. From aerial photos of Qumran, Jim noticed the limestone cistern had an uppermost opening. A 1,000-foot trough created from the mountains west of Qumran captured the water deposited by seasonal flash floods and directed it to the clustered buildings to supply them throughout the dry season. Jim conjectured that the sudden torrent may have caused the buildup of sediment. Once again, Jim found a set of fingerprints that matched perfectly to the ruins. The matches were jumping at him right off the page.

Rubbing his temples to calm his nerves, Jim moved on to location four. When Jim did his own translation of the text, he disagreed with Martínez's assumption that the Copper Scroll's lines eleven, twelve, and thirteen applied to location three. He interpreted them as an extended explanation of location four: *At the double entry pool, with the entrance at the north edge of the community, six cubits toward the white immersion (pool) of oblation rising from the soil, going down into the left, high above the sea floor; dig three cubits for forty silver talents.*

Qumran had one double entry *mikvah* (ritual immersion pool) which could easily be spotted at the northern edge of the complex. The mikvah was the highest pool at Qumran—both geographically and by elevation above the soil. Though there were other stepped pools in Qumran, the one on the northern edge was the only one that had two stairway entries which both went down several steps and then turned to the left. The residual white plaster that once coated the entire pool remained visible. Lastly, the sides of the pool were exactly six cubits long. This one site paired with all the specific details that the

Copper Scroll required. Jim was spurred on by the finding. The Copper Scroll was reaching through history; Jim felt its clutch.

In certain instances, the instructions in the Copper Scroll to would-be treasure hunters were so vague that they were deemed useless by scholars. For example, the scroll's location eleven gives the ambiguous instructions: *In the cistern which is underneath the east wall, in a spur of the rock: six silver bars in the entrance, underneath the large threshold.*[10] It seemed impossible to narrow down one *cistern* or *spur of rock* in all of Israel. Under the assumption that all the items were secreted to Qumran, however, Jim examined the ruins for clues. For location eleven, he searched the Qumran complex for a *cistern* that was underneath the complex's *east wall*. He found one.

Everything seemed so obvious that he oscillated between elation and doubt—elation that he had to be on to something, and doubt that no one else had seen the correlation before. A similar adrenaline rush usually overwhelmed him as an arson investigator, sifting through debris to find the first clue of the fire's origin. Though exposing blown out meth labs in Oklahoma trailers hardly prepared him for decrypting ancient Hebrew maps, his knack for analytical thinking had something to do with his self-confidence in approaching the Copper Scroll mystery. Jim was no slouch of an investigator. As fire marshal, he won the Oklahoma Arson Investigator of the Year Award and the International Arson Investigator of the Year Award from the International Association of Arson Investigators.

Laurie remembers the day Jim first identified the Copper Scroll with Qumran. She recounted to me, "I was in the kitchen with the grandkids when we heard Jim in the study whooping and hollering." Her grandson Seth asked how much coffee she had given him.

When Jim's son, Shawn, a graduate student in video production, came to the house to pick up his children, Jim jumped out of the study. "Son, I think I solved the Copper Scroll!"

Shawn replied, "Sure, Dad. But where are the kids? I gotta run."

What Jim's family knew was that when he got a hold of a thread, he followed it until the end, no matter what. For the next two months, Jim barely looked up from his desk. He found additional maps and online photographs of Qumran. He studied Vendyl's theories on the history of the Copper Scroll.

He tracked down archaeological reports from previous Qumran excavations. And he examined the penmanship on the published facsimiles of the Copper Scroll. After all his obsessing, he found matches in Qumran for the first twenty Copper Scroll locations. Only forty more remained.

GENIUS OR COPYCAT?

Jim was not the first researcher to assert a linkage between specific Copper Scroll descriptions and Qumran. It should be an obvious candidate considering the metal document was discovered in a cave complex only a mile away from Qumran's outer walls.

Allegro, the earliest Copper Scroll champion, believed the scroll's references to the biblical city of Secacah connected Qumran to the treasure. Secacah creeps up four times in the scroll's fourth and fifth column. Secacah was one of the six wilderness townships listed in the fifteenth chapter of the book of Joshua. Out of all the Iron Age vestiges in the Valley of Achor, Allegro believed Qumran was the worthiest contender for Secacah. Professor Jodi Magness from the University of North Carolina upholds Allegro's conclusion. She theorizes the Copper Scroll scribe used the site's scriptural name in an attempt to code its whereabouts.[11]

In a paper for the International Symposium on the Copper Scroll, Barbara Thiering proposed that the first twenty-one items in the scroll were hidden at Qumran, although she did not specify exact locations.[12] Pixner—one of the first scholars to methodologically localize all the Copper Scroll directions—determined caches 22 through 26 were hidden at or nearby Qumran.[13] Israeli scholar B.Z. Luria did not directly point to Qumran, but he proposed that all the valuables were buried around and between Jericho and the Dead Sea by the followers of second-century guerilla leader Simon bar Kokhba.[14]

Even though explorers and academicians had long tiptoed around the idea that Qumran and the Copper Scroll were intimately connected, Jim was the first to say that all of the locations had matchups within the confines of Qumran. His theory was more striking for its straightforwardness than its complexity. That's why Jim said no one proclaimed him a genius when he presented the report. "Most scholars simply thumped their heads," he said.

Thankfully, Jim did not follow the precedent of other explorers who said the vessels were all located in the caverns and tunnels underneath the Temple

Mount. The 35-acre nucleus of the Middle East's political and spiritual tension had been off limits to archaeologists for decades. A covert dig under the Temple Mount in 1981 almost set off World War III.[15]

Qumran was still an active dig site. The status of its ownership, though disputed, was not a flashpoint in negotiations between Israelis and Palestinians. From all appearances, digging at Qumran to test a rational notion, with enormous potential, seemed all together doable and warranted.

The problem, however, was that Jim had never actually been to Qumran. In fact, he had never even been to Israel. Jim told Laurie, "We have to go there. I want to make sure that I'm not imagining things." To determine the next forty locations, he needed to take measurements on the ground and make his own site survey. They got on a plane and flew to Israel in February 2007.

CHAPTER 5

LAND

Novice travelers on a meager budget, Jim and Laurie took a bus directly
from the Tel Aviv airport to the Old City of Jerusalem. As dusk descended,
they gulped down sahlab, a warm and creamy drink made from orchid, and
bought a couple of Jerusalem's famous oblong sesame seed bagels from a
street vendor. When they spotted a group of nuns in black habits, they decided
to trail them to the Christian Quarter.

The Old City of Jerusalem is composed of quarters: Christian, Muslim,
Jewish, and Armenian. Jim and Laurie wanted to find a hostel for the night
in the Christian Quarter, where rooms are generally cheap and more readily
available than the Jewish Quarter. Situated in the northwest part of the city,
the Christian Quarter houses the Church of the Holy Sepulcher. Eateries and
small shops are crammed into the narrow alley that runs up to the famous
sanctuary. In the daytime, palettes of color—in the form of hanging t-shirts,
honey-soaked desserts, and spice bins—spill out onto the walkways. By night-
time, all the color disappears as the Arab store owners pull down their shutters.
Stepping over streams of dingy mop water, Jim and Laurie happened upon the
hidden staircase of a hostel near the Jaffa Gate.

Run by two brothers, Palestinian flags adorned the reception desk. After
checking in, they filed past a small crowd of Canadian and European travelers camped out in the common area. Jim perceived a conformity in their
nonconformity: dreads, baggy cargos, dirty t-shirts, and top-of-the-line
backpacks. Though the hostel had great rooftop views, Jim and Laurie were
stuck in a windowless, fanless room, reeking of mildew. They had to pay
extra for towels.

"Welcome to the Holy Land," Jim whispered as they tucked into their stiff mattress.

Laurie giggled. She recited a Psalm which felt suddenly ironic. "The Lord loves the gates of Zion more than all the dwellings of Jacob," she whispered back.

The two agreed that even a smelly hostel was incapable of dampening their spirits. Jim and Laurie had dreamed for years of taking a trip to Israel. Never did they imagine that their first Holy Land tour would be on a reconnaissance mission.

After a night of rough sleep, they spent the morning strolling through the Jewish Quarter. The Jewish Quarter, in the southern part of the Old City, hosts high-end art studios with large glass doors and fixed prices, providing the city's most relaxed, cost prohibitive, window shopping. Laurie tucked into a kiosk selling cheaper Judaica souvenirs. She couldn't return to her grandchildren empty-handed. They followed the pressure-washed stone streets and stairwells, winding their way down to the *Kotel*, or Western Wall. Young Jerusalemite children ran about freely. Tourists bumbled around, losing all sense of direction in the stone maze.

After walking through metal detectors and showing a security guard the contents of Laurie's purse and Jim's backpack, they emerged into a large plaza. Jim held his breath. The five-story edifice loomed ahead. Wild plants and swift nests, protruding from the wall's cracks, brought the cherished stones to life.

Once the retaining wall for Herod's Temple, the Western Wall is the holiest place accessible to Jews for worship. A vast plaza leads up to the *Kotel*; the whole of it is branded an open-air synagogue. The courtyard spanning the front of the Western Wall is partitioned into a men's section and women's section. Orthodox men conducted morning prayer rituals, wrapping leather strips, attached to small leather boxes, on their foreheads and left arms. Young solitary IDF soldiers caressed the stones. On the women's side, Laurie nestled in among female soldiers and mothers with strollers. Rocking back and forth under the shadows of the *Kotel*, the women buried their faces in leather-bound prayer books.

On opposite sides of the partition, Jim and Laurie touched the *Kotel* with their foreheads and tucked their folded prayers between the cracks. The stones are not held together by cement, but rather their own sheer weight. Jim and Laurie's prayers were simple requests that they stay within God's will for their lives. Like the example set by the *Kotel*, they hoped that they would resist buckling under the enormous weight of their task. From Jerusalem, they soon began the short journey to Qumran.

QUMRAN'S RUINS

When Jim and Laurie arrived at the Qumran site, they paid the twenty-shekel entrance fee to a young Israeli girl with a Russian accent. With measuring tape and a camera weighing down his pant pockets, Jim soaked in the stillness of the valley and its aura of timelessness. To most passing travelers, the underwhelming site deserves no more than an hour in their itinerary. Jim, however, was jubilant to spend the day walking the same ruins that had rarely left his head for two months.

Qumran was exactly as Jim had expected from the Copper Scroll descriptions: the forty-cubit stairs, stepped cistern, snaking water channel, pantry and stable. Only, he hadn't anticipated a few site renovations. One Copper Scroll location—a burial site for a stash of gold—was covered with a recently built walkway. Another location was partially obscured by a viewing platform. In determining the accessibility of the treasure spots, Jim penciled notes on his map about the flooring at each location. The most promising floors were merely packed dirt; others were girded by flagstone.

Studying the ruins in three dimensions helped Jim identify locations described in the Copper Scroll that eluded him when working with two dimensional maps. For example, when tourists first enter Qumran, the main fortification on their immediate left is a watchtower. The tower once boasted a tall look-out to spot enemies converging from the north. Since the tower has no first level entry, it was likely accessed from wooden gangways stabilized on the surrounding buildings. In Qumran's final days, the site underwent a military confrontation with Roman legionnaires. In the tower's rubble, archaeologists found iron arrowheads and a surface layer of ash. Complex questions about the past buzzed around Jim's mind. He struggled to corroborate his First Temple history on the Copper Scroll with the evidence of Qumran's final phase of occupation.

Jim noticed that the watchtower's massive walls (over eight feet thick) left mounds of rubble slanting at 45 degrees. As he stood in front of the ruins, looking at his translation of the Copper Scroll, Jim had an epiphany. Descriptions for several locations in the Copper Scroll that seemed absurdly specific, he now understood were variously worded descriptions for the watchtower. If the copper tablet was inscribed by multiple authors, it made sense that each of the conspirators had different methods for describing the same spot. It was like the inscribers were playing a game of Taboo, giving out certain clues about the tower's physical characteristics but careful to avoid buzz words. According to Jim's premonition, the tower matched at least five different locations described in the scroll: *sloping walls, watch house, two-story building, thick lofty inclined fortification,* and *slanting guard post treasury.*

In addition to the descriptive references, Jim wondered if the watchtower had a code name in the Copper Scroll: *The House of Hakkoz.* Many translators agree that the Copper Scroll clearly lists the *House of Hakkoz* as a location for buried treasure. For example, Jim translated location 44: *Placed here and hidden, retrieved from the narrow (entry) House of Hakkoz (still) erect, is a wonderful fortune.* Hakkoz is a biblical name, referring to a priestly family that traced their lineage back to the First Temple. I Chronicles 24 describes the division of the priestly class into work groups. They were one of two dozen priestly divisions who rotated their services by a set calendar, each serving in the Temple for one week at a time.

After their return from the Babylonian exile, however, the Hakkoz family had problems proving their genealogy and were honorably disqualified from priestly duties.[1] Instead, the House of Hakkoz was appointed guardian of the Temple treasury.[2] Jim proposed that the Hakkoz family, at some point, transitioned from being treasurers for the Jerusalem Temple to standing guard of the surplus tithes hidden in Qumran's watchtower. For this reason, he conjectured, it came to be known as the *House of Hakkoz.*

To take a break from the midday desert sun, Jim and Laurie went inside the on-site Qumran museum. They watched a multi-screen video presentation that gave a bird's eye view of Qumran, complete with silent actors dressed in white linen tunics reenacting the daily life of Essenes. The Essenes were a splinter group unlike either the Pharisees or Sadducees, the two most well-known movements of the Second Temple period. After the Romans razed the Jerusalem Temple and condemned the Jews to exile, the Essenes faded from view along with the Sadducees. The Pharisee approach to the Torah evolved into what is now known as Rabbinic Judaism.

The *Community Rule* and *Damascus Document*—two of the most common manuscripts in the Dead Sea Scroll collection—are manuals for the sectarians' alternative society, listing out the group's rules for membership and conduct.[3] The name Essene is never denoted outright in any of the Dead Sea Scrolls. The Greek word is likely the transliteration of a lost Hebrew label. The authors take care to cloud their identity, referring to themselves as the "Yahad" (community). Still, the anonymous texts match what is known from contemporary historical sources about the Essene movement. Sukenik was the first to make the connection between the distinct theology presented in the scrolls and Essene authorship.

Separating themselves from the leadership of the Second Temple, the Essenes practiced a stricter form of Torah observance than their religious contemporaries. Josephus allegedly spent three years, as a teenager, with the Essene community. In *Wars of the Jews*, Josephus goes into detail about the Essenes' initiation processes, self-reliance, ranking system, purity laws, and communal finances. Members closely guarded the secrets of the community, or risked banishment. He believed the sect preserved sacred literature, and they were experts on medicinal herbs and the healing properties of stones. According to Josephus, even King Herod was impressed by the Essenes' integrity and piety, preferring them over the Pharisees and Sadducees.

Philo of Alexandria, a first-century Jewish historian in Egypt, affirmed several of the descriptions of Josephus in his manuscripts *Every Good Man is Free* and *Defense of the Jews*. About the Essenes, Philo wrote, "In no other community can we find the custom of sharing roof, life and board more firmly established in actual practice." Philo described a celibate male community of 4,000 members committed to the pursuit of holiness. Though they shunned wealth, the industrious community included farmers, craftsmen, and shepherds.

From what we can gather in the sectarian Dead Sea Scrolls and the witness of ancient historians, the Essenes held ascetic beliefs which led them to shun Jerusalem's priest-kings. Going to great lengths to live out their principles, they acted as much more than a protest movement. They initiated their own 365-day solar calendar, set up desert camp, and followed their own leader—referred to in the scrolls with the mysterious pseudonym, Teacher of Righteousness.

After the film, Jim and Laurie glanced over samples of archaeological finds from Qumran. The placards explained how worldwide interest in the Dead Sea Scrolls demanded a full excavation of Qumran. Roland de Vaux—chief editor of the Dead Sea Scroll publication team—led five seasons of excavation in Qumran from 1951 to 1956. The team uncovered rooms and expertly engineered water systems that had long been buried under the shifting sands. Though de Vaux never published a full archaeological report of his finds, he reconstructed many of the rooms at Qumran based off the room's artifacts.[4]

Qumran, for a sectarian settlement, had an unusually large number of coins plucked from the ground. Most of the coins were scattered here and there throughout the Qumran complex.[5] In one case, de Vaux unearthed three jars filled to the brim with 561 silver coins. Buried underneath the plaster floor in the doorway of one of Qumran's larger rooms, the jarred coins were mostly Tyrian shekels; all dated on or before 8 BCE. During the Roman Empire, Jews used Tyrian coins to pay the annual Temple tax, perhaps because coins from Tyre were a higher quality silver than the other Roman coinage.[6] The archaeologists were baffled by the presence of coin hoards in a settlement whose inhabitants were thought to have shunned wealth. Allegro was the only colleague of de Vaux to make a connection between the coin hoards and Copper Scroll treasure. Perhaps the Essenes maintained the habit of paying their Temple tax, but while the Jerusalem Temple was impure, they collected the taxes at Qumran.

The foundations of a few structures—mainly the deep round cistern, watchtower, and protective wall—left traces of Qumran's earliest occupation: the archaeological era known as the Iron Age. As extra proof of the early dating, de Vaux's team found a distinctive jar handle from the Israelite phase. The handle was buried at the deepest stratum, retaining the stamp *lamelekh* (Hebrew for "to the king"). They also found a pottery sherd with paleo-Hebrew writing, the script used before the Babylonian conquest. De Vaux determined that Qumran had been inhabited, off and on, since the reign of the biblical King Uzziah (783–742 BCE).[7]

De Vaux theorized that the first phase of occupation lasted until the Babylonian exile. For centuries, Qumran sat marooned. When the sectarians eventually settled Qumran again, around 130 BCE, they reinforced the first level of construction. They then destroyed, rebuilt, expanded, and fortified the settlement over the next 200 years. The site was permanently forsaken at some point during the First Revolt of 66 CE against Rome.

Jim scrutinized Qumran's site maps mounted on the walls. He overheard a passing tour guide say, "No other site in the region has plumbing as finely engineered as Qumran." When the guide walked away, Jim continued to eavesdrop. The guide continued, speaking in a British accent, "In the desert, a monastic group could only last as long as their water source." Qumran receives on average four to eight inches of rainfall a year.[8] Jim amused himself, thinking how several of those cisterns and dry gutters served as unsuspecting hiding spots for buried treasure. He wondered how tourism would increase when Qumran's best kept secret was revealed.

HILL OF KOKHLIT

The term *Kokhlit* appears twice in the Copper Scroll, once towards the beginning and again at the very end. Martínez translates location four of the Copper Scroll: *In the hill of Kokhlit, tithe-vessels of the lord of the peoples and sacred vestments; total of the tithes and of the treasure; a seventh of the second tithe made unclean (?). Its opening lies on the edges of the northern channel, six cubits in the direction of the cave of the ablutions.* Martínez also translates the very last lines of the Copper Scroll: *In the tunnel which is in Sechab, to the north of Kokhlit, which opens toward the North and has graves in its entrance: a copy of this text and its explanation and its measurements and the inventory of everything, item by item.*[9]

Because of the strange penmanship in the Copper Scroll and the slight spacing between words, it is especially difficult to distinguish between proper names and descriptive words. Copper Scroll scholars have long deliberated over translations for the letter combination *Kokhlit*. If the Copper Scroll authors were using a proper place name, we do not know of a locality named *Kokhlit* in ancient times. Since the word only comes up in a few other ancient sources, scholars are uncertain how to pronounce it, much less find its locale. The Babylonian Talmud refers once to a "*Kokhlit* that is in the wilderness." An Iron Age wine jug, most likely stolen from a tomb near Hebron, is inscribed with a place name with the same Hebrew root: *Wine of Kokhel*.[10] Even more significantly, the marble tiles with the *Treatise* refer to a hiding spot for Temple wealth that has the same root as *Kokhlit* (*Ein Kokhel*).[11] Pixner suggested *Kokhlit* was a nickname for a settlement of Essenes, possibly Qumran.[12]

The *hill of Kokhlit* was the only description in the Copper Scroll which Jim placed outside of the Qumran ruins. The Hebrew word for hill could also translate *mound of Kokhlit* or *heap of Kokhlit*. Prior to the trip, Jim spent hours studying a pixelated aerial photo of Qumran. His eyes were always drawn to a rocky outcrop 300 yards northwest of the complex. Exploring Qumran for the first time, Jim wondered if the authors were signaling the mound.

Jim rightly assumed that the tour group on their headsets would not detect when he and Laurie walked past the Qumran walls and headed for the barren hills. The mound demanded little consideration and had no reason to be included in a standard tour of Qumran. It was merely part of the scenery. They stepped around a chain post with a caution sign. Once they slipped behind the mound's bluff, they were sheltered from view.

According to the Copper Scroll's instructions, treasures were placed in a cavity near the *hill of Kokhlit*. Scouting around, he tried to determine the likelihood that the oddly shaped rock mound was hiding an entrance to a hollow cave. Standing astride the potential entrance, Jim thought its north side looked oddly like pictures he had seen of other Dead Sea Scroll caves. It had a spacious void filled with sloping loose debris. Many of the scroll-bearing caves in the cliffs of Qumran had been almost impossible to detect by visually scanning the cliff walls. Clearing out the debris was the only way to be certain.

Although Jim knew *Kokhlit* was more speculative than his other matches, identifying *Kokhlit* was his most pressing undertaking. The third and last locations in the Copper Scroll included the most valuable item: another scroll. The mysterious document, listed at the end of the Copper Scroll, is proposed as a complement to the Copper Scroll text, a second witness. Vendyl nicknamed that hidden scroll the "Silver Scroll," based on the assumption that its contents might also be preserved on precious metal. It's more logical to guess that a more detailed scroll was written on leather; the Copper Scroll may be a truncated version of an inked original. Many scroll buffs believe that only once the so-called Silver Scroll is found can the entire Copper Scroll be understood.

Although Jim could have spent an indefinite number of hours studying the layout of Qumran, he and Laurie had to catch the last bus back to Jerusalem. On the ride back, Jim confronted the big question. He slid closer to Laurie and asked, "Even if I figure out all of the locations, who is going to care? How am I supposed to get anyone to listen to me?"

Laurie put her head on his shoulder and answered with a smirk, "You usually keep talking until someone decides to listen."

As the sun set, the landscape became a kaleidoscope of color. From the bus windows, they watched as the rocky hillsides turned from tan to orange to brown. The top of the Dead Sea assumed a glass-like stillness, softly mirroring the crescent moon rising above.

GERSHON SALOMON

Jim did in fact have a friend in Jerusalem: Gershon Salomon, the founder of the Temple Mount Faithful—a veteran advocacy group for Jewish rights to the Temple Mount. Salomon was the one person Jim could think of that might take him seriously and know how to point him in the right direction. Before they got on a plane back to Oklahoma, Jim paid an unannounced visit to Salomon. It wasn't the first time. Years earlier, before Jim ever started researching the Copper Scroll, Jim met Salomon under stranger circumstances.

In 2001, a distant acquaintance named Stephen showed up uninvited to the wedding reception of Jim's daughter. As Jim choked back tears preparing for the father-daughter dance, Stephen slipped next to Jim at the table reserved for family. Stephen quietly insisted that Jim join him at a conference in Dallas the next day. Gershon Salomon was the featured speaker at a Christian conference on prophecy. Salomon founded the Temple Mount Faithful, a Zionist protest group fighting for Israeli sovereignty on the Temple Mount. Unlike other Temple Mount movement leaders, Salomon actively courted Christians to join him. Stephen wanted Salomon to see Jim's *Messiah Timeline*.

Starting off his story like he's opening a joke, Jim related the story to me. "I show up at Gershon's hotel room with the guy who crashed my daughter's wedding," Jim said. "With us was our mutual friend, a large Kiowa Native American named Screaming Eagle." Salomon was in the middle of saying his Sabbath prayers when the motley crew arrived.

Stephen had invited Screaming Eagle to the meeting because he believed he was a member of Israel's ten lost tribes. Screaming Eagle kindled the meeting by serenading Salomon, at the top of his lungs, with a traditional Kiowa song. He then presented Salomon with a silver clad lion's claw. Salomon graciously accepted. Below his snowy white mustache, he had a soft smile.

In the dimly lit hotel room, Jim walked Salomon through the excel document of his timeline. Salomon's irises grew from dots to discs when Jim got to the prophecies concerning the laying of the cornerstone for the Third Temple. Unbeknownst to Jim, his timeline synchronized with the anointing of the Third Temple cornerstone by Salomon's group, only ten months prior. Sitting on his hotel bed, Salomon told the story of how the Temple Mount Faithful dedicated the cornerstone in a public demonstration.

"Sensing the time had come," Salomon began, "my group was set to install a six-ton marble stone on the Temple Mount. Following Torah law, the stone from the Israeli desert was hewn by diamond, not by metal."

Salomon mounted the stone on the back of a flag-draped truck. The demonstrators—mostly older non-Orthodox Zionists—drove the truck to the Temple Mount gates. Priests, one in full biblical garments, and Levites, holding shofars, accompanied the procession. The participants believed they were making history, leading a practical campaign of restoration in the legacy of Ezra and Nehemiah.

Israeli police, in bulletproof jackets, barred the demonstrators from passing through the portal. The Israeli government was rightfully fearful of provoking Muslim sensibility. The former site of the First and Second Temples is now dominated by the golden Dome of the Rock to the north and the tarnished silver dome of Al-Aqsa Mosque to the south. Since the seventh century, Muslims have venerated the plateau as *Al-Haram al-Sharif*, the Noble Enclosure. According to the Quran, in a night vision, Muhammad flew on the back of a winged steed from Mecca to the "furthest mosque." Though Jerusalem is never named in the Quran, Muslim tradition anachronistically associated the "furthest mosque" with Jerusalem, gaining the city a revered status early in the Islamic imagination.[13] Though it is often labeled the third holiest site for Sunni Muslims, the Temple Mount hosts a tiny fraction of Muslim pilgrims each year in comparison to Mecca and Medina, far and away the most holy sites in Islam.

Today, Jews are forbidden by Muslim authorities in administrative control of the Temple Mount to show any religious observance in the area. If bringing a Psalms book to the Temple Mount breaks the rules, putting a six-ton cornerstone there, in preparation for the Jews' Third Temple, was clearly out of the question.

Salomon let out a prodigious sigh and massaged his bad leg. He vented to Jim, Steven, and Screaming Eagle, "The contemporary situation on *Har Habayit* is a far cry from the yearnings and dreams of all of us that fought in the 1967 war."

When Israeli tanks barreled through the Lions' Gate to liberate their holy capital on June 7, 1967, Israeli army Colonel Motta Gur made the historic announcement in his field radio: "The Temple Mount is in our hands! I repeat. The Temple Mount is in our hands!" Salomon was among the first paratroopers to enter the Temple Mount. Though the Israeli battalions sustained heavy losses breaking through the minefields and trenches separating East and West Jerusalem, by the time they reached the Old City, no shot was fired. The Jordanian snipers had fled. Salomon walked the area—praying, cheering, and crying with fellow soldiers. In that moment, Salomon remembers hearing a voice from *Hashem* tell him, "For this moment and most holy place, I saved your life. Build my house so I will again dwell among my people Israel, and among all my creation."

In their exaltation, paratroopers hoisted an Israeli flag up on the Temple Mount, replacing the Jordanian flag. The flag exchange symbolized what the paratroopers felt was a reversal of Jerusalem's fortune, a chance for the Jewish nation to reclaim what they lost in 1948. Within a few short hours, however, Israeli Defense Minister Moshe Dayan ordered the paratroopers to clear out and take the Israeli flag with them. Though Israel annexed the Western Wall and Old City, they feared the righteous indignation of the whole Arab world if they did the same to the Temple Mount.

Ten days after the war's end, Dayan went on his own to meet with Muslim authorities. Sitting shoeless in the Al-Aqsa Mosque, eyepatch aslant, Dayan ceded back all practical authority of the Mount over to the Jordanian *Waqf*—the Islamic religious council in charge of the Temple Mount since the twelfth century. According to their agreement, Jews were allowed to visit the Temple Mount, but Jewish prayer was forbidden. Israeli police would maintain security and accessibility at the site, but the Muslim authorities maintained their role as custodians; they got to keep the proverbial keys. Dayan generously announced, "We did not come to conquer the sacred sites of others or to restrict their religious rights, but rather to ensure the integrity of the city and to live in it with others in fraternity."

Salomon, an excellent narrator, concluded his history lesson: "There you have it. After almost 2,000 years of waiting, Jewish command of the Temple Mount lasted ten days." They had lost control of the Temple Mount at other points in their long history, but only in 1967 was it given away voluntarily.

Salomon wondered if he would witness the restoration of Temple worship, the apogee of Jewish hope, within his lifetime. "I am ready, God is ready, and Israel is ready," Gershon said. Stretching out his hands, Salomon thanked the men for their company and prayed the priestly blessing over them. Jim, Steven, and Screaming Eagle headed back to Oklahoma in silence.

After their first meeting, Jim and Salomon stayed in touch, always promising to reconnect. Still, Jim expected Salomon to be surprised when he made good on that commitment. On the last morning of Jim and Laurie's Israel trip, Jim waited outside Salomon's Jerusalem office. Salomon's office at the time was in an old unmarked building across from Zion Square, the center of Jerusalem's commercial life. A poor beggar stood outside selling red Kabbalah bracelets. Once Jim heard Salomon's cane clicking up the sidewalk, he knew they were in the right place.

Salomon recognized his "American firefighter friend" right away. With a quizzical look on his face, he invited them inside. In his dilapidated one room office, Salomon's desk was packed with floor-to-ceiling reproductions of menorahs, musical instruments, and utensils—used by the Temple Mount Faithful as props in their protest marches. Jim explained to Salomon the point of his trip, launching right into his entire theory on the Copper Scroll.

"At first, the whole thing soared over Salomon's head," Jim recalls. As Jim talked he noticed Salomon's frown of dim comprehension. Salomon was barely acquainted with the Copper Scroll or the architecture of Qumran. Plus, Salomon had his own ideas on the location of the Ark of the Covenant. Though excavations under the Temple Mount were forbidden, Salomon and fellow leaders in the Temple restoration movement strongly believed King Josiah stored away the Ark in a vault underneath the Temple Mount, perhaps concealed by the 570-ton monolith at the subterranean base of the Western Wall.

Salomon looked over Jim's maps and explanations for the first twenty sites at Qumran. Jim stood close to him in the cramped space, arching over awkwardly to avoid pressing against Salomon's crippled leg. Laurie stood flat against the wall. When Jim reached across the desk to point out the eastward facing stairs on the Qumran map, Salomon grabbed Jim's hand, turning it over to get a better look at his palm. "Well would you look at this," Salomon exclaimed. "Your palm line matches mine!" He held up his own palms, pointing to the crease that parallels the knuckles. Jim and Salomon both had a deep crease extending across their palms in a perfectly straight line.

Salomon pushed aside Jim's research. He was too bewildered by the palm comparison. Laurie searched Jim's face for any sign of frustration, but he smiled blankly and shook his head. He politely held out his hand for Salomon's amusement.

Despite his disinterest in the details of Jim's theory, Salomon instructed Jim, "You should keep working on this. It just may head somewhere." As the director of a protest movement which routinely fought the Israeli Supreme Court and Jerusalem authorities, Salomon understood the obstacles. He had plenty of suggestions for Jim on who and what to avoid.

Jim and Laurie started to say goodbye. They had to catch their flight and Salomon had a Temple Mount rally to attend. Salomon looked intently at Jim and told him, "Do this the legal way so you don't lack legitimacy. You really need to go through the IAA." Jim nodded. He decided whatever rough edges his pursuit might bring, he would hold to that counsel.

CHAPTER 6
GATEKEEPERS

B ack in Oklahoma, Jim eagerly renewed his Copper Scroll research. Treating his investigation like a full-time job, he set out to identify the remainder of the locations. Losing sleep and skipping meals, Jim was absolutely absorbed by the process of documenting his research. For weeks, he shut himself up in his study, buried in pictures, maps, and measurements of Qumran. What would seem like a tedious chore to most was a life-giving task for him. To illustrate his points, Jim used every program in Microsoft and every satellite image of Qumran available. What followed was a highly professional, articulate report.

Jim organized the report in an easy to follow manner: one location presented at a time, in the order they appeared on the scroll. Each explanation began with the location's English translation from Martínez. After the Martínez translation, Jim inserted a facsimile of the Hebrew lines, as they appear in the Copper Scroll strips. Under everything, Jim offered his own unique translation.

When first studying the Copper Scroll, Jim had no partiality to any of the various scroll translations. He utilized the Martínez translation, as opposed to Allegro or Milik, simply because that was the most up-to-date translation he had on hand in his home office. The Martínez version was more than sufficient in matching the first five sites on the scroll. Once it became overwhelmingly apparent to Jim, however, that all the locations were at Qumran, Jim realized he had a problem. The Martínez translation was completed under the assumption that the descriptions given on the Copper Scroll were all over Israel, to include Jericho and Jerusalem. Jim needed a new translation, working under the rubric that the verbiage in the scroll should be limited to reflect what was available in the confines of Qumran.

He found a facsimile of the scroll online. Tediously combing through his Hebrew-to-English concordance, he compiled a letter-for-letter comparison—using the Martínez translation only for reference and context. As the Hebrew letters formed words, he compared them to biblical words in the *Strong's Concordance*.[1] Most of the time, he had to rearrange the word order to make the descriptions intelligible. Many of the words were misspelled, spelled phonetically, or spelled in a manner customary to that region or timeframe. Copper Scroll experts had long complained of the same problem in their analysis of the text. With trickier translations, Jim based his word choice off architectural studies of Qumran, as if the Copper Scroll served as a map legend for the ancient site. For example, Qumran has a watchtower, sheep's pen, and pottery refuse—all which Jim found words for in the Copper Scroll.

He also employed historical information about the Essenes. First-century sources tell us that the reclusive Essenes had peculiar religious and social habits. How they ate their communal meals, when they ritually immersed, and what types of prayer routines they followed all fed into Jim's conclusions as he built his translation. For this reason, Jim found it logical for the scroll to denote a scriptorium, prayer room, and mikvah.

Jim held a sober view of his unusual translation: "My method is vulnerable to attack, as well it should be." Paleographers and epigraphers study for decades every nuance of ancient Hebrew letters and words, identifying the tiniest spelling, script, shape, and vocabulary differences between centuries and regions. The retired Oklahoma firefighter could conjure up only a little conversational Hebrew he learned from Miriam. Still, he could work a concordance to death, compensating for a paucity of Hebrew expertise with sheer grit. As a result, what he produced was not a translation, but instead an "investigator's comparison," a compilation of words suited to test his inkling that Qumran was the exclusive hiding spot for Copper Scroll treasure. When Jim's location translations differed markedly from that of Martínez, the report provided a page of clarification for how and why he matched the textual depiction to a specific area of the Qumran ruins.

Jim was careful to stay true to the scroll's intent, but he felt justified when his investigator's comparison differed from the official academic translations. Even among experts, John Allegro observed, "There are so many alternatives to the reading of a word, each dependent on the true interpretation of another, itself perhaps resting on one or two indeterminates, that, failing the discovery of new evidence, the rendering can only be a succession of possibilities."[2]

THE AUTHORS

After months of intense study, Jim wore out the spine on his concordance. He eventually wearied of sitting alone in his study, and he started going daily to his local Starbucks, sprawling out his maps and translations, alternating between espresso and chai lattes. Though he told no one that he believed the items were buried at Qumran, he was happy to chat with baristas and other patrons about the Copper Scroll and its implications. On any given day, he could be found sitting at a table with retirees or hipster teenagers. Because of Jim, coffee lovers in Lawton were well-versed on the First Temple period and the Dead Sea Scrolls.

At night, his tired mind played out possible scenarios that led to the creation of the copper treasure map. He was intent on unlocking the method to the inscribers' madness.

The scroll, to even the inexpert eye, has obvious alterations in penmanship. Jim detected five different handwritings, all of them suggesting the handiwork of a rushed amateur. Jim believed the accomplices operated in sequence, hiding items and recording their locations on the copper plate, before passing the baton—or in this case, the hammer and stylus—to the next hider. Because of the sheer weight of the fortune, the items had to be secreted out of the Temple in separate operations. An extended caravan of treasure-laden animals trudging through the desert would have been too conspicuous.

In his research, Jim looked for patterns and techniques peculiar to each of the compilers of the Copper Scroll. Dividing the facsimile of the manuscript according to the disparate handwritings, Jim realized that the first and second conspirators hid at twelve locations; the third writer hid at eleven places; the fourth at seventeen locations; and the fifth hid at only five locations. He concluded that the last hider's objects were the most important.

Accompanying the explanations for each location in Jim's report were two graphics: one pinpointing the burial spot on a modern aerial photograph of Qumran; the other marking it on a graphic diagram of Qumran. The graphic diagrams were rendered by Jim with the help of Shawn, his tech-savvy son. At first Jim used red dots to identify the targeted sites. Once the red dots started to look clustered, Jim decided to color-code the locations, according to each writer, to trace any obvious patterns of movement. He noticed that the hiding areas allocated to each author divided Qumran into quarters. Jim postulated that they did it this way to cut down on the chance of duplicating hideaways. Conducting their labor in separate cycles was also the only way of maintaining secrecy. The first writer hid in the northwestern quadrant of Qumran; writer two and three had the southwestern quadrant; and writer four hid in the northeastern section of Qumran. Writer five was not confined to any quadrant. His strategy of burying his five troves appeared random, until Jim made a closer examination.

For the last writer, Jim mapped out his five locations by pushing tacks into a satellite map of Qumran, careful to not poke through the paper and scratch his Starbucks table. According to Jim's translation, the last five locations include a trading encampment, a basin, the kitchen, ascending steps, and a fountain. Jim plotted the tacks one after another. When Jim pushed in the last of the tacks, he got chills all the way down his spine. He let out a yelp and turned to see if any other patrons heard. Writer five hid his items in a straight line. Like the stars in Orion's belt, the pins marking the burial spots ascended the hill, bisecting the complex. The constellation of pins led right to the rock mound—the *hill of Kokhlit.*

Up until this point, Jim was still uncertain about the *hill of Kokhlit* matching the Copper Scroll's description. After all, it was the only location outside of the Qumran complex. Since it was a natural formation, not man-made like the rest, it seemed harder to narrow down with specificity. But seeing all five sites line up perfectly, Jim believed they were far too exact to have occurred by chance. Writer five must have intentionally lined the locations in ascending order to direct the finder to the *hill of Kokhlit.*

A Starbucks buddy in a leather biker vest with sleeve tattoos plopped down at Jim's table. They sported similar low ponytails. Jim was eager to share. In a hushed voice he said, "It seems that whoever penned the Copper Scroll was telling whomever figured it out in the distant future: If you can find these last five sites, they will point you to the most important location of all: the cave." The patron hadn't a clue what map Jim had on the table with pushpins, but he imitated a quiet golf clap. More comfortable with self-deprecation, Jim backtracked, "It's like the ancient writer was saying 'Jim, I know you aren't a bright firefighter, but simply follow the little dots.'"

To grasp a better understanding of the word *Kokhlit*, Jim drove home and phoned Professor Kenneth Hanson, a Judaica scholar at the University of Central Florida. Hanson has a host of videos on YouTube, created for his online students but available for all. In them, he combines his training in theater with a vast knowledge of Jewish history. It is not unusual for him to lecture in full costume. Jim hoped Hanson's enthusiasm also extended to non-students. It did.

Hanson explained to Jim that when scholars encounter an obscure Hebrew word, of which there are many in the Dead Sea Scrolls, the first question they ask is: what is its grammatical root? Every word in the Hebrew language boils down to a root of just three letters which, through various permutations, can be expressed as a verb, noun, adjective, or just about anything. In the instance of the word *Kokhlit*, there are three Hebrew letters equivalent to the English "k," "kh," and "l." Hanson said, "When I see the word, I immediately think of the word *k'khol* meaning 'blue,' but it makes little sense in the context of the Copper Scroll."

The verb *kokhel* appears in the book of Ezekiel for applying eye makeup. "What if we add the equivalent of the Hebrew letter "t" to the front of the word?" Hanson asked Jim. "Now we can conjure up another grammatically linked and kindred word: *t'khelet*." Jim was excited by Hanson's thought train. *T'khelet* was a very special term indeed. It referred to the blue or turquoise dye referenced forty-nine times in the Hebrew Bible. The dye was used to color the clothing of the high priest, as well as the tapestries of the holy Tabernacle. It was also used on the tassels attached to the corners of a person's prayer shawl. Could it be that the mysterious language of the Copper Scroll was linking a specific hill with an aura of holiness, symbolized by the turquoise blue threads in the holy garments of the high priesthood? In calling the hill *Kokhlit*, the text might be referring to a "holy hill." "In other words," Hanson said, "something very holy may well be sequestered within."

TELLING VENDYL JONES

Once Jim identified locations in Qumran which matched most of the descriptions in the Copper Scroll, he felt like he had to meet again with Vendyl.

After all, Vendyl was the one who first triggered Jim's interest in the Copper Scroll, and he desired his approval. Plus, Jim was using his unique history on the scroll to pinpoint somewhere close to Vendyl's excavation. Though Jim's approach and conclusions were different, he wanted to make sure Vendyl understood it that way, not as intellectual property theft. Jim knew Vendyl was quick to assume he had been double-crossed.

On the day Vendyl agreed to meet, Jim arrived fifteen minutes before expected. Jim stood outside the door knocking when a slightly pot-bellied Vendyl casually answered in a button-up shirt and his underwear. "Well," Jim said feigning apathy, "go put some pants on, and I'll give you a hug." Vendyl first poured them a cup of cardamom flavored coffee and then got dressed.

In the year that passed since their last visit, Jim sensed that the health and memory of the elder explorer had deteriorated significantly. They went to Vendyl's study where the walls were decorated with Israeli art and panoramic photos of Jerusalem. Above his bookshelves was a reproduction of the Copper Scroll on parchment. Vendyl gestured for Jim to have a seat on the other side of his desk.

Light came from a single desk lamp, illuminating Vendyl's face, leaving Jim in the shadows. Pulling out the first draft of his Copper Scroll report, Jim told Vendyl, "I've been doing research and have reason to believe that all of the Copper Scroll treasures were buried under the ruins of Qumran, or right outside of it."

Relentlessly single-track minded, Vendyl paid enough attention to hear Jim say the words "Copper Scroll" and "Qumran." Hearing his favorite two words opened the abyss. He leaned back in his ergonomic chair and went into a tailspin, recounting his theory on the *Cave of the Column*, his past excavations, and his intention to get back to Israel.

Jim respectfully repeated: "Vendyl, I think I have solved the Copper Scroll." Pushing forward his report, Jim nodded to Vendyl, encouraging him to study the maps.

"Oh, I see," Vendyl said, "this is very interesting." He stroked his white beard with his age-spotted hands, flipping through the graphs and images as Jim's theory sank in. The lines on Vendyl's forehead became more pronounced, the deeper he squinted. Unlike Jim, Vendyl had never produced an extensive report of his theories or translation. He disbursed it piecemeal through his newsletters and lectures.

Minutes passed before Vendyl looked up. He surely noticed that Jim's report made no mention of the *Cave of the Column* nor made use of Vendyl's translation. Still, Vendyl finally locked his hooded eyes with Jim and was geared up to dispense the advice for which he assumed Jim had come. "Go out to Qumran at night and dig with no one watching," Vendyl instructed, pointing his index finger at Jim. "Try to dig as much as possible and then when the IAA inspectors show up the next morning, it will be too late for them to derail anything."

Vendyl and Jim walked outside to his back porch. Pulling out his pipe, Vendyl talked about an upcoming excavation he was planning in Israel. He was certain he had identified the biblical site of Gilgal at the north end of the Dead Sea.[3] Vendyl intended to mark out the exact parameters where the Tabernacle once stood. In preparation, he was sharpening his skills in locating ancient objects with what looked like dowsing rods. He instructed Jim to bury his wedding ring anywhere in the yard; he swore he could find anything. Jim obliged. After Vendyl muddled around the backyard for forty minutes, with the rods giving no hints, Jim dug back up his ring.

Since embarking on the Copper Scroll mission, Jim had only shown his research to Salomon and Vendyl. Salomon told Jim to take a straight course, play it safe, and cooperate with the Israeli agencies. In direct contrast, Vendyl instructed him to keep the IAA out of it. Despite their contradictory advice, Jim took their words as reassurance to press on, one way or another.

LETTING THE SECRET OUT

Once the research report was fully polished, Jim got fidgety. Though he wasn't content to merely sit on the information, he had a problem: Only academics or archaeologists could apply for excavation permits in Israel. "I'm from the south side of the tracks in Lawton, Oklahoma," Jim vented. "I don't have a Ph.D. I have zero chance of the Israelis listening to me."

Jim cold-called anyone he thought could help get his foot in the door with the IAA: Christian authors, professors in biblical studies departments, and well-known rabbis. They had a difficult time taking him seriously. In lieu of total strangers, Jim reversed his strategy and started talking to everyone in his orbit. Without revealing the exact whereabouts of the treasures, he told friends that had never so much as heard of the Copper Scroll about his methodology for solving it. Person after person, Lawtonians walked away from conversations with Jim tipsy with excitement as they weighed the potential of his discovery.

In short order, the gossip about Jim's quest spread, and he elicited inquiries from local media. The *Lawton Constitution* featured his story in an article with the tantalizing title: "City man may have solved Copper Scroll riddle." Next, Oklahoma's Channel Four News aired an interview with Jim. The anchorman opened the segment with a teaser: "Retired Oklahoma fire marshal says he's unwrapped a mystery that is reminiscent of a Hollywood blockbuster." The program showed Jim at a conference table going between a Copper Scroll facsimile and his research report. Spliced in were graphics plucked from the internet of the Ark of the Covenant and Herod's Temple.

After the local news episode, Jim was invited as a frequent guest on podcasts and radio shows. He made a pledge never to turn down an opportunity to get the word out, but he didn't always know the audience size or quality of the broadcast beforehand.

What Jim lacked in high profile connections, he made up for in cheerleaders. Laurie and his three kids—Shawn, Heather, and Michael—were eagerly supportive. He also had a decent following among Messianic groups of all stripes. He did interviews with Messianic teachers for radio, television, and print. Jim visited Messianic megachurches, home groups, and holiday events. In August 2007, Jim was asked to share his research with friends at an annual Sukkot gathering.

Sukkot, also known as Feast of Tabernacles, is a weeklong festival where Jews reflect on their ancestors' forty years of wandering in the desert. The years of wandering came after they were freed from slavery in Egypt and before they could enter the land God had promised by covenant to Abraham. Though the desert wandering was a punishment for one generation's scarcity of faith, it fulfilled God's plan to unite the former slaves as a free and consecrated people. In the desert, they learned how to think and act as a people, a nation capable of being a light to the world. The tradition of congregating in sukkahs—temporary dwellings—allows believers to strip their modern comforts and focus purely on God's provision.

Messianic communities often have their own take on the holiday, celebrating it communally by setting up sukkahs at national parks. Campers spend their days like a G-rated Messianic Woodstock: barbequing, dancing, hiking, and playing music. Unlike Woodstock, they also do a lot of Bible study and sober theological debate.

Long before Jim made the Copper Scroll discovery, he attended week-long Sukkot celebrations with his family. Jim's tent was a familiar icon in the sukkah circles at Oklahoma's Lake Murray State Park. Stitching together used canvas drop cloths—destroying Laurie's sewing machine in the process—Jim designed a medieval-themed tent with tassels along the border and roof. It looked less like a sukkah and more like a prop for a Steampunk expo.

Per their annual tradition, Jim and his family set up camp at Marietta Landing on the lake. They also provided space for their friend Chris Knight. Chris was a middle-aged single guy with a compact tractor business in Dallas. He usually camped with a different set of friends in an area known as Buzzard's Roost, but in 2007 he had specifically asked to join the Barfield family for Sukkot. Chris was much less gregarious than the Barfields, but staying up late around campfires, Chris proved to be their intellectual match in Bible studies.

One morning, after Jim gave a short introduction to his Copper Scroll research for a breakfast crowd at Lake Murray, he realized that he was tired of telling his solitary story: "*I* deduced this" and "*I* discovered that." He wanted to use the proverbial "we." Harkening back to his military and firefighter days, he needed to be part of a brigade with a mission. Isolation did not befit the extreme extrovert. Jim decided right then to put a purpose and an organization behind his investigative report. He would create a team of people, the *Copper Scroll Project*, with the shared mission of helping the nation of Israel recover the items of the Copper Scroll. Jim realized he needed an aide-de-camp in his battalion.

Jim left the breakfast meeting and stormed into Chris's wobbly sukkah. Chris was awake, sipping on chai tea and reading in the shade of his palm branch covering. Jim asked, "Chris, will you be my number two in command of the *Copper Scroll Project*?" Chris took another swig of tea, smiled and nodded affirmatively, as if he had been expecting the question. "I don't think you understand," Jim reiterated. "If I must choose only one person, besides Laurie, to help with me with this, it's got to be you." Chris chuckled at Jim's insistence and nodded again.

With Chris on board, Jim made his rounds to other tents. He asked his sons and friends to fill in the rest of the ranks. Jim said he didn't want to take their favor for granted; he wanted to include them in the project. With a camp spirit in the air, his friends readily agreed, their chests visibly inflated from their renewed sense of purpose. Jim couldn't tell them yet how he might need them in the future, but he felt relieved to have company.

AIDE-DE-CAMP

Chris is a bit of a mystic. Gentle and introverted, one way that his spiritual consciousness manifests itself is in dreams. He pays close attention to his dreams, mining them during his waking hours for appropriate guidance or warnings from God. When he speaks about God he consistently refers to him as "Father." Though Chris is known among his friends for being acutely sensitive to the still small voice of his Father, Chris's first thirty years were anything but inspired.

His father abandoned him when he was young and his mother struggled as a result. Growing up in an unstable, impoverished home, where he often felt responsible for providing for his younger brother, Chris learned to steal food at an early age. This upbringing lent itself to a life of drug and alcohol abuse. As an adult, he held down a steady job as a bartender, but he was often in trouble with the law for drunken driving, check fraud, and credit card theft.

In 1987, Chris moved from Dallas to Austin. He had his grandmother's gas card and enough money for one night at a cheap hotel. He was afraid of getting arrested in Dallas after a night of partying with a stolen credit card. Within the week, he found a landlord who let him do odd jobs at an apartment complex until he could afford the rent. He soon scored two part-time day jobs. As he was beginning to think his luck had finally changed, he got pulled over for speeding. When the officer ran his license, a warrant came up. Chris went straight to jail.

For the first two weeks, Chris's survival instincts kept him sane. It wasn't until they moved him into a single cell in the back of the facility that he finally broke down. In his despair, Chris recalled one night, months earlier, when he was watching Christian cable programming, high on drugs. He had repeated the words of a televangelist and asked God to forgive his sins and grant him eternal life in heaven. Unlike what the television preacher promised, Chris did not feel "born again" after the prayer. In fact, he had hit rock bottom and worried his destiny was to repeat the mistakes of his absentee father. Lying on his cot in the dark lonely cell, he whispered an anguished challenge to God: "If any of that is real, please show yourself!"

The next morning Chris was transferred to a county jail to participate in a prisoner worker unit. As he got settled, a guard pushing a library cart came by asking the inmates for book requests. Chris asked for a Bible. After the guard handed him a paperback King James, Chris plopped down on an aluminum bench, drooping his head. He hardly noticed a large African American cellmate who perked up when he overheard Chris's request.

"I was sitting on a bucket in my own house when the cops came in out of nowhere and apprehended me," the cellmate said by way of introduction. "I have been trying to figure out why I am here," the cellmate continued. Poking Chris in the chest, he declared, "I think I am here because of you. Now tell me brother, why did you ask for that Bible?" He motioned for Chris to scoot over and sat down on the bench next to him. The stranger grabbed Chris's new Bible off his lap and started flipping to Isaiah. Although Chris desperately wanted to be left alone, something in the man's searching eyes encouraged him.

Chris told the man his entire life story and the series of bad decisions that led to his arrest. Reading Chris passages from the prophets, the cellmate explained to Chris that the only one who could redeem him was the God of Abraham, Isaac, and Jacob. Chris peppered the man with all the questions he had been carrying around for years. Chris and the man talked almost the whole day and into the evening in that dingy gray cell. A young homeless man, who also shared their cell, listened to their conversation and silently wept in a corner—his tears forming a small puddle on the bleached floors.

Chris woke up after a foggy sleep. His teacher was gone. The homeless man stood along the wall, leafing through the Bible. Chris asked the officer on duty where his African American cellmate had been taken. The officer looked at him strangely. He said there had never been anyone else in the cell. No one had gone in or out all night. Whatever happened that night in jail, the track of Chris's life was permanently altered.

Several months before Jim began researching the Copper Scroll, Chris had a dream where Jim, all dressed in white, rushed through the door of a tent. In the dream, Jim motioned for Chris to leave the tent and kept repeating, "We have to go." Jim pointed to a desert region that was filled with holes and a hill, like a desert golf course. Chris heard an authoritative voice in the dream saying, "He is ninety-five percent accurate." When Chris first awoke after the dream, he wondered what the dream could mean, especially since Jim had never stepped foot on a golf course. Only months later when Jim told Chris about his Copper Scroll theory did Chris realize the meaning of the dream. For that reason, Chris didn't hesitate when Jim asked him to join the *Copper Scroll Project.*

Since becoming a man of faith, Chris renounced his previous days of bad living. He now reads a never-ending supply of books about overcoming addiction, rejection, and sin patterns—keeping an extensive journal about his personal revelations. Chris has been single since his conversion. He has pale blue eyes and a still unlined face. Although Jim often teased Chris, a life-long partnership crystallized that Sukkot. From that point on, Jim shared all the credit, and the burden, with Chris.

CHAPTER 7

CONNECTION

A fter retiring from the fire department, Jim worked a couple of days a week at the Comanche Nation College teaching a fall course on investigative report writing. Juanita Pahdopony, the Dean of Academic Affairs at the college, heard rumors of Jim's side venture. According to Jim, Juanita volunteered him to give an informal brown bag seminar in the school auditorium for the faculty.

"We want to hear about the investigative report of all investigative reports," Juanita told him.

"You're the boss lady," Jim agreed with comical deference.

Juanita is a small-framed Comanche woman with spikey hair. She is an active poet and artist with a reputation for being persuasive and bold. During the brown bag seminar, Jim noticed that she acted especially excitable. As soon as the hour-long question and answer time was over, she motioned for Jim to follow her to her office.

Standing by her desk, Comanche art decorating the walls, she explained to Jim how she and her Jewish husband were once a host family for an Israel Defense Forces officer. Jim felt tired from the seminar, but he remained standing to match her gaze.

"Foreign military from friendly nations used to come to Fort Sill to train at the post's artillery school," Juanita explained. "American sponsors helped the overseas officers adapt to their temporary life in Oklahoma. In the 1970s, my husband and I hosted one Israeli officer named Shuka Dorfman. I have kept in touch with Shuka and his wife, Talmah, for thirty years."

"Wow, that is really interesting," Jim said. He leaned against the arm of a chair to signal his preference to sit. Juanita was too excited to pause.

Juanita continued, "Jimmy, I'm telling you about Shuka and Talmah because Shuka now works for the Israel Antiquities Authority."

"He is an employee there?" Jim asked, a little stunned. "He's like the janitor, right?" he added sarcastically.

"No, Jimmy," she replied. "I think he is the head of the whole thing."

Jim's eyes flashed. Now he gripped the chair to stabilize himself. He couldn't believe what he was hearing. Juanita was his kids' art teacher when they were in high school. They had enjoyed friendly collegial banter for years.

"Juanita, are you pulling my leg, trying to convince me you happen to be good friends with the Director General of the IAA?"

"I'll prove I'm serious!" she retorted. "I'm calling him tomorrow."

Juanita kept her word and phoned Dorfman the next day. She explained to him that she had a friend for him to meet who had done some thought-provoking archaeological research. Dorfman insinuated that if Jim came to Israel, he would oblige his former host's request.

Juanita interrupted Jim's class to give him the good news. He shook his head in disbelief and announced to his students, "While I am trying to teach you how to write persuasively, Mrs. Pahdopony just proved that volcanic energy is the best trigger for a positive response. No one can say 'no' to this woman!"

It had only been seven months since his trip to Israel with Laurie, but Jim wasted no time cashing in on this momentous, and potentially only, opportunity to speak directly to the IAA. Jim and Chris were on a plane to Israel within weeks. Chris had planned to be free at a moment's notice; the notice came even sooner than he had anticipated.

SHUKA DORFMAN

Dorfman arranged for Jim and Chris to meet him and his wife at the David Citadel Hotel in Jerusalem. Dorfman's son was the assistant manager of the hotel. It was early Friday afternoon, and the city was bustling as Orthodox Jewish men, in fur hats and satin robes, briskly walked to the Western Wall for prayers. Orthodox women, in floor-length cotton skirts and scarf-covered heads, darted out to the produce stalls for last minute items for the Sabbath dinner. The Jewish sages taught that the Sabbath should be welcomed like the coming of a beautiful bride. Being in Jerusalem before the sun sets on a Friday is like observing frantic wedding preparations.

Sitting out on the balcony of the hotel, with a majestic view of the Old City, Dorfman and his wife talked with Jim and Chris about their mutual acquaintance, Juanita, and the couple's fond memories of their time living in Oklahoma. Dorfman had been a young officer during his training at Fort Sill, but the experience helped to launch his long and successful military career. He eventually rose to the rank of IDF brigadier general and chief artillery officer. After his military service, however, he desired to serve Israel in the cultural arena. He welcomed his appointment to the IAA in 2000. Dorfman, on the surface, was an odd choice. He was the first non-archaeologist, non-academic to hold the position of Director General.

A son of Holocaust survivors, Dorfman brought a tough outer shell to the job. He maintained immunity from the plethora of criticisms that his position naturally faced. If construction workers accidentally uncovered artifacts or old graves in the process of building storefronts, Dorfman decided if the real estate development could continue. When he opted for preservation over development, the entrepreneurs accused him of costing millions in the name of old bones or broken pillars. On the contrary, when he favored development over preservation, ultra-Orthodox Jewish groups—like the Haredi organization, Atra Kadisha—assailed Dorfman for allowing the desecration of Jewish graves.

Disturbing buried bones is prohibited under *halakha*, Jewish law. Atra Kadisha members are the self-appointed guardians of Israel's Jewish graves. They offer little mercy to whoever violates their conviction. Atra Kadisha members have been known to start street fights with IAA archaeologists, and graffiti threatening messages at IAA excavations. Talmah Dorfman was hospitalized after a large group of Haredi Jews attacked her in front of her home. The revenge attack on his wife provoked Dorfman to end any overtures of conciliation with the group.

Mostly, the fact that he had many enemies was a badge he carried proudly. He told a reporter, "When the leftists think you are a rightist and when the rightists think you are a leftist, when the Haredi Jews think that you are not even Jewish, and when everyone attacks you—then you know that you're doing a good job."[1]

Dorfman's son took a break from his hotel management duties to say hello to his parents and introduce himself to Jim and Chris. "You missed your Secretary of State, Condy Rice," he said. "She was staying here at the Citadel but left yesterday."

Jim retorted with a riff: "I'm sure she left me a note at the desk, angry that I hadn't come by to say hello."

After more small talk, Dorfman got to the point, "Well, Mr. Barfield, what can I do for you?"

"It's not what you can do for me," Jim replied, pausing for emphasis, "but what I can do for you."

"That scares me," Dorfman retorted, wincing a little.

Jim told Dorfman, "I believe I have identified all of the locations in the Copper Scroll."

As soon as Jim mentioned the Copper Scroll, Dorfman scratched his mop of curly hair, sighed deep, and said, "Well, go ahead then." He had clearly come to the meeting as a favor to an old friend and thought that old friend had sent him a crackpot.

"Show me what you have," Dorfman said with the most tolerant tone he could muster.

Jim laid the report on the patio table in front of them. He spelled out his research, starting with the explanation of the Valley of Achor, and how the scroll indicated that all the artifacts were buried at the same location. Jim illustrated how he had found locations in Qumran that fit every description offered in the Copper Scroll. Wisely, Jim withheld his beliefs on the background of the Copper Scroll, its link to II Maccabees or the *Treatise*, or any reference to being First Temple items. Planting biblical phraseology in an archaeological thesis was walking a minefield. One misstep and the entire argument could blow up in his face. Besides, Jim believed his First Temple views were irrelevant to his conclusions on the locations.

Flipping pages, Jim read the Copper Scroll's first location and pointed out on a map of Qumran his match for the *steps leading to the east forty cubits*. Jim explained his logic about the third location with the *cistern of the courtyard of the peristyle*. Dorfman's disposition softened. Uncrossing his arms, he was assuaged that the firefighter wasn't insane. What Jim showed him, up to that point, could perhaps have been a coincidence. But at least Jim's methodology was impressive. His proposition that every location was in Qumran seemed reasonable.

Jim planned to go through as much of the report as possible. When he got to his fourth location, the *double entry pool*, Dorfman leaned forward for a closer look. He blew out his cheeks. Seeing that Dorfman agreed that the pool was a convincing match, Jim went on, "There are nine matching fingerprints between the Copper Scroll and the *double entry pool* at Qumran. With nine matching fingerprints, as an investigator, we would throw a guy in jail."

Dorfman put his hand up, telling Jim he had no need for him to go further. Still looking intently over the map of location four, he pulled out his cellphone and called up the two main Israeli archaeologists for Qumran: Yitzhak Magen and Yuval Peleg. Dorfman said to the men on the other line, "I have something you need to see."

Jim and Chris left the Citadel Hotel with a plan to reconvene at the IAA offices in a few days for a meeting with Magen and Peleg.

BUREAUCRACY OF ARCHAEOLOGY

Even if Dorfman believed Jim's theory was worth testing, Jim still had to lobby the other shareholders. Technically, the IAA does not have jurisdiction over Qumran. Qumran falls under Israel's Archaeology Department of the Civil Administration (ADCA), a separate institution. Qumran is part of the "West Bank"—known to Jews as their historic Judea and Samaria; to Palestinians, it is illegally occupied land.

Qumran is nestled near the rocky sandstone cliffs where the West Bank meets the Jordan River. Different archaeological rules apply to areas in the West Bank than to Israel proper. Although Israel wrested control over the West Bank in 1967, the international community deems it disputed territory. Unlike Jerusalem, Israel never annexed the West Bank; instead, they held on to the swath of land as part of the government's strategy to trade "land for peace."

Under the Oslo Accords—the Israeli-Palestinian peace process which started in 1993 but has since run aground—the West Bank was split into three areas. Area A was under exclusive Palestinian control; Area B gave Palestinians civilian control and Israelis security control; Area C was under both

Israeli civil and security control. Qumran was part of Area C. Since 1967, Qumran, like the rest of Area C, has been completely controlled by Israel. Still, if negotiations for a peace agreement ever produced a two-state solution, Qumran could possibly be drawn into the new Palestinian state. For that reason, Israel's conservative political factions promote annexation of Area C.

Palestinian sympathizers occasionally attend international exhibitions of the Dead Sea Scrolls to protest Israel's title to the cultural property, never mind that the scrolls are Jewish texts written in Hebrew. Near the final stages of the Oslo Accords, Palestinian negotiators demanded a freeze on all active excavations in the Judean Desert. In turn, the Institute for Islamic Archaeology issued a position paper demanding that Israel relinquish all artifacts excavated in the West Bank during the previous three decades.

Considering the rich Jewish history in sites sprinkled all over Judea and Samaria, Israel regards it as essential to conduct explorations while it is still in control of the contested territory, even if the awkward political situation muddies the archaeological waters. Since 1967, over 3,000 archaeological sites in the West Bank have been surveyed by the ADCA. When an artifact is found, it goes to military storage facilities, the whereabouts of which are kept under wraps, and visitors are prohibited. Only select artifacts make it to Israel's museums and universities. This is because international law[2] prohibits archaeological digs in disputed territories and judges the siphoning of disputed cultural property equal to antiquities theft. The warehouse contents await a season when their discovery is less controversial. (Note: The British Museum in London—the greatest benefactor of imperialist archaeology—would be stripped bare if antiquities laws were enforced retroactively.)

Yitzhak Magen was the Staff Officer for Archaeology (SOA) in the ADCA for 25 years. The assignment is a lifetime term and allows limitless power. No archaeologist wanting to dig in the area did so without first going through Magen. Critics accused Magen of turning the area into his "personal sandbox."[3] Vendyl first warned Jim, "Yitzhak has all the keys, to all the doors."

Only outsiders to the ADCA required excavation permits. Magen's staff was free to dig without the burden of applying for a license. What transpired from this situation was that an overworked and busily excavating staff often neglected to fulfill their publishing responsibilities. In 2007, Israeli researchers sued the ADCA—and won—for withholding data about their findings that should have been made public. In Magen's defense, because of the tense political situation, many foreign scholars were hesitant to dig in the West Bank.

Jim was clueless about the nuances of Israeli archaeological agencies.

MAGEN AND PELEG

Jim and Chris took advantage of the days leading up to their meeting. They caught a morning bus out from Jerusalem to Qumran. It was Chris's first trip. Jim ran into the cafeteria to grab them breakfast while Chris shadowed a group of American tourists starting their tour. The guide was summarizing the collection of Dead Sea Scrolls found in Qumran caves. Chris happened to walk over as the guide was elucidating the mysterious Copper Scroll—a scroll that most of the tourists had never heard about. One man, wearing a wide-brimmed straw hat, asked the guide, "Why hasn't anyone ever tried to find the Copper Scroll treasures?"

Chris strained to hear the answer. "One man continues the search: Vendyl Jones," the guide responded. "He has been looking for the items for most of his life. I think he is getting close."

"If he hasn't found anything already, then maybe the Copper Scroll items aren't real," stated another male tourist with a heavy Southern accent.

An older woman replied loud enough for Chris to hear, "I think they are real, and I think it will all be found soon." By the time Jim returned with eggs poached in spicy tomato sauce, Chris was smirking with satisfaction. The tour guide moved on to the topic of the Dead Sea's shrinking shoreline.

Jim and Chris ate under a shaded pavilion while Jim pointed out the watchtower, great cistern, and other key locations. Chris marveled over the modesty of the ruins. The tour groups struggled to find an emblematic background for their group photo.

Before Qumran got too crowded, Jim snuck with Chris up the path out of Qumran to show him the *hill of Kokhlit*. Scouting around the rock formation, Jim noticed a sinkhole. The sinkhole had developed since his last visit to Qumran, most likely a byproduct of the tumultuous floods during the 2007 rainy season. Four experienced rappelers had been swept to their deaths by flash floods in the area. Jim put both palms down inside the sinkhole. He guessed it was the size of a basketball. It formed at the exact spot where Jim believed the cave entrance was buried. A dozen cracks, emanating from the hole like sun rays, sloped up toward the cave entry.

Jim looked at Chris and said, "You know sinkholes form when a void lies below. Why else would this be here?"

Chris fanned the back of his shirt to keep it from sticking to his back. He recalled that in his dream, Jim had showed him a desert landscape filled with holes and one hill. Only once Chris climbed up the rocky mound did he understand that the locations inside Qumran were represented by the holes, and *Kokhlit* was the hill.

Jim snapped several pictures of the sinkhole. If the hole got bigger, he wanted photo documentation. They walked back down the craggy decline to the Qumran complex. Since the last time Jim was at Qumran with Laurie, he had identified forty more of the locations, all of which he needed to verify. He and Chris carefully walked over each site, confirming measurements of walls and common rooms. They reenacted traffic patterns that the Essenes likely followed, according to belief structures described in sectarian scrolls like the *Community Rule*. When necessary, Jim modified his investigator's comparison. He also came prepared with calculations estimating how much space was needed to bury dense hordes of gold and silver.

After a drink break, Jim wanted to confirm how the last scribe's five sites made a flawlessly straight line, not just on a satellite map, but on the ground. Jim stood at the first of the five locations and had Chris stand back at the *hill of Kokhlit*, the final scribe's last location. In their pockets, they each had one of Laurie's compact mirrors. Luckily, it was a sunny day. When they held up the mirrors, a ray of light reflected off Jim's mirror, passed in a straight line through each of the fourth scribe's locations, and hit Chris's mirror at the cave. Jim recounted the moment to me later, "We were crazy happy. I don't know what the Qumran workers thought when Chris and I started jumping up and down, holding lady mirrors."

As scheduled, Jim and Chris went on a Tuesday to the Rockefeller Museum in East Jerusalem—the headquarters for the IAA—to meet with Dorfman, Magen, and Peleg. The fortress-like compound encircles a rectangular courtyard and reflecting pool. The smell of jasmine wafted from the gardens. With its hexagonal tower, the museum combines the architectural style of the Ottomans with Jerusalem's signature white limestone.

In 1938, American philanthropist John D. Rockefeller Jr. financed the museum's construction to house the large volume of antiquities surfacing during the British Mandate. Ten years later, after Israel's War of Independence and an uneasy cease-fire, Jerusalem stood divided. The compound—then named the Palestine Archaeological Museum—landed on the Jordanian side of the barbed wire border. By default, the Jordanian Department of Antiquities took full ownership of the growing collection of Dead Sea Scrolls. They nationalized the museum in 1966. Only the scrolls from Cave 1 were under Israeli ownership.

During the Six Day War, in a clash to reunite the Israeli capital and reclaim Jewish history, an IDF paratroop brigade commandeered the museum. Bullet holes riddling the compound's edifice pay tribute to the raging night fracas with Jordanian snipers. While shots were still being fired, three Israeli archaeologists accompanied a military escort to the compound. Securing the Dead Sea Scrolls was their first order of business. At the same time, the famous Israeli archaeologist and military commander Yigal Yadin sent Israeli intelligence officers to Bethlehem. After a day of interrogations, the officers coerced Kando to hand over a shoebox containing the *Temple Scroll*. The keynote manuscript was held hostage under Kando's bedroom floor tiles for two decades.[4] Kando was fully reimbursed for the forced transaction. He secretly transferred the rest of his scroll collection to a safety deposit box in Switzerland.

Israel transferred the complete scrolls to safer territory in the Israel Museum in West Jerusalem. Thousands of unpublished fragments stayed in the Rockefeller Museum and continued to be studied by the primary international team of editors. Though the Israeli authorities tried not to interfere with the ongoing work of the text editors, they soon moved the IAA's offices into the compound. (Then the IAA was known as the Israel Department of Antiquities and Museums.) They found a quiet home in the turf once off limits to them as Israelis and as Jewish scholars. However, it took another fifteen years for the first Israelis to wedge their way onto the international team.

Compared to the Israel Museum, the Rockefeller Museum brings few tourists, primarily because of its location in the predominately Muslim side of Jerusalem, right outside of the Old City walls. During the spike of suicide bombings that started in 2000 and left over 800 Israelis dead and 4,000 injured, the museum was almost ghost-like. The haphazard displays of noteworthy artifacts, representing all three of Jerusalem's faiths, linger among aging architecture. Some of the archaeological material from de Vaux's excavations of Qumran still languishes in the museum's basement.

The five men took their seats at a conference table in Dorfman's office, sipping on Nescafé in Styrofoam cups. After a short introduction from Dorfman, Jim thumbed through his thick report to the first map of Qumran and launched into his theory. Magen—with sunglasses perched on the end of his nose despite the room's dim lighting—made clear from his dour expression that he had no interest in research pertaining to the Copper Scroll. Chris prayed silently as he tried to keep from withering under Magen's gaze.

Though explorers looking for the Ark of the Covenant were so common they tripped over each other in Israel, treasure hunters rarely made it inside the IAA offices. They are mockingly nicknamed "ark-eologists." Until Jim could prove himself, Magen automatically pegged him in the ark-eologist camp. Jim went into the meeting understanding there would be an academic prejudice against him. Magen pushed the report across the table to Peleg, his second in command. Peleg was younger, and more inclined to think outside of the box.

As Peleg listened closely to Jim and examined the maps, he seemed to care less about Jim's lack of credentials and more about the bizarre correlations Jim identified between the Copper Scroll and Qumran ruins. Few people knew the site more intimately than Peleg. During Magen and Peleg's years-long excavation at Qumran, they verified an early Iron Age occupation, for which Peleg had yet to find an adequate explanation.[5] Perhaps the Copper Scroll held the answers.

Jim prudently explained his matches for the scroll's first five sites and last five sites. Magen sat with his arms folded. Peleg studied each location description carefully. After Jim finished his exposition, Peleg leaned into Dorfman and mumbled something in Hebrew. Dorfman nodded in agreement. Though Jim didn't understand him, Chris was surreptitiously recording the meeting with a small digital audio recorder in his pocket.

Leaving the building, Dorfman asked for a copy of the report on compact disc. Jim wanted to give it to him but asked that he sign a nondisclosure statement. Dorfman demurred. Archaeologists loathe signing anything that limits their publication rights. In the end, Jim relented and gave Dorfman and Peleg a digital copy of the research. If they ever tested Jim's research without him, he had the audio recording of their meeting as evidence. Also, Chris carefully took a picture of all the men at the table looking at Jim's maps.

Jim reminded the men, "Our objective is to restore the treasures and artifacts of the Copper Scroll to the nation of Israel by operating directly with you all to recover any artifacts that may exist at Qumran."

Magen replied, "We have been digging all over Qumran. I swear this stuff isn't there."

"Don't forget, though," Jim said politely. "The Copper Scroll says the items were stashed twelve to eighteen feet underground. Have you ever dug at Qumran below virgin soil?"

Magen shrugged and looked away. Peleg shook his head "no."

After the meeting, Jim and Chris went for lunch at a quiet café in a hidden courtyard, *Tmol Shilshom*. Amid stacks of books lining the perimeter of the cobblestone walls, they debriefed. The anticipation of the week left Jim feeling drained. As they recounted the meeting and tried to determine the reason for Magen's overt hostility, they kept coming back to the observation that the research clearly resonated with Peleg. Because of his reserved expressions, however, they were unsure of the extent.

Jim had an idea. Flagging down their waiter, he asked him if he could listen to an audio recording and translate the Hebrew for them. Chris had it cued to the final minutes of the meeting when Peleg mumbled something to Dorfman. The waiter listened to the recording twice, without knowing the context, and told Jim, "The man said, 'I think he has done it.'" Jim's eyes went wide and his jaw went slack.

CHAPTER 8
SLEUTHS

Although the first meeting with Dorfman and the ADCA went better than expected, Jim left Israel with no indication that anything further would be done. Still, Jim hoped that if Peleg genuinely thought, in his own words, that Jim "had done it," perhaps it wouldn't matter that Magen had a dim view of Jim.

For months Jim anticipated a phone call from the Israelis. A call never came. Jim reached out to Dorfman several times but heard no response. He interpreted their silence as disinterest, but not a total rift in the relationship. Perhaps to the IAA, Jim was a harmless dreamer, captured by his own naiveté.

Laurie, tired of feeling her restless husband toss in bed each night, told him to get back on a plane to Israel to see what he and Chris could do in person. And that's what they did. Jim and Chris arrived in Israel in December 2007. It was Jim's third trip to Israel in a year. They tried to secure a follow-up meeting with Dorfman, Magen or Peleg. Preoccupied with other excavations, all three were elusive. Jim got so antsy that he went to Qumran to make sure they weren't secretly testing his research without him. Qumran was exactly as he left it, including the sinkhole. Frustrated at his own hastiness to buy a flight to Israel, and the ADCA's lack of response, Jim rang Tamar Yonah.

Yonah, a religious Zionist with gladiatorial opinions, is the hostess for Israel's most popular radio talk show in English, hosted on Israel National News. Yonah's listeners are mostly Orthodox English-speaking Jews, on the right of Israel's political spectrum. Jim included himself among her fans. He emailed her on occasion about her programs, to which she always replied. When he told her he was in Israel, Yonah invited her out-of-town listener over for dinner with her family.

Yonah lived in Beit El—an Israeli community in the West Bank, also known by the contentious term of "settlement." A little north of Jerusalem, the Jewish settlement is sandwiched between populous Palestinian areas and protected by a large IDF base. Driving with Yonah into Beit El, past the towering cement security wall, Jim and Chris were surprised to find pristine roads lined with white block houses and slanting red tile roofs. Under the bright blue sky and long stretches of cirrus clouds, billboards advertised Israeli cellphone plans and soft cheeses. Children rode scooters in the street.

On the other side of the settlement fence was Ramallah, the de facto capital for the Palestinian Authority. From a hilltop, Yonah pointed out the late Palestinian leader Yasser Arafat's compound with its rooftop satellite dishes, a stone throw's away. In 2004, she heard on the news that Arafat was being airlifted out of Ramallah for emergency medical treatment. "I stepped out on my back patio to yell curses at the terrorist in his helicopter, one last time," Yonah laughed.

Touring her home, she showed them her nine-year-old son's backyard archaeological dig. He had roped off the parched earth in a small square where he found a few first-century coins. Growing up in a country with such deep historical roots, it's said that if anyone so much as sticks a shovel in the ground, they'll find something. Amateur archaeology is a clandestine Israeli past time.

Already apprised of Jim's theory on Qumran, Yonah was keen on the *Copper Scroll Project*. She, like many religious Israelis, expected archaeology to be the catalyst for a national revival, putting aside any doubts about the land's spiritual heritage or ancestral roots. Yet she was still curious about Jim's religious status.

"Jim, what the heck are you? A Noahide? A Christian?" Yonah wondered. She had interviewed Vendyl on her radio program and thought perhaps Jim, like Vendyl, was involved in the Noahide community. The daughter of a Holocaust survivor, she was dubious of non-Jews, as a rule.

"I am a guy who wants to see your nation whole again," Jim replied.

Yonah sighed, scratching her head under her covering. She glanced at Chris who gave a shrug and said "same." Yonah accepted that they were a paradox.

Serving chopped salads and bland white cheese, both local passions, Tamar got straight to the point. "Jim and Chris, you have come along way. How can I help your project?" she said.

"I can't get the archaeological authorities to call me back," Jim groused. He reached for the fresh lemonade with mint. "We are desperate and want to meet someone at the Temple Institute."

Jim explained to Yonah and her husband that although he deeply respected Gershon Salomon at the Temple Mount Faithful, he also desired to show the Temple Institute his research. With two different leaderships, the Temple Institute had a similar mission as Salomon's group but was much larger, moderate, and influential—the giant of the Temple Mount movement.

Salomon was less Orthodox but more controversial than other Temple Mount devotees. He advocated for the immediate dismantlement of the Muslim shrines atop the Temple Mount. The Temple Institute was more diplomatic, focusing on readiness for a Third Temple rather than its immediate construction. On the question of timing, the Temple Institute cited the Talmudic tradition that the Temple could only be rebuilt when the people merited it.

In Jim's last conversation with Salomon, he told him of his intention to reach out to all the major players in the Temple Mount movement. Jim believed strongly in the value of cross-organizational communication. On the fateful day in 1995, when the Oklahoma City bombing left 168 people dead, Jim happened to be the chair of the board for the Red Cross's disaster services. Jim oversaw coordinating between the military and civil rescue responders at the site. What he called "the hardest 72 hours of my life" shaped forever his prioritization of having all relevant parties toiling in sync.

"On the chance that a holy object is found at Qumran, I don't want to catch the Temple organizations off guard. I want to know that they can reinstate the vessels as required, without quarreling or competition," Jim told Yonah.

Jim guessed rightly that Yonah possessed the connections to make an introduction. Yonah happened to be acquainted with an important leader in the Temple Institute. The rabbi had his own radio program at her station. Yonah agreed to set up a meeting but insisted that Jim keep the arrangement confidential.

TEMPLE INSTITUTE

The Temple Institute acts as a cultural and educational center in the heart of Jerusalem's Old City. While the Temple Institute's long-term goal is to rebuild the Temple, in the meantime, they've assembled what one spokesperson calls a "Temple in waiting." Fulltime research staff and able artisans reconstruct Temple elements from gold, silver, and other valuable material, as stipulated in the Torah. Should the event ever arise that the Temple Mount had a vacancy, blueprints for a Third Temple are prepped to launch construction. Vitrines at the Temple Institute's gallery are stacked with ritually qualified flasks, lavers, pitchers, decanters, lyre, and trumpets. They have designed custom-fitted priestly garments, including the gem-encrusted breastplate for the high priest. Members of the priesthood take classes at the institute on the meticulous laws and rituals of Temple service, including animal sacrifice.

The institute's presence is felt near the Western Wall by passersby who pause to take selfies with the golden menorah in its glass showcase. Six feet tall, overlaid with pure gold, the three-million-dollar lampstand is the most popular example of their Third Temple collection. In the visitor center, a gilded replica of the Ark of the Covenant is prominently displayed in the last showcase, dramatically revealed behind automated curtains. Mounted paintings depict the Israelites transporting the consecrated repository through the desert on their shoulders. Sparks launch out from between the cherubim to clear the way, killing snakes and scorpions. In other prominent art, the Ark is featured as Joshua's weapon of war, a critical player in bringing down the walls of Jericho. A smaller painting portrays the colorful account of David's half-naked dance for the Ark's homecoming to Jerusalem, an act of veneration that endears the flawed king to every Bible believer.

Most of the institute's reproductions are kosher and ready for use in the Third Temple—like the copper wash basin and table of showbread. The Ark is a mockup for research and instruction only. Only the real Ark—the symbol of Israel's covenant with God—will suffice for the Holy of Holies. The institute has a gift shop for tourists to load up on *ephod* aprons, paperweight menorahs, snow globe Temples, and three-dimensional Ark of the Covenant puzzles.

Unlike Salomon, the Temple Institute was traditionally reticent to accept Christian encouragement or even financial help in their costly endeavors. Jim knew the idea of a gentile locating Israel's lost vessels would likely be an awkward pitch.

After Yonah made the arrangements for the meeting, Jim and Chris made their way to the rabbi's office near Zion Square, on the upper floor of a surprisingly modern building by Jerusalem standards. Like most public spaces in Israel, guests had to open their bags for a security officer and submit to a metal detector scan before getting past the entry. After taking an elevator up and finding the unmarked office door, Jim and Chris were buzzed into the waiting area. Once inside, the secretary warned Jim that the rabbi was on a tight schedule. She ushered them into his office.

The rabbi motioned for them to sit. The American-born rabbi was clad in the uniform of the Orthodox, a holdover from eighteenth-century Europe: baggy suit with a black hat. Jim began his introduction by asking the rabbi if he was familiar with the Copper Scroll. As soon as he alluded to the Copper Scroll, the rabbi rolled his eyes, stood up and slipped off his black jacket. He revealed that he was carrying a Glock pistol on a holster.

Before Jim showed him the research, the rabbi—unremittingly humorless—interrogated Jim on his intentions. Israel's antiquities laws say that when an artifact is found legally, the finder gets five percent of the value. Assuming Jim was another enterprising explorer in the Holy Land, the rabbi tried to bait him. "What do you expect to do with the finder's fee?" he asked.

"I am not a treasure hunter," Jim answered. "My central desire in getting involved with the Copper Scroll is to return the items to the rightful owners: the nation of Israel."

"If God has selected me to do this," Jim went on, "He gave it to a guy that doesn't give a darn about wealth. I want to return these items to Israel and what they do from that point is up to them."

The rabbi looked pleased with Jim's answer, until Jim added offhandedly, "As far as I'm concerned, Israel could give the finder's fee to all of the Jews who were kicked out of their homes in Gaza." Two years had passed since Israel unilaterally pulled its citizens out of their homes in Gaza, a tiny strip of land on the shore of the Mediterranean Sea bordering Egypt and Israel. Israeli news was filled with stories of how the evacuees had yet to be resettled into permanent communities. Half the staff in the Temple Institute offices still donned the orange wrist bands representing opposition to the Gaza disengagement.

The rabbi misunderstood Jim to be saying that Israel was right to evacuate settlers from their homes. Jim immediately recognized that he had somehow hit a raw nerve for the rabbi, but it was too late. In response the rabbi spit at Jim, like an Old Testament prophet. He got up to escort Jim out of his office.

"Wait, wait. You don't understand," Jim stammered, bemused by how quickly things went sour. "I'm really sorry about the Gaza disengagement. That's not at all what this is about."

Jim quickly pulled out his report. "Let me explain to you my theory," Jim said, then added, "after that, you can decide if you want to kick me out." The rabbi sat down, slightly pacified but arms folded.

Jim showed the rabbi the first five and last five sites on the map of Qumran. The rabbi hunched over the maps and research, repeatedly glancing at Jim as if he were surprised by Jim's rich knowledge of the Temple inventory. The rabbi's manner soon warmed; he settled down, knowing he was among like minds. Chris pulled out the audio recording from the meeting with Dorfman, Magen, and Peleg. He put the small device on the table and asked the rabbi to listen. After hearing Peleg say, "I think he has done it," the rabbi smiled and stroked his beard.

Jim's theory, in all its simplicity and obviousness, clearly stirred the rabbi. Although the Temple Institute had research staff that spent an inordinate amount of time deliberating the locations of hidden Temple artifacts, they had made little headway in comparison to the gentile American firefighter. Getting up from his desk, the rabbi walked over to Jim, grabbed him by the shoulders and kissed him on both cheeks.

"We boys in Oklahoma aren't used to the cheek kissing thing," Jim laughed. He felt dizzy from the rabbi's quick transition from umbrage to affection.

"Jim, tell me this," the rabbi said. "If it is all as obvious as you are presenting here, why hasn't anybody else figured it out already?"

"I don't know. That's the vexing question I keep mulling over." He gesticulated as he tried to come up with an answer. "Maybe, sometimes the simplest solution is the hardest to come by."

"These items are our birthright," the rabbi mused, running his fingers through his beard.

"Yes, they are, sir," Jim stated, "and I believe I can find them." His eyes moistened along the edges.

Chris intervened and added, "For now, we want to be good stewards of the research."

The rabbi, suddenly gregarious, explained the messianic process to Jim and Chris. He referred to the Temple as the crown jewel for world peace, divine peace. He lamented that the loss of the Temple created a void for the whole world. If even one artifact from the Temple could be unearthed, then humanity might awaken to the source of her collective ache. The Temple Institute based their positivity on the message of the prophets. The rabbi quoted from Isaiah 2: "In the last days, the mountain of the Lord's temple will be established as the highest of the mountains; it will be exalted above the hills, and all nations will stream to it."

As soon as they left the Temple Institute offices and were out of sight, Jim bent down and sobbed uncontrollably. He hadn't cried that hard since the first breakfast he had with Laurie after several sleepless days and nights working the aftermath of the Oklahoma City Bombing. Then, as now, he bore the yoke of a tremendous commission.

DESERT SLEUTHS

With two days left on their Israel trip, Chris and Jim went to Jerusalem's Café Aroma to brainstorm how they could make the remaining days productive. There was still no word or even sign of life from the ADCA. Sitting in intermittent silence as they sipped their iced coffee and broke off pieces of bagel, they both tinkered around with the previously unthinkable idea of an illegal excavation.

"You know," Chris said, "we can't afford many more trips to Israel to push them to action."

Jim nodded. Even a simple peek into the buried cave had seemed unthinkable, but he was getting impatient with their limited options.

"Digging inside Qumran, with locked gates and an armed after-hours security guard, is out of the question," Jim said.

"But the *hill of Kokhlit* is unprotected," Chris countered. "It's outside the fence and hardly considered a cultural heritage site."

Under the premise that poking around the *hill of Kokhlit* was technically legal, Jim and Chris agreed on a scheme that seemed the least risky. They left the coffee shop to buy a piece of PVC pipe from a local hardware store. If they could stick the PVC pipe into the ground, by the sinkhole, they could then funnel a small camera through it and take pictures inside the cavity. They figured they would barely even have to break ground.

The following night, with butterflies in their stomachs, Jim and Chris rented a car to drive to Qumran. When Jim was a helicopter pilot in the Army, he was trained as a combat scout pilot; identifying paths of approach for attack was his milieu. They parked on the side of the road, several miles from Qumran's visitor center. The landscape around Qumran made finding a concealed route easy. Two *wadis* (dry ravines) weave their way to the site, one on its north and one on its west side. They knew they could easily navigate their way through the dry watercourse without being spotted from the ground.

Carrying headlamps and backpacks, Jim and Chris began their hike up the wadi as soon as the sun began to dip behind the Dead Sea. Intentionally, they gave the impression of two guys on a rappelling trip. As the extending shadows of Qumran started to come into view, Jim's butterflies turned into total regret. He worried that in one fell swoop they would spoil the integrity of the *Copper Scroll Project* and the legitimacy of any potential find. He cranked around to face Chris and said, "Jimmy D is about to sissy-boy out." Chris looked relieved.

The two marched back in silence. As the darkness of the desert deepened, they could barely see the silhouette of their parked car. After the impish mission, Jim understood his sensitive conscience prevented him from going outside of the law. "All is lost if I veer from the official path," he told Laurie when he got home. "I have to believe that the Israeli authorities will eventually come through and provide a controlled excavation."

CHAPTER 9

PREDATORS

Jim and Laurie had limited savings. They mostly lived off their retirement pensions. The money had been enough for their humble lifestyle, but two trips to Israel in one year stretched the family budget. Jim knew he couldn't afford to keep flying to Israel to knock on doors. He also knew that if even if somehow, he got permission to dig with a willing archaeologist, he didn't have the finances to subsidize the project.

Jim reluctantly started doing speaking engagements with the intention of fundraising. Although he loved the teaching aspects of public speaking and naturally connected with audiences, he felt uneasy asking for donations. He had always been turned off by "health and wealth" televangelists—preachers that stylize the Christian gospel to focus on financial blessings. He wanted to avoid any resemblance of that message, so much so that he never brought himself to make direct appeals for financing during his talks.

A friend, who knew of Jim's dilemma, gave him a card for a man named Blake Foster. The card indicated that Blake was a consultant for faith-based organizations—a "philanthropic professional." Blake's website touted his ability to train and transform ministry leaders. Jim wasn't sure how Blake could consult him to success, but he left no stone unturned. To be sure, he never would have expected his online Hebrew tutor, Miriam, to be the longtime secretary of Vendyl Jones. Never would he have imagined that his coworker, Juanita, had a long-term friendship with the Director General of the IAA. His journey had proven the dictum that help often came from the most unexpected places.

Taking the card, he called Blake Foster. After only talking to Jim about the *Copper Scroll Project* for twenty minutes on the phone, Blake was already a whole-hearted fan. Jim offered to meet with him to walk him through his Copper Scroll research. Blake said he didn't need to see the written report to be convinced. Believing that he had a spiritual gift for connecting people, Blake swore he would help find both an archaeologist and funders.

BISHOP EATON

Blake arranged for he, Jim, and Chris to meet a potential patron named Barney Eaton for coffee in Dallas. According to Blake, Barney had connections in Israel at the highest levels. He was a philanthropist and nonprofit consultant. At their first meeting, Barney introduced himself to Jim and Chris as "Bishop Eaton." He was short and squatty with wide-set eyes, a toothy smile, and hair combed in a side part. The back of his thick neck bulged over his collar band. What Barney lacked in stature, he made up for with panache.

While the three men waited for Blake, delayed by rain, Barney explained how he and his wife started their own nonprofit organization with the goal of bringing faith-based organizations together. Though he had yet to see Jim's report, Barney said Blake had given him the gist of it over the phone. Barney told Jim in a nonchalant manner that his group of benefactors would fully finance a dig. As for the archaeologist, Barney explained, "I'm well connected with plenty of archaeologists working in Israel. I can get one of those guys to do it."

Jim was taken aback by Barney's immediate offers of sponsorship. Without sharing the research behind his Copper Scroll theory, he hardly felt like he had earned Barney's patronage. Jim had to ask, "What motivates you to fund this dig?"

"Are you kidding me? I want to be involved with something that has world-changing implications!" Barney exclaimed. "As payment for my efforts, I merely ask to have the right to a video crew at the site to take documentary footage."

"You have a documentary crew?" Jim asked.

"This video will be top-notch," Barney replied, "complete with high definition cameras and three-dimensional rendering." Chris noticed that Barney didn't give a direct answer to Jim's question.

Right then, Blake walked into the coffee shop, shaking rain from his jacket. After he ordered an Americano, he announced to the men that he had good news relating to their phase three: public relations. Blake explained how he had gotten in touch with a social media executive that had launched a new startup company in Bedford, Texas. According to Blake, the company was on its way to being "bigger than Google." Blake explained his hope that the *Copper Scroll Project* could be used to buttress the upstart tech company, and vice versa.

"Right after the discoveries at Qumran are made, we will orchestrate all the press releases and images of the artifacts," Blake said. "When we release footage or announcements, they should only be available through a portal on the new website."

Jim and Chris simultaneously furrowed their brows. Though only Barney was nodding affirmatively, Blake ticked off ideas as fast and steady as a heart rate monitor. "People will have to login with all their contact information before getting the story about the dig and its finds. Millions of people will visit the site!"

Jim questioned how a social media website was relevant to his primary goal of securing a permit to dig. Blake demurred, "I'm only an old farm boy from Missouri, but when I hear from the Lord, I know he is up to something."

Over the next month, Barney and Blake's zeal continued to surge. The consultant duo brought Jim and Chris to several meetings with various media specialists. When talk of one website idea would fade, a new design on how to harness the press emerged. Before long, all the consultant speech left Jim weary, and the ideas all sounded the same. Jim was indifferent to most of what Barney and Blake were advising. Their focus was on how to handle the distribution of information after discoveries were made. Jim was less worried about the handling of press releases than he was the handling of the artifacts.

It eventually got to the point that when Blake's number appeared on Jim's caller ID, Jim felt his every muscle go weak. Blake and Barney's verbosity was taking too much of Jim's time. All the same, if the consultant and patron didn't threaten the sanctity of the artifacts, or the goal of restoring the relics to Israel, Jim acquiesced. He needed an archaeologist, permit, and resources; they pledged to be his ticket for all three.

Sensing Jim's uneasiness with nonstop public relations talk, Blake tried to spiritualize the connections he offered Jim. One evening, he picked up Jim and

Chris and told them they were going to meet a prophetess named Melanie—a friend of his from church who was known for her dreams and visions. Melanie was a petite woman with an intensely charismatic faith. When Melanie first met Jim, she clapped her hands and in a singsongy voice began spouting out prophecies. "A year ago, I had a vision," she told Jim. "Every time I prayed for Blake I saw him in a cave. The cave was filled with lots of gold and sacred items." Because of that dream, she was certain Blake was meant to be part of the excavation.

Melanie added, "I also had a vision of you, Jim. In my vision, you stood with a group of people. You were all being recognized. But you, you were being crowned by a gleaming black angel. The angel put rings on your fingers and cloth over your hands."

As the relationship progressed, Blake and Barney labored to present themselves as men of wealth and importance. The more time Jim and Chris spent with them, however, the veil of their image began to fall off. When Barney presented Jim with a leather Italian briefcase as a token of appreciation, Jim noted the used briefcase was broken and torn in places. Blake and Barney, themselves, lived in small rental apartments and drove old vehicles. After a lunch with some of Barney's supposedly high-profile media contacts, Chris gave a ride to one of the men who, according to Blake, was an esteemed television producer in Dallas. Chris was surprised a successful professional lived in an old shack with his mother. At one point, Jim overheard Blake explaining to someone on the phone that he had to postpone a payment because he lost a significant amount of investments. Jim later learned Blake had followed Melanie the prophetess's financial advice and been burned. Whether the men were intentional hucksters, or innocently naive, Jim was becoming less comfortable with either scenario.

One night, after meeting again with Melanie the prophetess and hearing more of her strange dreams, Chris had a meaningful dream of his own. In the dream, he, Jim, Laurie, and their son Shawn were running through ankle-deep water in a ravine. The maze of the riverbed brought them to a dead end, much like Wadi Qumran. All four clambered out over the sides to escape. Perched from above, they peeked into the crevasse. A Tyrannosaurus Rex, wearing a bishop's hat, jerked around his repugnant head, roaring, and stomping. In Chris's dream, the creature was too short-necked to spy them from its lower position.

Jim and Chris were about to tell the Blake-Barney band that the alliance was done, and the *Copper Scroll Project* was going back on its own, when Barney made a pronouncement. In a month, he promised, he was going to fly Jim and Chris to Israel. Barney was also going to bring his sister, wife, and son.

Jim expressed hesitation about going to Israel merely for a goodwill tour. Barney assured Jim that the trip was with the intention of getting the excavation started. A respectable archaeologist would secure the permit by the time they arrived. If for any reason the dig was delayed, Barney said they were going to be attended to by one of Barney's contacts, an IDF general named Avi Sandler.

"General Sandler will be picking us up at the airport and making arrangements for the excavation," Barney clarified. "When we are with the General, there will never be a time that we aren't surrounded by tight security, so be expecting it. At barricades, Avi's black suburban will bypass the waiting cars. The IDF will salute him as he goes by."

Barney guaranteed that General Sandler had the contacts to introduce Jim to Israel's Prime Minister Ehud Olmert—just in case things with the IAA needed a little push from the top. Barney said he was positive that after Israeli dignitaries understood the implications of the Copper Scroll, they would cut the red tape and expedite dig plans.

Jim consented to going on the trip, even though he had a gnawing feeling in his gut. At least, Jim reasoned, he would find out, one way or another, what Barney and Blake were up to. If Barney couldn't deliver something in Israel, their affiliation would be over and Jim could strategize. "It's time for them to poop or get off the pot," Jim told Laurie. If Barney and Blake delivered on even a quarter of their big promises, this trip had the potential to be Jim's big breakthrough.

VIP TOUR

Jim asked to bring Laurie and Shawn with him on the trip. Barney readily agreed and paid for all their tickets. For reasons that Jim didn't know, Barney didn't invite Blake. Much to his chagrin, Blake stayed in Texas.

Getting off the plane in Tel Aviv, Jim's entourage got their first red flag. General Avi Sandler, in fact, looked like a run-of-the-mill Israeli tour guide.

He stood at the arrival gate with a poster scribbled with black sharpie: "Welcome to Israel, Eatons and Barfields!" The vehicle fetching them from the airport was no suburban motorcade; it was a standard Israeli passenger van meant for tour groups.

Loading their luggage into the van, Jim whispered to Barney, "This is not what I was expecting. When are we going to dig?"

"I've been promised that the permit will be here in a couple of days, and we can start the excavation," answered Barney. "Until it arrives, let's enjoy a little tour of Israel."

"Who is General Sandler?"

"Don't say anything to Avi, but he is procuring the permit right now," Barney said in a hushed tone. "He's in the Mossad, so he is naturally very secretive about stuff. He is in the middle of negotiating with archaeologists."

Jim seriously doubted an Israel intelligence agent was posing as a tour guide, but he held his tongue and boarded the van to head for the hotel.

For the first several days the group traversed all over Jerusalem and Bethlehem. They stopped at each religious landmark, which are as plentiful as the rocks on Jerusalem's hillsides. Avi clearly specialized in touring Christian groups, and true to his alleged rank, he conducted his tour like a miniature boot camp. They often had to don biblical era clothing while reading the relevant scriptures at the holy sites or singing hymns. Barney and his wife wept when they tried on the clothes of the high priest.

Every morning, over a lavish Israeli breakfast, Jim asked Barney if he had secured the permit. Every morning, Barney gave him the oft-repeated assurance that the permit would be in their hands by the end of the day. On day four, there was an upturn in events. Avi, striding into the breakfast room with a purposeful air, announced to the tour group that there was a sudden shift in the agenda. He said he had attained unprecedented permission for them to be involved in an official archaeological dig. In addition to packing plenty of bottled water, Avi wanted everyone to wear good work shoes and clothes they didn't mind getting dirty. Interest peaking, Jim thought maybe Barney had come through.

Barney's wife got excited, whispering to Jim, "Does this mean we finally get to go dig?"

"I have no idea," Jim replied, "but I sure hope so."

Instead of going to Qumran, however, the van pulled up outside the City of David, a humungous and controversial archaeo-tourist site right outside Jerusalem's Old City walls.[1] Ushering everyone out of the van, Avi said, "I want my group to get the matchless opportunity of participating in an actual Israeli excavation." Right as Avi was explaining the history of the site, another tour bus rode up for their "privileged" dig-for-a-day experience. The site soon became so crowded that the tourists were broken up into crews. Staff members walked from group to group teaching about the process of excavation, and double-checking discoveries. One child, barely tall enough to hose the mud from his screen, found an ancient nail and several mosaic tiles.

The Barfields and Eatons shook their wire screens, like they were panning for gold. Jim strolled under the shade to stretch his back. He spotted an employee with a familiar face giving instructions about how to classify glass or potsherds. Jim recognized the archaeologist from the Rockefeller Museum. They had been briefly introduced in the hallways, on the way to the meeting with Peleg and Magen.

Checking over his shoulder to keep an eye out for Avi, Jim approached the archaeologist and introduced himself. "Shalom, nice to see you again. I haven't been in touch with Peleg since that meeting. Do you happen to have Peleg's phone number?" Without hesitation, the archaeologist jotted down Peleg's direct office line on a piece of paper. Jim thanked him and quickly tucked it away in the pocket of his jeans before anyone noticed.

The next day, the tour van drove to a site along the Jordan Valley, north of the Dead Sea. The most popular baptismal site on the Jordan River is the northern site near Galilee, but Avi notified the group that archaeologists had proven that the exact site of Jesus' baptism was on the eastern bank of the river, across from Jericho.

"Normally, no one can enter this site," Avi warned. "However, I have pulled some strings and arranged for special IDF protection while we are here." As they climbed out of the van, Avi gave each traveler a white robe. Jim rolled his eyes, and Shawn groaned when a huge tour bus rolled up to the allegedly secret baptismal site.

The Jordan River baptism is often a formative climax of Christian tours, despite which site the tour guide chooses. Yet most tourists are alarmed to see that the once mighty flowing river is now a murky stream. Running from the Sea of Galilee in Israel's north to the Dead Sea in the south, the Jordan River is blocked by an aging dam. In a region where water is scarce, most of the river's tributaries have been diverted by Jordan, Syria, and Israel for farming. What is left forms sluggish brown waters. Baptismal sites were shut down for testing in 2010 to be certain that the water posed no risk to human health.

Thinking it odd that Avi had yet to talk to him directly about the supposed excavation plans, Jim cornered him after the baptisms, while Barney was shimmying out of his wet robe.

"How is it coming for you in getting the dig permit at Qumran?" Jim asked.

Avi replied, "Oh, you're the guy wanting that permit?"

"Yes. You mean, you didn't know it was for me?" Jim asked, stupefied.

"I'll have to get back to you, but I'm talking to the right people about it," Avi replied. In fact, we are going to have lunch with two Israeli dignitaries right now."

"Who?" Jim asked.

"I can't divulge their names or positions, but they will meet us this after-noon," Avi said. "We are making a little detour." He waved Jim back to his seat.

Jim recalled Barney promising a meeting with Prime Minister Olmert if the excavation was held up. He understood the alleged Prime Minister meeting was now reduced to two unidentified Israeli "dignitaries." The van stopped at a large restaurant alongside the highway. When they sat down to order off the American-style menu, two Israeli officials walked in and started making the rounds to everyone's table in the restaurant. The men gave each group of tourists a standard talk about the importance of the Jewish nation and then left. As the dignitaries rushed by Barney and Avi, their faces showed no sign of recognition. Shawn mumbled, "Avi must think we're idiots."

The next day, they reached the point in the tour requiring a day trip to Qumran. Still, with no permit in hand, they were going to the site as regular tourists. When they arrived at the ruins, Barney asked Jim to give his family and Avi a walking tour of all the sites at Qumran that he had matched up with the Copper Scroll. Barney explained that it would be a distinctive highlight of the trip if Jim showed the research in its real-life application. Jim refused. The tour now felt like a prison to him. He was plotting an escape route.

Barney stormed into the Qumran guest center, and his family followed. Jim, Chris, Laurie and Shawn broke away and scurried up the hill to the *hill of Kokhlit*. Hiding behind the cliff line, Shawn filmed the potential buried cave site and the growing sinkhole. Jim had anticipated this trip to bear more fruit than documentation. Yet, he didn't want to leave empty-handed.

Back on the bus, after an hour of walking aimlessly around Qumran, Barney was fuming but silent. Jim acted cool. Avi, for his part, glared at Jim. He had lost track of them when they were behind the *hill of Kokhlit*. He announced on a microphone, "You guys who think that you're Indiana Jones need to knock it off."

Only once they were at the hotel, did Barney approach Jim. He hissed, "You really got us into trouble at Qumran. While you were poking around in the cliff, the Mossad approached Avi. They said a high level Palestinian terrorist was spying out the place and you guys were talking to him. We had to fill out a report to keep you out of trouble."

Jim, with a contorted smile and bulging eyes, leaned in and told Barney, "Well, you can tell the Mossad, plllbbbbb," sticking out his tongue and almost spitting in Barney's ear. The usually playful Jim was desperately hanging on to his last vestige of tolerance.

After dinner, Jim asked Barney to meet him in the lobby. Jim demanded to know what was going on. Jim learned that Barney's nerves lent themselves to a kind of verbal mania; contradictory words poured out of him. One exaggerated pledge led to lie upon lie—all without any connection to each other.

"General Sandler is taking care of us. There are only two generals over him to the top of the Israeli army," Barney sputtered. "In fact, he is a war hero. In 1967, Avi was the tank battalion commander who developed the plan to liberate Jerusalem. His tank hit the Lions' Gate storming into the Old City. He jumped out to assess the damage, and he was hit by a bazooka. He was dead for two days in a body bag at the morgue. When they came to process him, Avi jumped up and started breathing. After dozens of emergency surgeries, he is truly a six-million-dollar man."

"Enough! I don't want to hear anymore. I don't want to wait anymore," Jim snapped. "Produce something or I'm out!"

"We need to keep things as secretive as we can. Once the excavation begins, we will have to lock down the site and have an armored military presence and continuous security to protect the finds," Barney continued. Troubled by his own chatter, he was visibly shaking, struggling to steady his hands by pressing his fingers into his overgrown eyebrows.

"And if this supposed permit does come through, what about the finances? How will we pay for the cost of the dig and archaeologist?" Jim asked. The deceptions were becoming so blatant that Jim was poking Barney like a piñata; the harder hitting the question, the more the lies spilled out like cheap candy.

Once again, Barney promised that the permit was imminent. "I've got the capital that will kick start the excavation. My money is literally floating its way bank to bank," Barney said.

"Goodnight, Barney," Jim interrupted, standing and flipping around on the heel of his boot. He had to leave. He was on the verge of punching the man except for the pity he felt for him for believing his own lies.

The next morning Avi's tour agenda included a trip to Eilat, Israel's beach town on its southernmost tip, butting up to the Red Sea. Israelis hold Eilat in the same mixed esteem as Americans do Vegas. After traveling for hours through the barren beauty of the Negev desert, Eilat creeps up like a mirage. The small shoreline is packed with barely clad European tourists, Israeli students playing paddle ball, and kiosks selling kitsch trinkets.

When they got to their beachside hotel, Barney and Avi huddled together by the doorway to the hotel dining area. Jim assumed they were discussing the fiery argument he and Barney had the night before.

Avoiding eye contact with Jim, Avi gathered the group to tell them of the day's plans to hike at the border between Egypt and Israel. Jim informed Avi that the Barfields and Chris were skipping the day trip. Before Avi had a chance to respond, they escaped outside to the beachfront. Now that over a week of touring around Israel had gone by, with one bait-and-switch trick after another, Jim's gang was physically and emotionally spent. Barney had given them the figurative runaround; Avi had *literally* run them around.

Jim, Laurie, Chris, and Shawn took a walk on the abnormally quiet beach to finally debrief in private what had been mulling around their heads. Grumbling, however, required more strength than they could muster. Together, they collapsed on hotel beach chairs under the shell of what normally held a canvas canopy for shade.

Jim and Chris worried that Barney was conspiring to take the research out from under them. Laurie and Shawn couldn't bear to watch everything fall apart because of the evil intentions or, possibly, the grandiose delusions of a couple of men.

After several minutes of sitting on the beach chairs passed in silence, Jim let his head collapse in his hands. One by one, they prayed, asking God to cool their fears and orient them in the right direction. They offered up their most heartfelt pleas. Two turtle doves flew down from the date trees to perch on the canopy railing above. While the birds darted overhead, Laurie cried, resting her cheek on Jim's shoulder and mopping her tears with her hair. The creased lines in Jim's forehead softened.

After their Amens, the group contemplated their next steps. They could go through Juanita to try and arrange a second meeting with Shuka Dorfman at the IAA. Dorfman had made it clear, however, that when it came to Qumran, the ADCA was in charge. That meant the decision was in the hands of Magen or Peleg, and Magen had yet to return a call or email.

They decided to bypass Magen and contact Peleg directly. In the pocket of his unwashed jeans, Jim was still carrying Peleg's direct number that he had gotten from the archaeologist at the dig-for-a-day site. As one of the only men with full archaeological reign over Qumran, Peleg was their last hope. They got up to walk back to the hotel. The turtle doves startled and flew away.

Jim bought a calling card and called Peleg from a local payphone. He doubted Peleg would be in his office on the eve of Shabbat, but he waited for the voicemail to pick up. Instead, Peleg answered.

"Yuval, this is Jim Barfield. I met with you about the Copper Scroll research. Do you remember me?" Jim dropped his shoulder, rubbing the muscles in his neck and back.

"Yes, of course I remember," Peleg said. "I'm glad you caught me. I was walking into my office to pick something up that I had forgotten."

Jim got straight to his point. "I'm in Israel right now," he said. "I know this is spur-of-the-moment, but I was wondering if you could meet me to talk more about doing an excavation at Qumran to test my research."

Without a moment's pause, Peleg replied, "Yes, I would love to."

Still on the phone, Jim signaled a thumbs-up but his hands were trembling. His voice caught in his throat and he struggled to get the next words out. Shawn and Chris punched the air. Laurie, with her mascara stained face, let out a shriek.

"Can you meet me in two days at the Rockefeller Museum in Jerusalem— the same place we met last time?" Peleg said.

"Absolutey," Jim said, finally able to force a reply.

Jim couldn't believe it. After a disastrous trip, the prospects for excavation were suddenly brighter than ever. He was so stunned that he felt more numb than elated.

As they walked back to the hotel, Chris almost ran right into a small sign that said in Hebrew, Arabic, and English, "Go in Peace." Shawn pulled out his camera and snapped a picture of it.

ESCAPE ROUTE

After the phone call with Peleg, the Barfields and Chris agreed to hide their excitement and act as if nothing had changed. The tour still had a few days to go. Jim worried that if Barney and Blake found out he had circumvented them and gone directly to the Israeli authorities, they might try and sabotage his meeting.

The next morning Avi had the group wake up early to travel to another biblical body of water at the opposite end of Israel: The Sea of Galilee. Jim used the long hours in the van to sit in silence and plan. They all stared out the windows as the landscape gradually faded from shades of brown and desert sands to green and rolling hills reaching heavenward.

Josephus described the Galilee as "the ambition of nature." While Jerusalem often jolts first-time pilgrims because of its modernity, the Galilee has morphed very little in two millennia. Only the most superb imaginations can call forth mental pictures of Jerusalem the way it once looked, when the Temple stood erect, and the paths of ascent were not lined with stalled buses and honking cabs. The blue skies, still water, lonesome boats, and lush valleys of the Galilee, in contrast, make an idyllic backdrop. The pre-modern scenery properly evokes every miracle in the gospel story: Jesus directing the raging storm to be still; calling his disciples to cast their nets on the other side; and feeding 5,000 followers on a hillside.

Avi booked rooms at a stunning shore-side resort, once the proposed site of a forty-million-dollar Christian theme park. On the first morning after their arrival, the group planned to visit the remains of an ancient fishing boat from the first century, known as the Jesus Boat. Jim stayed back from the excursion. He needed time to figure out how to secretly get his whole gang to Jerusalem the next day to meet Peleg. At the start of the trip, Barney told Jim, "At any point, if you need to leave the tour to take care of a task for the excavation, you can." Jim decided to retroactively take advantage of that permission. At four in the morning, Jim left a note with the hotel desk clerk. The note told Barney not to worry, but something had come up. Jim promised that his gang would meet him in Tel Aviv for their scheduled flight home.

The four of them stealthily caught a taxi to the Tiberius bus station. They sat on benches watching the sun come up as they waited for the first morning bus out. A column of migratory storks flew overhead. Chris broke the silence. "Guys, I know now what my dream meant," he said. "In my dream, the bishop-dinosaur, Barney, was looking for us. He was angry because we ran off from the Galilee, but he had no idea where we went. When we peered over the sides of the wadi and looked down, we had a bird's eye view of the situation for the first time."

Jim downplayed Chris's dream of a bishop-dinosaur. He was too sleepy to over spiritualize the role of con-men. In his eagerness to see through an excavation at Qumran, he latched onto the first people who gave him promises of immediacy. He was fortunate that, despite his misguided judgment that landed him on a tour circling Israel, events had taken a dramatically positive turn. His feet felt light as he ascended the steps onto the bus.

Jim found Peleg sitting alone in a shady spot of the Rockefeller Museum's courtyard. He was relieved he came without Magen. The Barfields and Chris had puffy red-rimmed eyes. Attempts to sleep on the long bus ride were unsuccessful. Peleg, snacking on peanut-flavored chips, inquired politely about how they had enjoyed their tour of Israel. Their venting overlapped as they all shared the surreal story of what they had been through over the last week and a half

"Our tour guide was somehow a member of the Mossad, an archaeologist, and a famous general," Jim recounted.

"If I had to dress in biblical garb one more time or visit one more 'off-the-trail' site, I was going to keel over," Shawn added, sticking his tongue out to the side in mock death.

"It did feel like the twilight zone at times," Chris said.

Peleg got lost in the details, but he was entertained by their manner. A quiet introvert, Peleg was put at ease by the realization that he wouldn't need to fill any empty space of conversation, especially in English. After they relayed their journey, Jim confessed to Peleg that even though he didn't think Avi or Barney had much power to do anything, he worried that they might try to hamper an excavation that didn't include them. Peleg shushed Jim's concerns: "My office gives the permits. It all comes through here."

"That is a relief," Jim replied. "Does this mean you are really willing to be the archaeologist?"

"I am happy to do it," Peleg said. He didn't offer his reasons or motivations. Jim didn't need him to. He thought of the audio recording he had of Peleg quietly telling his boss that he thought Jim "had done it." And Jim also knew that Peleg was likely going against the wishes of Magen. It was best to avoid any topics that might induce Peleg to rethink the offer.

Moving on to solve logistics and discuss excavation dates, Peleg told Jim that rainy season was coming up and after that, for the next four months, it would be too hot at Qumran to dig. Peleg suggested December 2008 which would also give him time to handle the permit. Jim assumed there would be little paperwork since the ADCA made things easy for their own staff.

Arriving at the airport in Tel Aviv to return home, Jim was too elated to fret about the awkwardness of seeing Barney. Barney didn't show. Barney's wife, clearly irritated with the Barfields and Chris, told them that Barney had a stomach virus. He was not flying home yet. Later Chris overheard her on the plane telling her son that she expected Barney to stay in Israel and "accomplish everything he needed to do." Chris wondered what a supposedly sick man had to accomplish, but he let it go. It didn't matter anymore.

CUT TIES

When the group got back to the United States, Jim and Barney were mutually done speaking to each other. Their last form of communication was the note Jim left at the Galilee hotel. Since Blake hadn't been present on the Israel tour, Jim presumed Blake innocent of the whole affair. After all, the other-worldly promises about the trip had come from Barney. Jim assumed Blake's worst offense was his naiveté.

Once the Barfields and Chris were back stateside, Jim met with Blake in Dallas to explain what had happened during the trip. Jim informed Blake of the good news: they had an Israeli archaeologist, with full access to Qumran, and a December dig date. Unexpectedly, Blake fell apart.

"You have to renegotiate with the Israelis," Blake pleaded.

Wringing his hands and avoiding eye contact, Blake uncovered a complicated scheme. He explained how he hoped that in the event of a Copper Scroll find, the Israeli government, grateful to have their legacy unearthed, would form an agreement with him that would allow his bank to tie into the Copper Scroll's gold.

"Can you contact Peleg to renegotiate a contract, so my bank can get a foothold in the plans? I will never actually have to use the gold. It's only collateral for our investments," Blake sniveled.

In their months of discussing plans, Blake had presented himself as a consultant for nonprofits, never a bank manager or bank employee. Jim sat silent in open-mouthed disbelief. Blake's plans sounded even more corrupt than anything Jim had ever heard from Barney.

Later that week, after avoiding Blake's calls, Jim investigated the website that Blake had sputtered off for his Sovereign Nation Bank. What he came across was a shoddy two-page site that had clearly been created by an amateur. Beset with mostly broken links, Jim clicked on the site's contact page and found one phone number for the bank president. Jim called up the number. A man answered who sounded like he had been woken out of deep slumber. Jim thought it odd that a banking professional would be sleeping in the middle of the day. The man answered, "Who is this? Is this law enforcement?"

Jim explained that he had gotten the number from a website for Sovereign Nation Bank. "What website? What bank?" the groggy man asked. As soon as Jim named Blake Foster, the man spouted a litany of curse words and hung up. The website was taken down soon after Jim made that call.

After the bank revelations, Jim cut Blake out of the *Copper Scroll Project* completely. When Blake introduced Jim and me at the conference in Dallas, their relationship was hanging on its last thread. Jim blocked Blake's calls. "He was like a leech, always worried I was leaving him out. It's true. I was leaving him out!" Jim told me. I suddenly understood Blake's obsession with the gold standard in our first conversation.

Melanie the prophetess emailed Jim with a warning vision. "In a dream," Melanie wrote, "You were waving a paper agreement that you made with the Israelis. Murky eyes crept up behind you and turned into an evil presence." The gory vision had Chris decapitated and Jim's hands chewed off by wolves. She warned that Jim and Chris were headed toward self-immolation.

Blake sent Jim a follow-up email warning him that he knew of a pastor who entered a written agreement with a leader in Israel. After being given a prophetic warning to withdraw from the contract, the man refused and suddenly died of a brain aneurysm. Blake demanded, "Take immediate action to get out of this agreement and renegotiate it, or you are on your own."

Jim ignored the threats from both Melanie and Blake. He felt as though he finally saw clearly after a long drive in the fog.

Burned by the months he had wasted hanging around with a trifecta of miscreants, Jim was raring to go out on his own. Now that he had the permit and the archaeologist, all Jim had to do was raise the cash to cover the minimal costs of the dig. Since the IAA was heading the dig, he only had to raise ten thousand dollars to cover plane flights, a rental van for volunteers, and food.

Jim had to confront his demon: directly asking for financial help. Blake's final warning to Jim was that he was forbidden from reconnecting with any of his donor contacts. Jim had no problem obliging. Instead, he went to his local community.

At the Lawton Public Library, Jim held a meeting for anyone interested. He gave a public seminar about his Copper Scroll research. He told the gathering of friends, family, neighbors, firefighters, and teachers, "It looks like we have a permit and an archaeologist, but we need some help with the financing." That night the *Copper Scroll Project* raised five thousand dollars.

Several months later, I met Jim in Dallas for his talk at the *Etz Chayim* Messianic congregation. A member of *Etz Chayim* called Jim's cellphone after the talk. A soft-spoken successful cattle rancher named Mack Kizer asked Jim directly: "How much more do you need?"

Jim told him, "Five grand."

Mack replied, "I'll mail you a check."

The two were inseparable from that point on.

CHAPTER 10

HOPE

With the excavation under the auspices of the Israeli authorities and the fundraising complete, Jim had little to do other than show up on the dig date with his research in hand.

Doing nothing, however, was an impossible task for Jim. As a helicopter pilot in the U.S. Army, he often heard the five P's of planning: Proper Preparation Prevents Poor Performance—an adage he lived by. Jim kicked into planner mode out of habit more than necessity. If holy Temple treasure was going to be found after thousands of years, he wanted to be ready.

First on his agenda was preparing a crew of people to accompany him and Chris to Israel. Usually, excavations at Qumran required a few hired laborers to move and haul dirt while the ADCA archaeologist closely observed. Though a few diggers were sufficient for excavations at normal depths, the Copper Scroll specified depths of twelve feet or more. Jim imagined Peleg would be unprepared for the magnitude of the work load. Worried the excavation might get stalled because of a manpower shortage, Jim asked four friends, who knew their way around a shovel, to come to Israel as standby volunteers: Don and Linda Thomas, Todd Hubenthal, and Mack Kizer. He also thought to bring along a few other team members with different areas of expertise.

Ken Colvin, a truck driver and distant cousin, called one day, out of the blue, to tell Jim he had engineered a remote-controlled robot car with an infrared camera on top of it. Calling it Robo-Cam, Ken made a special trip to Lawton to demonstrate the robot's capabilities. Outfitted with caterpillar tracks, an on-board light source, and a mounted camera, Robo-Cam looked like a small army tank on reconnaissance. The design of Robo-Cam was weighted to easily maneuver in a winding cave without falling over. Jim recalled what a terrible time Vendyl had in proving anything was inside the impenetrable *Cave of the Column.* He wondered if a gadget like Robo-Cam might have served Vendyl well. To avoid the elder explorer's mistakes, Ken and his Robo-Cam earned an invitation to join the group in Israel.

After months of hearing about the importance of media from Barney and Blake, Jim thought it worthwhile, at least for history's sake, to bring a cameraman to Qumran. Without having documented footage of the artifacts being unearthed, Israel's enemies would likely accuse the Jewish state of a subversive plot to reclaim the Temple Mount. The ADCA did not like media presence at excavations, however, and Jim wanted to avoid stepping on Peleg's toes. Still, Jim saw no harm in his son Shawn—who happened to be a graduate student in film production—bringing his personal video camera to the site. Casey, another aspiring documentarian and acquaintance of Chris, was invited to rotate camera duties. Their video equipment was too high-quality to be inconspicuous, but they planned to play up their amateur cards. I tagged along as a journalist; all I required was a moleskin notebook and pen.

As word spread about the upcoming excavation, Jim was approached on a weekly basis by friends, and even strangers, who begged to play a part in the potentially historic dig. Some told him they *had* to go: They experienced specific dreams or visions from God, verifying they were to be a part of it. "Often the dream included me paying for their ticket to get there," Jim told me in a sarcastic tone.

One charismatic woman told Jim she had known her whole life that she was supposed to be involved in the return of the Ark of the Covenant. A police officer told Jim he could conduct security for the operation. An airline stewardess insisted that she and her husband would be great assets because of their flexibility with air travel. On one occasion, a construction worker quit his job after hearing Jim speak at his congregation. After the fact, he called Jim to tell him that he was free to help dig. Jim told him to get his job back. All who could not dig at least wanted to observe.

"We can't have so many people that we need stadium seating and buckets of popcorn," Jim told Chris.

Even still, Jim had a tough time turning anyone down. After one of Jim's revival-style speaking engagements, Laurie politely jotted down the names and contact information of people who asked to volunteer. In an unpromising voice, she told them she would call if Jim needed the assistance. No one ever got called from the list. When sending out email updates, Jim had to be vague about the exact date of the dig. He harbored a legitimate concern that stragglers might show up at Qumran unannounced.

SETTING UP CAMP

Once Jim had what he called "the advance team" in place, he had to consider the cheapest and most practical way to house and feed almost a dozen people for potentially a month or longer. In the early twentieth century, European Egyptologists stayed for months in rustic tent camps at remote excavation sites along the Nile. Qumran was too big of a tourist attraction to transform into a campground and too close to modern comforts to justify it. Even still, in the way of lodging, there are few options in the immediate vicinity of Qumran. The Dead Sea coast is lined with luxury hotels but renting six rooms seemed cost prohibitive. The Kibbutz Kalia Hotel bumps up next to the Qumran ruins, offering a lower budget lodging option, but the rooms had no kitchenette.

"I went from laboring over my research report to forecasting a dozen people's laundry and cooking needs," Jim recalls.

As Jim researched the possibilities, a man named Flynn Bloom from North Carolina stepped into the picture. Flynn was a small businessman, owning a few convenience stores in his home state. He had been involved years before with Ron Wyatt's excavation at the Garden Tomb, but when the dig came up short he refused to let the anticlimax dampen his faith. He heard about Jim's housing woes from a mutual friend and was compelled to aid a fellow rogue explorer. He called Jim and offered for the group to stay in his four-bedroom, three-bathroom house in a quaint Israeli neighborhood in the small town of Arad. It was Flynn's second home which he lent to many a friend. Jim was only the friend of a friend, but no matter. Flynn told Jim it would be an honor to turn his home into the *Copper Scroll Project* headquarters.

Jim quickly agreed to Flynn's generous offer. Jim never had a reason to visit Arad but liked that the Negev town was convenient enough to make a daily commute to Qumran. Jerusalem was also just over an hour's drive from Arad. Arad had a hardware shop, a mall with a decent café, and a medium sized grocery store. A few team members would have to sleep on air mattresses in the living room and basement—a small nuisance compared to the giant plus of free rent.

Jim told Flynn, "You are taking a risk letting your house get crammed with Okies. By the end of the month we'll have old cars on cinder blocks outside."

Five months out from Peleg's suggested dig date, with most of his team and logistical plans in place, Jim decided it was time to start a website. He had found a physical place to house the *Copper Scroll Project* in Israel, and now he needed a virtual one. "Everyone was always asking me if I had a website," Jim explains. "I was starting to feel like an underachiever without one."

A family friend, who happened to be a young and hungry web guru, volunteered to design a high-quality website for the *Copper Scroll Project*. He did so well optimizing the site for internet search engines that anytime someone Googled "Copper Scroll," Jim's website ranked in the top three links. On most days, it outranked Wikipedia for the search term.

With an online presence, Jim could make information about the *Copper Scroll Project* available to anyone in the world—well beyond the reaches of his travel. Although he withheld his theory on Qumran, he offered other valuable information on the website. He made versions of his first love, the *Messiah Timeline* in Excel, available for download. He ran regular video updates, proving himself to be confident in front of a camera. As a teaser, he posted graphics on the website of the buried cave and the sinkhole at Qumran. The pictures were intentionally too close-up for anyone to make heads or tails of the location. Most readers imagined the photos were taken in Jerusalem, and Jim did not dissuade the notion.

Analytics proved that only a few months after the website's launch, the *Copper Scroll Project* gained a significant viewership in Israel.

CONTAGIOUS EXPECTATION

In the months preceding the dig, Jim continued doing speaking engagements, even though he was finished fundraising. He liked speaking to groups. At his core, he was a teacher—albeit one who deployed unusual tools of instruction. The Copper Scroll research, like the *Messiah Timeline*, provided Jim with the opportunity to teach people about his passions: The Dead Sea Scrolls, the prophet Jeremiah, the wilderness Tabernacle, and the First Temple period.

Jim had a knack for painting biblical history with a wide brush. Every time he threw out a new theory about the order of Melchizedek; or made a side comment about the practices of the Essenes; or quoted a passage from an obscure ancient manuscript, I was afterwards knee deep in books cross-referencing him. Because of the originality of his theories, trying to fact-check Jim was almost impossible. All I could say with certainty was that before I met Jim, I did not rightly appreciate the implications of the Dead Sea Scrolls. But soon, the Dead Sea Scrolls and Copper Scroll consumed me as well. I was a Christian prior to my new passion, but my faith had experienced a cerebral revival. And I wasn't the only one.

Everywhere that Jim spoke, the *Copper Scroll Project* bred a contagious hope among Bible enthusiasts—a hope that the Bible would definitively be proven true. A hope that laying eyes on the Temple's lost treasures would restore the faith of all unbelievers. And a hope that Israel, a nation that has known its share of persecution, would, upon receiving remnants of its glorious past, be reassured of God's fidelity to her exceptional covenant.

I witnessed the hope that overtook every unsuspecting victim that happened to meet Jim. When I observed him speaking to audiences, I came to anticipate the listeners' palpable spiritual elevation. Trying to maintain the proper distance of a journalist following a story, I was hardly immune to the antiquity's influence. Whether I admitted it or not, my sagging bookshelves, stacked with Copper Scroll research, were a vain attempt to mask my own impulsive hope with intellectual reasoning.

The opening line of the Copper Scroll is a coded message of hope. The Copper Scroll begins *In the Valley of Achor*—a familiar reference to students of the prophets. The Bible first introduces the Valley of Achor as a place of punishment and death. Achor means "trouble." According to the seventh chapter of the book of Joshua, after Joshua's army handily defeated Jericho, a Hebrew named Achan defied God's proscription to restrain from plundering the city. God warned: "All the silver and gold and the articles of bronze and iron are sacred to the Lord and must go into his treasury." (Joshua 6:19)

When the Hebrew army suffered an unexpected defeat in their ensuing campaign, Joshua understood that his people were being collectively punished for one man's sin. Through a process of divination, he identified Achan as the perpetrator. Achan's family and even his livestock were summoned to the Valley of Achor and stoned to death. Jim took the lesson of Achan to heart. When it comes to the misappropriation of spoils, the punishment is death.

In a beautifully poetic twist, the prophet Hosea,[1] writing almost 700 years after Achan's stoning, promised that Israel's future hope and redemption would spring forth from the Valley of Achor: "There I will give her back her vineyards, and will make the Valley of Achor a door of hope. There she will sing as in the days of her youth, as in the day she came up out of Egypt." (Hosea 2:15) Redemption from an unlikely place was also part of Isaiah's prophetic message. Isaiah prophesied that in the time of salvation God would make the "Valley of Achor a resting place for herds, for my people who seek me." (Isaiah 65:10)

The story of the *Copper Scroll Project*—staged in the Valley of Achor— awakened expectation in hearts where it had long gone dormant. Thoughts of the scroll's possibilities gave many people bone-tingling chills. That's why Jim had more invitations to speak than he could accept, why people begged to join the adventure, and why his website was going viral. And as Jim antici- pated, hope may have been why Peleg, a secular Israeli archaeologist who fig- ured Qumran had zero spiritual importance, was willing to take a professional risk on an amateur's research.

FALSE ALARM

In September 2008, Jim and Chris returned to Israel to meet with Peleg and finalize plans for a winter excavation. With almost sixty locations identified in Jim's research, they had to decide which sites to prioritize. Peleg came to their hotel in Jerusalem on the first night of their arrival.

Like many Israelis, Peleg only knew one mode of dress: casual. He wore dusty work boots, frayed cargo pants, and stretched out cotton t-shirts. He looked the part of an Israeli reservist officer—which he was. What he didn't pass for was a published academic—which he also was. Despite his accomplishments, he much preferred being out in the field than the classroom or office.

Mild mannered, Peleg lacked fluency with his English; he spoke warily. He rarely initiated jokes in English but often snickered. In the quaint hotel lobby, as Peleg scanned Jim's report, his cellphone buzzed in his pocket. "Jim, why don't you pick the top few locations you would like to make the initial test sites," Peleg suggested, glancing at his phone to screen a call. "In two days, we'll go over to Qumran together and look closely at each of your preferred sites."

"Sounds like a plan," Jim replied. His head was already abuzz with possibilities, but he tried to match Peleg's composure.

"Have you been to Qumran lately?" Jim asked.

"Qumran is like my second home," Peleg replied.

The next morning Jim and Chris went to Qumran on a scouting mission. They wanted to imagine how the locations would look through the protective eyes of Peleg. By walking through each of the locations, they aimed to find which sites were the easiest to access with the least threat to the ruins.

Digging at the *hill of Kokhlit* was Jim's top priority. He thought Peleg would agree since the heap was set away from the Qumran complex. Although the *hill of Kokhlit* was the most speculative of Jim's locations, it potentially held the most hallowed Temple vessels, including another scroll. Jim told Chris, "If we find the Silver Scroll, we'll call in another firefighter to solve that one!"

Jim also prioritized a twenty-foot-long stone pipe, or gutter, that sat on the edge of the Qumran complex. The gutter began inside the ruins and ran underneath Qumran's outer wall on the way to the edge of the plateau. When Qumran's water system was functional, the pipe channeled waste water out of the complex. Jim was confident that treasure was buried somewhere along the widest part of the pipe, specifically a stash of gems.

According to Jim's concordance-based translation, location eight and nine gave the Hebrew word for gems: *The gutter at the cliff eastward is a hundred-fold fortune. Enter, remove two cubits, look inside. Slid back are vessels with gems. Bring up again ten talents.* None of the academic translations of the Copper Scroll indicate that gems are part of the buried items. The scroll's weighted items are usually listed as gold or silver, but several times the cache isn't identified at all. In those cases, the catalogue gives the location of an item and sometimes its weight, without identifying it materially. Allegro assumed unspecified bullion pointed to a mixed stash of gold and silver. Other academics proposed that they were bronze.

Jim speculated that the unspecified deposits were gems. In all his research, this was the most imaginative leap of logic. Believing the Copper Scroll fortune included gems came from what Jim thought to be the historical background of the scroll and its connection to the gem-rich Temple. In the *Treatise of Temple Vessels*, the author described enormous and various amounts of hidden gems.

Jim and Chris stood straddling the eastern end of the drainage channel, analyzing the best approach for excavation. The dig test would be complicated. The scroll did not specify where along the twenty-foot tunnel the stash was concealed. Chris put down his thermos of green tea. On a whim, he powered on his digital camera, reached inside a small opening to the shaft, and snapped a couple of photos. Chris wanted to catch a glimpse of the murky debris which had blown inside over twenty centuries. He needed the camera's flash to illuminate things. When he looked at the image on the camera's electronic visual display, he did a double-take. At first glance, he thought a glass soda bottle was thrown inside the gutter. On closer inspection, a dream-sensation came over him. He put the camera's display right in front of Jim's nose and cupped his hand to block the sun's glare.

"Chris, am I crazy or is that the biggest diamond I have ever seen in my entire life?" Jim asked. A nervous laugh caught in his voice.

"That's sure what it looks like to me!" Chris agreed.

Jim got down in the dirt and peered through the tunnel. He spotted the top of the gem, but he restrained himself from grabbing a stick and funneling out the object. Under Israeli law, it is illegal to remove artifacts from archaeological sites. If they disturbed an artifact, they risked being arrested for antiquities theft. Besides, they only had to wait one day to show it to Peleg.

Waiting at the bus stop to return to Jerusalem, they sat staring at the display on Chris's camera. They zoomed in and zoomed back out again. No matter which way they viewed it, it always looked like a giant diamond. "We waited for that bus for two hours, but we didn't feel a second of it pass because we were giggling like little school girls," Jim recalls. They wondered why anything from antiquity would be on the top layer of debris but explained it away as the work of a flash flood.

As soon as they arrived at their hotel room they called Laurie and Shawn and emailed them the pictures. Shawn jumped on his computer and started using his graphic design skills to examine the diamond-like object. Shawn made a three-dimensional rendering of the gem and emailed them back an animation of the object. It had thirteen sides and looked to be about seven inches long and one inch thick. A dozen times during the night Shawn got out of bed to study the picture. Across the ocean, Jim and Chris couldn't stop staring at it either.

Jim and Chris tried to remain casual when they met Peleg the next morning at Qumran, but they strode right through the main ruins to lead him to the gutter. Yuval knew the area well. He and Magen had excavated all around the tunnel's stone exterior in 1998, but they never opened the tunnel to excavate its interior. Jim felt awkward divulging to Yuval that he knew a gem was inside the pipe. Getting down on all fours, he didn't waste much time on explanations. He pulled Peleg down to be eye level with the glittering object.

"Yuval, we happened to spot something intriguing when we were scoping things out yesterday," Jim began. He pointed inside.

Carrying a folded wire hanger in his back pocket, Jim handed it over to Peleg and motioned for him to try and fish out the gem. Peleg's flat affect livened. He stretched out the hanger and locked the hook around the gem. After sliding it out to the entrance, Peleg picked it up and wiped away its thin layer of dust on his pants. As he held the gem up with both hands, rotating it for examination, the sunlight rays made dancing sparkles. Chris excitedly drew out his camera to take a selfie of his beaming mug with the gem in the background.

Peleg said laconically, "Oh, this is nice. It's not old, but it's nice."

"What do you mean? Are you sure it's not old?" Chris asked. He felt like Yuval had taken a pin and with one poke completely deflated the balloon of excitement he had been cherishing in his belly for the last 24 hours.

"Yes, it is a crystal. It's made from glass. I think some spiritual people left this out here," Peleg explained. "How do you call them in English? They love crystals and chants."

"New Agers?" clarified Chris.

"Yes, that's it. I think they had a wedding here or something." Peleg spoke with an accent common to Israelis when they speak English. When he pronounced "that," it came out "zat," and "they" sounded like "zey."

Sure enough, Jim looked and saw burned-out candles lining the trail going all the way from the edge of Qumran and up to the mountains. Since the popularization of the Dead Sea Scrolls, Qumran had become a superlative place for fringe religious sects seeking the divine. New Age practitioners felt Qumran had immense spiritual qualities, the Essenes being the ultimate cosmic teachers.

From the gutter, Jim walked with Peleg up to the *hill of Kokhlit*. He showed Peleg the expanding sinkhole. Peleg agreed that the *hill of Kokhlit* and gutter were good places to start the excavation. Before finalizing the dig date, Peleg said he still had a few details to iron out, like getting approval from the other shareholder, the Israel Nature and Parks Authority (INPA). This government organization was responsible for the protection of all the national parks and nature reserves in Israel. Technically, the *hill of Kokhlit* was outside of Qumran, in a declared nature reserve; Peleg needed their approval for an excavation.

"We can't do the dig now," Peleg began. "It's the hottest summer in the past twenty years, and it would be miserable. For you at least. I'm used to it." He continued to think aloud. "In October, I only work eight days because of the Jewish High Holidays. After that I have army duty. Let's do December. Everything will cool off and settle down by then."

Peleg put the crystal in a bag on the passenger's seat of his truck. He promised to take it to the lab for testing. "Why not?" he shrugged.

Back at the hotel, Jim and Chris researched thirteen-sided crystals used in New Age ceremonies, and learned the crystal was called a Vogel. Vogels are made of quartz and are known for their extreme clarity and precisely cut angles. They are alleged to help adherents resolve their inner trauma by extracting negative energies. Valued at around a thousand dollars or more, Jim couldn't imagine why anyone would leave it in a tunnel at Qumran.

On the flight back, Chris clicked through the pictures of the Vogel on his camera. He couldn't shake the daydream that even if the crystal was a false alarm, it was not a one-off but a harbinger of real discoveries to come.

Jim playfully pushed Chris's elbow off their shared arm rest. He cracked, "I bet Yuval sent the crystal for 'lab testing' on his wife's dresser."

FRIENDS AND ENEMIES

As word spread in Lawton about the upcoming dig, Jim became somewhat of a hometown hero. Locals clamored to officially endorse his undertaking.

Oklahoma State Senator Don Barrington asked Jim to make a special visit to the capital. Barrington was once the chief of the fire department and a long-time friend of Jim. On the phone, he explained that many of the Christian senators wanted to know more about Jim's potential discovery. They had a regular Bible study while Senate was in session. Don asked Jim to come as a guest speaker.

On the morning of the Bible study, Chris filmed Jim giving an update for the *Copper Scroll Project* website right outside the capital. They were still trying to populate the website with content, a task new to them both. In the video, an oil rig jutted out into the skyline behind Jim. Oklahoma has the nation's only seat of government parked on an active oil field.

In the Senate chamber, Jim presented to the legislators his usual Power-Point slides. Most of them had never heard of the Copper Scroll and knew little about Israeli archaeology. However, they were all intrinsically pro-Israel. Their conservative Christian faith inspired their political support for the Jewish nation. By the time Jim was finished with the prepared portion of his talk, they jumped to their feet and gave Jim double back slaps. Several of them expressed their strong hope that a discovery would neutralize the international political pressures placed on Israel. They sent him off with a prayer for the *Copper Scroll Project*'s success and a request to keep them posted.

Next, a Kiowa Native American man from Oklahoma nicknamed Skeeznix came across the story of the *Copper Scroll Project* on a special program on a national Christian cable network. He couldn't believe the coincidence when the program host noted Jim's hometown. He got Jim's number from the phone book and called him. He shared how the Messianic movement had spread among the Kiowa, some of whom considered themselves part of Israel's lost tribes. He asked if he and his friends could pray for Jim, Kiowa style. "I never turn down prayers," Jim replied. A week later he was in a bona fide Kiowa sweat lodge. Two hours of invocations swirled around Jim while he focused intently on not passing out.

Not all of Jim's friends, however, viewed the news of the upcoming excavation positively. Once Vendyl found out that Jim was cooperating with the Israeli agencies, their relationship soured. Vendyl still believed the IAA intentionally obstructed him when he was on the verge of a find. He felt betrayed by Jim, who was supposed to be his fellow maverick driving against the IAA, not working alongside them.

Natan Mor—Vendyl's former aide—informed Jim of the extent of Vendyl's grudge. Vendyl had told Natan, "If Jim and the IAA find the Copper Scroll treasures, we can say goodbye to any hope of the nation of Israel ever seeing the precious artifacts again. This will be the end of it." Vendyl asked Natan to organize an angry mob to meet Jim at the airport in Tel Aviv.

When I questioned Jim about why Vendyl turned on him, he admitted that losing the mentorship of the elder explorer stung. But he empathetically defended him: "Vendyl had focused on the Copper Scroll since 1967, pouring his heart and soul into locating these items. I understand why he would be cranky about me stepping onto the scene, out of nowhere, and then suddenly collaborating with his enemies."

CHAPTER 11

TEASER

Come December, Peleg still lacked permission from the ecologist at the INPA to dig legally at the *hill of Kokhlit*. The ecologist was withholding permits because it was the rainy season, and he was concerned about the unintended ecological impact. The Dead Sea region only rains a few times a year, between November and April. What little it does rain at Qumran is often accompanied by flash floods funneled east from the western highlands. Even an inch of rainfall can turn the wadi bordering the Qumran plateau into a raging torrent.

Although the dig at the *hill of Kokhlit* was temporarily postponed, Peleg told Jim and Chris that they could still dig at a few test sites inside the Qumran complex, like the gutter. Jim and Chris flew to Israel by themselves and told the rest of the team to be on standby. They arrived in Tel Aviv early on a Friday afternoon. The airport in Tel Aviv was quiet. No Vendyl-inspired mob greeted them.

The earliest excavation day they could hope for was Sunday, the first day of the workweek for Israelis, but they had yet to hear a final plan from Peleg. In the meantime, Jim and Chris took a bus to Jerusalem. Sabbath keepers themselves, the two men followed the throngs of Orthodox—*datim* in local parlance—walking to the Old City. Before going through the metal detectors at the Dung Gate, they filleted open their backpacks for Israeli security officers. As he was putting away his camera, Jim thought he heard someone over his shoulder whisper, "It's the Copper Scroll guy."

Once he and Chris got inside the plaza affronting the *Kotel*, an Orthodox Jewish couple pushing a stroller walked up to them. "We have to know something," they said. "Are you Jim Barfield?"

"I am. Have we met?" Jim asked.

Apparently, the couple had come across Jim's website and had been keeping up with his email updates. They had most recently watched the video update from the Oklahoma State Capital. It helped that Jim was easily recognizable in a crowd. Almost three years into his Nazarite vow, his long hair gave him an increasingly biblical air.

"We are so excited about what you are doing. Please don't give up," the wife said. The husband shook Jim's hand. The wife, who couldn't make physical contact with Jim, gripped the stroller tighter. Tears formed in the corners of her eyes.

Meeting Israelis who were rooting for him was life-giving to Jim. Everything he had been working toward was intended for the people of Israel, even if it was unbeknownst to them. Only at this moment, standing in front of the Western Wall, did Jim feel like he was anything more to the common Israeli than an invisible nameless servant, working on their behalf to find their lost dowry. He tried to lock the faces of the Israeli family into his memory; they personalized his muse.

Looking out from the plaza and up to the Temple Mount—vastly overshadowed by the glinting gold and shimmering blues of the Dome of the Rock— Jim soaked in the sound of the faithful. The soft murmuring of Jews quietly reciting from the Psalms soon fell away as the Muslim high-pitched call to prayer crackled from the loudspeaker above. Startled swallows, nesting in the crevices, took flight.

The Dome of the Rock was built in the seventh century shortly after the armies of Islam captured it from the Byzantines. Built as a shrine, not a mosque, it has no match in Islamic architecture. The Dome's octagonal base is beautified with blue ceramic tile; the cupola was gilded with 24-karat gold in the 1950s. Historians believe the conquering caliph Abd al-Malik was at least partially motivated in commissioning the shrine to symbolize Islam's victory over her Christian and Jewish enemies.[1] The structure was built directly atop the area identified with Solomon's Temple. It was designed to eclipse the nearby Church of the Holy Sepulcher. The impression is still chilling today. The glinting Dome dominates panoramic views of the Old City. Five times a day the Muslim crier silences the competing prayers of Jerusalem's Jews and Christians.

In its lower level, the Dome enshrines the "foundation stone," an exposed bedrock which has long been a focal point for Jewish adoration, in Plexiglass. Jewish tradition says the foundation stone was once part of the Garden of Eden. It was the place that Noah built an altar to God after the flood and the location of the intended altar for Abraham's near sacrifice of Isaac. During the First Temple period, the Ark of the Covenant rested directly on the bedrock inside the Holy of Holies, a perfectly square inner sanctum—the nucleus in a series of concentric courts. Rabbinical literature best summarizes the stone's centrality: "Palestine is the center of the world, Jerusalem the center of Palestine, the Temple the center of Jerusalem, the Holy of Holies the center of the Temple, the Ark the center of the Holy of Holies; and in front of the Ark was a stone called *Even Shetiyah*, the foundation stone of the world."[2]

Islam morphed certain Jewish traditions about Mount Moriah and the foundation stone into Islamic ones. They agree that the site was where God tested Abraham's obedience. In Islam, however, Abraham almost sacrificed Ishmael. Muslims believe the foundation stone was touched by angels 2,000 years before Adam and Eve and that the angels will return to the spot to announce the final day of judgment. Muslims maintain the enshrined rock has an embedded hoof print from the takeoff of Muhammad's winged horse.

WAR TRUMPS ALL

On Sunday, Peleg called Jim and left him a message saying that he was leaving his office to oversee an emergency salvage excavation. A construction crew had made an accidental antiquities discovery. Building new parking lots are a common source of archaeological progress in Israel. Archaeologists have love-hate relationships with bulldozers. In this instance, workers were adding on to an industrial complex in the town of Ma'aleh Adumim, right outside Jerusalem, when they stumbled upon Byzantine era ruins. One of Peleg's roles with the ADCA was to be on call for such emergencies and provide archaeological supervision.

Jim and Chris went to the Ma'aleh Adumim site to meet with Peleg. They spotted his hulking physique right away, pacing the edge of what looked like a dirt quilt—perfect rope squares marking off strata. By the time Peleg trudged over to them, his breath was panting and short. He had good news and bad news. "The ecologist refuses to let me dig at the cave before April," Peleg explained. "However, I see no harm in starting to excavate at the other test sites inside Qumran."

"We'll take it!" Jim and Chris chimed.

"I need a few days to finish out this emergency excavation," Peleg continued. "Then I'll call you, and we'll meet in Jerusalem for dinner to finalize all the arrangements."

"We'll talk to you then. Don't worry about us. We're comfortable and staying at a house in Arad," Jim said.

"Arad?" Peleg asked with a look of condescension. "Why are you there?"

"Because it's free," Jim said.

Jim and Chris rented a car with a GPS to get them to Flynn's house. They were charmed to find a modern home with a supreme view of the Negev desert from the back patio. The house was located on a cul-de-sac. Most of the neighbors were friendly new immigrants from Russia. The dining room had an eight-seater kitchen table. Jim set up the table as a temporary work station and called Laurie.

As trips to Israel became more frequent, Laurie chose to sit them out. Laurie cared for her grandchildren daily. Still, the couple had a difficult time being apart, and they talked on Skype at every chance.

On their fifth morning in Arad, Jim was on Skype with Laurie and mentioned his concern that Peleg had not yet called. Laurie distracted him with stories of the grandchildren. Jim listened as he dined on hummus and pita for breakfast. Suddenly, Jim heard the buzz of jets overhead. He went out on Flynn's balcony and spotted two jets flying in a holding pattern at high altitude. As soon as the jets dived west, Jim knew they were flying in the direction of Gaza.

Israel had been threatening for months to retaliate against Gaza's Hamas—a Palestinian terrorist group committed to Israel's destruction. Since 2005, when Israel fully disengaged from Gaza as a peace overture, Hamas had continually attacked the Jewish state. With weapons being smuggled into Gaza from Egypt, dozens of Qassam rockets fell daily on southern Israel. Many times, the rockets narrowly missed school classrooms and playgrounds. The trajectory of the rockets was improving, hitting inside larger Israeli cities in the Negev, like

Beer Sheva and Ashkelon. Israeli children in the south were accustomed to interrupting their games and running for bomb shelters. By the looks of things, the Israeli Air Force was geared up for their response.

Watching the jets disappear, it dawned on Jim why Peleg never called to confirm their Jerusalem dinner plans. Peleg, as a tank commander in the IDF reserves, was outside Gaza preparing for a ground invasion. Known as Operation Cast Lead, Israel launched an all-out assault on the Gaza Strip from the air, sea, and ground. The Operation had one goal: rendering Hamas impotent. No one knew how long that might take.

Jim and Chris decamped home. To his friends and family on standby, Jim sent out an email announcing their return: "This is such a small country, and things change quickly as the political situation flounders. One minute I was waiting on a phone call from Peleg to go to dinner and the next minute Peleg was preparing for battle. *Hashem* has his own timing. Right now, my prayers are with our Israeli friends and their families. We are coming home."

CHAPTER 12

HUNT

By spring 2009, Operation Cast Lead was long over. The ecologist issued the nature reserve permit. Peleg cleared his schedule. Rainy season passed and Qumran was hot, though not yet blistering. The excavation was likely to commence. Jim sent news to his advance team that "all systems are go," and we flew to Israel. The team got to Flynn's house a few days early to sleep off jet lag, fill the fridge and pantry, and study up on the details of Jim's report.

Everyone on the advance team was from either Oklahoma or Texas; each was as improbable as the next to be included on an archaeological dig in Israel. Mack—gored by a bull the day before leaving for Israel—had never been on an airplane. Blood stains seeping through his shirt, his nearly seven-foot frame made for an awkward contortion in economy class. Ken brought Robo-Cam, and a friend of his named Larry Owens. The last time Larry was in an international city was Saigon during Vietnam. Linda, a surgical nurse, and Don, a retired mechanic, were the only married couple on the trip. Tall and lanky with a Moses beard, Todd professed to be one-part hippie and one-part hick. Casey and Shawn looked the part of serious videographers, but their boyish sense of humor kept the group dynamic light.

Each person had a vague notion about his or her role in the *Copper Scroll Project*. Mack and Don were good with shovels and logistics, should Peleg need volunteers. Ken operated Robo-Cam. Larry entertained Ken. Linda and Todd liked to cook for big groups. And Casey and Shawn oversaw all media documentation. No one overestimated their value for the project. They were keenly aware that they were there mostly because Jim prized company. As the tagalong journalist, I mostly felt like a member of the team, but I also played the role of outside observer.

On April 20, 2009, the team awoke while the sky was still grey, and the morning sun had yet to introduce itself. Rubbing the sleep from our eyes, we set out to Qumran in a rental van for the first day of the dig. Driving from Arad to the Dead Sea required us to take Highway 31, a roller-coaster of a road where the navigator has no option but to ride the breaks all the way down the zigzagging descent. Worried about being late, Chris still refused to speed. His cautiousness was justified by the mangled wreckage of abandoned vehicles at the base of the steep cliffs which the highway overhung.

The group came to life as we spotted the Dead Sea in the distance. The salt pillars marking the edge of the water reveal the Dead Sea's unusual composition. Because of rapid evaporation rates and a scarcity of outlets, the water is nine percent saltier than the ocean. Chemical plants make a fortune extracting the trove of sulfur, gypsum, magnesium, chlorine, sodium and potassium.

Floating in the buoyant Dead Sea is a must for every tourist in Israel, but they rarely last long. The slimy brine has the added effect of making a small scratch burn like fire. When Roman General Vespasian was dispatched to the Jordan Valley to lock down the Jews' First Revolt, he was curious to confirm the reports about the salty sea. He tied the hands of a few soldiers and tossed them into the water to see if they could float; they did, much to their delight.

While the team made a car game out of spying the ubiquitous caves passing by on the cliff lines, everyone chatted about the day's possibilities.

"I am psyched to finally be doing this," Shawn said. "I feel like it's taken forever to get to this point where shovels break ground." He had come a long way since the day he blew off his dad's first announcement that he had solved the Copper Scroll.

Jim sat shotgun, chain-chewing gum. "I've been waiting eagerly too," Jim added. "But this whole time I've been so focused on pushing to make it happen that the last two years have actually gone by pretty fast."

Looking out the window, the group saw a lone Bedouin woman, draped in heavy black robes with shiny embroidery, walking along the side of the road. They passed two shoeless boys in the hills, hustling their flocks to an unseen destination. Shawn stuck his camera out of the window to take a picture of the roadside monument: "Lowest Point on Earth, 394 Meters Below Sea Level."

As the group piled out of the van, Peleg was in the Qumran parking lot waiting—unusually prompt for an Israeli. Wearing a pair of fake Oakley sunglasses and a dingy white t-shirt tied to the top of his bald head, Peleg was much more prepared for the blistering heat than Jim's crew.

Jim did not warn Peleg that such a colorful cast was accompanying him to Israel. Despite the conspicuous cameras and tripods, he introduced them to Peleg as family and friends who wanted to observe. Jim explained that if assistance with digging was needed, they were more than happy to help. Shawn and Casey were the only ones self-aware enough to feel embarrassed by the group's intrusion. Peleg suppressed any sign of disapproval and politely shook hands with the team. Chris gave him a quick hug and said, "The last time we saw you, you were off to war."

Peleg replied, "Yes, we know when they start, but we never know when they will end. At least it's over for now." He then introduced his work team: three sunbaked Bedouin diggers who did not speak English.

Walking into Qumran in its pre-tourist hours, Chris exclaimed in a chipper voice, "This is the first time we have come here and been able to walk past the ticket counter. We have paid that twenty-shekel entrance fee a dozen times by now!"

ESSENE DEBATE

Had it not been for the Dead Sea Scrolls, Qumran wouldn't need a ticket counter. The tiny site hardly stands out from other nearby ruins. The Israelis started billing Qumran as a tourist attraction in the 1980s. Even still, many tourists on a tight schedule skip Qumran for the desert's more visually appealing sites. They make the day trip from Jerusalem to visit the much grander neighboring site at Masada—an ancient palace turned rugged fortress roosted on a high rock plateau. Or, they opt to visit Ein Gedi where historic ruins are bedecked with lush greenery, wandering ibex, and spring-fed pools and waterfalls.

Peleg—despite being one of Qumran's foremost archaeologists—contributed to the belittling of the compound's importance. After ten years of intermittent excavations at Qumran, Peleg and Magen published a much-anticipated paper promoting the divisive idea that the site in the second century BCE was a forward observation post; in its latter occupation, during the Roman phase, it was nothing more than a pottery factory. The academic duo proposed that the site had no religious purpose, only commercial, and in fact had nothing to do with the Essenes. The proximity of the hidden scrolls was mere coincidence. They based their revisionist thinking on their excavation of Qumran's pottery kilns, pottery rejects, and the thousands of pieces of stacked pottery in the pantry. The two archaeologists were struck by the tons of high-quality potter's clay sitting on the bottom of two Qumran water basins. Their rogue theory became harder to defend when a wide range of pottery samples from Qumran underwent a neutron activation analysis. The tests concluded that well over half of the pottery originated outside Qumran. The critique naturally followed: If Qumran was once the hub of the region's pottery industry, why did they import utensils from Jericho and Hebron?[1]

Although a near consensus about the origins of the Dead Sea Scrolls once existed, the argument has overheated to the point that normally composed professors have reduced themselves to lawsuits, identity theft, and defamation. Experts revel in contradicting experts; Sigmund Freud labeled it the "narcissism of small differences." Among scroll scholars exists an Essene camp and an anti-Essene camp. The Essene camp approaches Qumranology by merging the textual record with the archaeological. The anti-Essene camp adopts a post-modern methodology, insisting that the physical record must be analyzed apart from ancient textual sources. Both camps growl that they are being silenced by the other. Magen liked to refer to the Essene camp as "a guild with money and conferences."[2]

The association between Qumran and the Dead Sea Scrolls developed soon after their discovery. The most obvious reason had to do with proximity. Out of eleven caves, six were within a quarter mile of Qumran. The cave which stored the largest cache of scrolls was only a few hundred yards from the ruins and could only be accessed by walking through the complex. The caves in the cliffs surrounding Qumran are natural, but the larger caves in the Qumran plateau are man-made.

Archaeological evidence at Qumran also pointed to a linkage between the ruins and the scrolls. The type of pottery jars that stored many of the parchments in caves were cylindrical containers with bowl-shaped lids. The same uniquely shaped lidded jars were unearthed inside Qumran. Plucked from the soil of Qumran were several inkwells—a rare find at comparable sites from this era—indicating that a surprising proportion of occupants might have been scribes. The Dead Sea Scrolls must have made up a voluminous religious library for the inhabitants of Qumran. That presented the next riddle to solve: what highly literate and religious community inhabited Qumran?

The kind of community described in the sectarian materials matched what historians knew from ancient sources about the Essenes. For example, the charitable and equitable practices of the Essenes described by Josephus and Philo, like the pooling of personal property, paralleled the requirements laid out in the scroll *Community Rule*. According to *Community Rule*, initiates at Qumran had to yield their private property to the communal fund. Josephus idealized the ascetic group for shunning wealth and pursuing humble lives of religious study and worship.

In addition, the *Damascus Document*, another sectarian scroll, profiles a religious community obsessed with maintaining a strict standard of purity. While the *Damascus Document* standards far outpace the requirements of Sadducees and Pharisees, the scroll parallels many of Josephus' descriptions of the Essenes laws and rituals.

Josephus and Philo wrote about the Essenes living in communities all over Israel, but they never specifically referenced an Essene settlement near the Dead Sea. Pliny the Elder, a first-century Roman geographer, is responsible for providing a geographical clue about the Essenes' headquarters. In Book V of his *Natural History* (77 CE), Pliny described a religious community that, prior to the destruction of the Second Temple, lived "to the west of the Dead Sea," at a necessary distance from "the noxious exhalations on the coast." Pliny described the "solitary tribe" as settling above Ein Gedi. Qumran is the strongest candidate, by far, to comply with Pliny's account.

Qumran's architecture matches the needs of an ascetic group focused on intense study and ritual cleanliness. The ruins show evidence of ten stepped pools, many of which served as ritual immersion pools, a necessity for the Essenes' purity laws. No other site in Israel has that many immersion pools within a dense complex. Qumran's one kitchen and large pantry, with an abundance of tableware, points to the existence of communal meals, a sacred rite for Essenes. A large assembly hall in the ruins may have hosted the kind of group study and prayer which, according to Josephus, was a regular part of the Essenes' daily ritual.

For over thirty years, the question of the scrolls' authorship appeared settled. Biblical scholars widely accepted the Qumran-Essene hypothesis. De Vaux cemented the viewpoint.[3] Based on his archaeological discoveries, de Vaux constructed a historical narrative with Essenes living at Qumran during Second Temple times. The sect came under attack by Vespasian and his Roman legions when the Romans were sweeping the area clean of Jewish strongholds in the first century. The Essenes hid their scrolls in nearby caves before they fled or were killed.

De Vaux originally estimated that no more than 200 sect members lived in the Qumran complex. Because Qumran has almost no sleeping quarters, de Vaux supposed that the separatists only worked, ate, and worshiped inside the complex. During the summer, they converted the surrounding caves into living quarters; during the winter, when the caves were more prone to collapse, they dwelled in tents on the hillsides. Israeli archaeologist Hanan Eshel located the contours of ancient tracks leading from the settlement to the caves. A scant amount of archaeological evidence was acquired to indicate that the environs once hosted an encampment: old sandal nails, broken pottery, circles of stones, and a tent peg. Granted, archaeologists wouldn't expect to find many artifacts on the exposed windswept hills. Qumran possibly housed around twenty residents in upstairs dormitories. Nothing remains today of a second level.

By the late 1980s, cracks in the Essene theory emerged. Scholars began to challenge the prevailing assumptions about the origins of the scrolls and the purpose of Qumran. They wondered if de Vaux faulted in interpreting the archaeological remains at Qumran. If the archaeology was decoupled from the scrolls, the artifacts and architecture could point to other possible uses for the site.

De Vaux died of a heart attack before he completed a final report from his Qumran excavations. Belgian scholars Robert Donceel and Pauline Donceel-Voûte were tasked with cataloguing and publishing de Vaux's field notes; they took the opportunity to rethink the conclusions of the priest-archaeologist. What they determined, rightly or wrongly, was that the original excavations failed to establish a concrete archaeological link between Qumran and the Essenes, or even Qumran and the scrolls.[4]

For starters, the Donceels were struck by the lack of scrolls or scroll fragments found inside the Qumran complex. No records of community life were found in the ruins to give Qumran context. The husband and wife academic duo focused on the insufficient number of private dwellings for a place assumed to house a religious community. The Donceels interpreted the remains at Qumran, particularly some sophisticated ceramics and a reclining couch, to indicate the site was once a manor home for a wealthy Jerusalemite family. Religious sectarians, the logic went, did not own such nice things.

Qumranologist Jodi Magness is the most convincing critic of the conclusions of the Donceels, and the anti-Essene camp to which they belong. After carefully synthesizing de Vaux's raw data, Magness determined that the Qumran-Essene connection held up. Magness argued that wealthy Jerusalemites were unlikely to choose the remote Qumran as a winter getaway. Because the Donceels had never actually excavated in Israel, they overstated the presence of Qumran's luxurious wares, modest in comparison to contemporary sites. Unlike the pageantry of other villas in the region contemporary to Qumran, Qumran lacks frescoes, mosaics, fine furniture, or marble.[5] It abounds in mortar stone walls, packed dirt floors, and utilitarian dishes. The Donceels' flawed theory did not account for the plethora of immersion pools at Qumran nor the sprawling cemetery attached to the settlement with mostly male interments.

Professor Norman Golb of the University of Chicago was the shrillest dissenter from the Essene theory. He believed Qumran was a Judean military fortress, as evidenced by its tall watchtower and strategic location on a major transit route. Never mind that Qumran is built at the bottom of an overhanging cliff, a vulnerable location for a supposed stronghold. Golb insisted that the archaeological data from Qumran must be divorced from the scroll corpus. By his calculations, a small sectarian community like the Essenes could not sustain the number of scribes sufficient to produce volumes of manuscripts. (Paleographers note little similarity between the handwriting styles of the various Dead Sea Scrolls. By some estimates, the 800 manuscripts represent the labor of 750 different scribes.)

Golb also supposed too many Jewish viewpoints and textual traditions were represented in the scroll corpus to be the product of one rogue Second Temple sect. Although some of the legal views in the scrolls align with Sadducean thought, they contain other theological ideas about fate and the afterlife that are closer to that of the Pharisees. Golb imagined that the scrolls were safely removed from Jerusalem libraries during the First Revolt against Rome. A retinue of Jews fleeing Roman forces between 66 and 73 CE made their way to Qumran—a day's march. In haste, they borrowed pottery jars from an already abandoned Qumran to store their scrolls and hide them in caves for safekeeping.[6] From there, they likely fled to Masada or Ein Gedi, hoping to one day retrieve their holy texts.

The Temple Scroll from Cave 11 was a rare instance of finding a scroll in its full state of preservation: thin parchment, wrapped in bleached linen, inside a jar covered with a bowl-shaped lid.[7] The linen cloths, in their own way, support the theory of Essene ownership. Josephus describes the Essenes' custom of white linen clothing, unlike the more popular woolen clothes that usually incorporated vivid patterns found at other first-century archaeological sites. The IAA's textile expert, Orit Shamir, proposes that the Essenes repurposed pieces of their linen tunics to wrap their scrolls.[8]

It's the job of archaeologists to take all data into account, and when it comes to Qumran it seems like bad science to ignore the vast scroll libraries so close to the site. According to Devorah Dimant, a textual expert on the Dead Sea Scrolls, the identification of Qumranites as the scroll authors grows more convincing, not less, as research techniques advance.[9] Handwriting on a pottery sherd unearthed at Qumran has been determined to match the handwriting of a scroll author. Chemical tests have proven that some scroll jars were manufactured at Qumran. A test sampling of scroll ink was produced with water from the Dead Sea.

Despite the best efforts of the anti-Essene scholarly camp, the Essene hypothesis is still the most popular and long-held; even if it is now accompanied by a degree of skepticism. As for Jim, he entertained no doubt: Qumran was inhabited by Essenes, and the Essenes were the authors of the Dead Sea Scrolls. In his research, Jim argued that the Essenes were uniquely positioned, as an ascetic community incorruptible by riches, to be the best keepers of Temple wealth. Qumran made a logical hiding spot since, to the Essenes, Jerusalem and the Temple were defiled. Qumran, Jim believed, was more than a desert monastery; it was idealized by the Essenes as a New Jerusalem. As their spiritual nucleus, it was the only place outside of Jerusalem that was sacred enough to entomb holy ritual objects, perhaps brought there by disaffected priests sympathetic to the Essenes. With that in mind, Qumran's layout was Jim's interpretive key to the Copper Scroll. One had to be studied in conjunction with the other.

Surprisingly, conversations about the origins of the Dead Sea Scrolls never came up in Jim's meetings with Peleg. Jim knew that opinions on the scrolls' authorship were irrelevant to his theories on the locations of the caches. All that mattered was the current architecture of Qumran and how well it matched the descriptions of the Copper Scroll, even if it was an ancient pottery factory. Small wonder, therefore, that scholarly rivalry among scroll scholars has created tunnel vision for decades regarding the Copper Scroll. Jim saw the forest for the trees.

By default, archaeology is more the art of serendipity than the science of prediction. As a merciless discipline, new archaeological discoveries often turn academic theories on their heads—granting historians only a short grace period to catch up. If even one of the Copper Scroll relics was located at Qumran, the entire paradigm of scroll study would tilt. Jim hoped his theory, if proven right, could finally unlock the secrets of the Essenes.

POTENTIAL CAVE

Fishing through his oversized pockets for the keys to the gate, Peleg asked Jim if he still wanted to start at the *hill of Kokhlit*. Haunted by what might be inside the Copper Scroll's most important location, Jim tried to keep his nod casual. Jim guessed that Peleg was drawn to the area because it was an undisturbed site. A student of archaeology, Peleg understood that, when it came to the Dead Sea region, no stone should go unturned.

Jim suggested that the dig start right on top of the sinkhole. Peleg, who had already given it some thought, countered with his own instructions. The diggers would dig a six-foot trench right along the rock edge and then begin digging out away from the rock. The goal was to identify a possible cave opening. "We'll burrow our way to the sinkhole in no time," Peleg assured.

Within fifteen minutes, the Bedouin diggers dropped four metal poles into the sun-scorched ground and created a canopy of shade with a faded black mesh tarp. The shading was adequate, despite the tarp's gaping holes. They then laid out the equipment. For all the technological advances of the modern world, the archaeological process looked surprisingly primitive: picks, shovels, spades, wheelbarrows, and buckets. The whole of their equipment was worth no more than a hundred dollars.

Signaling for Jim and Chris to follow his lead, Peleg stood close by the diggers, watching carefully as their shovels set to work. Peleg made no indication that the rest of the team was invited to help with the digging. Each person found his or her own non-imposing perch, opposite from the tarp—close enough that we wouldn't miss anything, but far enough that we could only hear the echo of the picks hitting occasional rock.

After forty minutes, before the diggers broke a sweat, a strange lip appeared in part of the rock, indicating an opening of some kind. Peleg jumped down into the hole to get a better look. Todd chopped the air so hard with excitement that his hat fell off. Peleg instructed the diggers to carefully follow where the rock lip curved under with their trowels. Chris, standing next to Jim, snuck the group a thumbs-up. Shawn adjusted his camera for a better angle and whispered to his dad, "Maybe after this we can go search for Atlantis." Jim stayed quiet, bent forward with his gaze locked on the rock.

This day, like every other day, Jim wore his battle dress uniform—a white V-neck shirt, camouflage pants, boots, and a leather fedora. Chris looked his opposite with a baseball cap, khaki cargo shorts, and old tennis shoes. Shawn had a director's goatee and the regulation hipster glasses with thick black frames. His black hair was carefully groomed.

One bucket at a time, the diggers removed the dirt and large rocks and walked them down to the bottom of the hill. I waved for Casey, who was moving in and out of the tarp with his camera, to give me an update on what he overheard. He came and squatted next to me. "All we know so far is that Peleg is taking interest in how the rock is curving under," he reported. "Don't get too excited yet." With Peleg visibly intrigued, adrenaline pumped through the team's veins. We took our only real task, sitting and waiting, extremely serious.

After pulling out thirty buckets of dirt—and three live scorpions—the diggers hit solid rock. Peleg brushed the rock lip off and reported without emotion, "It's nothing." Peleg said the digging would continue at the cave, down deeper, but romantic hopes of an early discovery were dashed. A few team members went back to the van to get chairs and ice chests. Shawn and Casey turned their cameras off to conserve battery.

The sudden disabuse of our fantasies reminded me of a scene in the iconic 1968 film, *Funny Girl*: Barbara Streisand, playing Fannie Brice, got a telegram notifying her that she had an audition for a Broadway play—her dream job. Fannie threw her head down saying, "Where's all the suffering before you click? And the hard knocks, the setbacks you're supposed to learn from? This is too quick. I haven't suffered enough yet." Archaeology is not known to yield fruit after forty minutes of excavation. As much as Jim and the team wished that to be true, like Fannie, we hadn't suffered enough yet.

The strange rock curvature was a small portion of the potential cave site. The three diggers continued to remove dirt for three more hours, wrapping around the *hill of Kokhlit* to a depth of about three feet. When the tarp no longer protected them from the midday sun, the work pace slowed and breaks increased.

Those of us sitting on a pile of rocks, away from the dig, were roasting by midday. Larry and Ken's polyester pants showed sweat stains. Linda, who dressed like a conservative Jew, regretted her layers. Todd, despite his giant straw hat, was crimson. One by one, the team members crept under the tarp, figuring that if we stayed quiet we could enjoy the shade without bothering Peleg or the diggers. If we had been allowed to dig, we would have jumped on the chance. Thus far, no invitation was forthcoming. Everyone settled with making ourselves as invisible as possible.

The Americans drank gallons of cold water to quench their thirst; the Bedouin and Peleg opted for hot tea with mint. During a break, one of the diggers—curious as to why they were digging outside the ruins—asked, "What's in here? What are we digging for anyway?" Peleg ignored the question and gathered up the small glass tea cups.

The Bedouin were right to question the purpose of an excavation outside the compound. The most recent attention the mound received was from a 2006 report by Israeli archaeologist Joe Zias and American biblical scholar James Tabor.[10] Noticing the discoloration of the soil a few hundred feet north of the mound, the scholars theorized that the area served as the Essene community's open-air latrine. From the writings of Josephus, Tabor and Zias knew the Essene bathroom rituals required them to go at least 1,500 feet outside the camp, dig a trench with a hatchet, and cover their feces. The report noted that the rocky outcrop, Jim's *hill of Kokhlit*, provided a natural barrier to block the Essenes from view. Jim's concept stood in direct contradiction to Zias and Tabor. The area could not be both a holy repository and a communal toilet.

At four o'clock, after the diggers finished a four-foot trench along the rock face, Peleg answered a call on his cellphone. He looked at Jim and walked away to talk out of earshot. Jim noticed that when Peleg returned, he seemed anxious, declaring that it was time to close out the dig at the *hill of Kokhlit*. "There are no signs of human activity here—no pottery in any of the stratum," Peleg told Jim. Picking up a handful of dirt to let it seep through his fingers, he added, "Its natural dirt, virgin soil."

Jim dreaded those words. He knew that for his theory to be fully tested, they needed to dig an additional six feet down and ten feet back. Not wanting to get the excavation bogged down, but also wanting to leave the door open to return to the *hill of Kokhlit*, Jim negotiated. "That's fine," he said. "All I ask is that the dirt not be filled back in." Peleg nodded. Jim and Peleg made plans to meet back the next day to excavate the drainage channel where they found the Vogel.

The van was quieter on the way back to Arad. A few in the group felt deflated, but Jim was unfailingly optimistic. "For now, the *hill of Kokhlit* doesn't mean anything to Peleg or the ADCA," he said. "To them, it's nothing more than a weird rock formation disconnected from the ruins. We need my research to be verified by finding at least one Copper Scroll artifact inside Qumran, and then Peleg will feel warranted in revisiting the *hill of Kokhlit*."

Despite his upbeat attitude, the experience from the day was a wakeup call. Jim hadn't anticipated how long the digging would take with only three people doing the labor. To get any closure on whether the *hill of Kokhlit* was an actual cave required more time and laborers than Peleg was willing to initially commit. And Peleg showed no interest in asking any of the Americans with Jim to operate as volunteers. If Jim questioned his own judgment in bringing along so many observers, he never admitted to it.

GUTTER

The next morning Jim made sure that the team arrived at the site on time by getting Ken, the retired trucker, to drive. "Archaeologists have the hours of morning talk show hosts," Casey said, trying to wipe the sleep out of his eyes.

Peleg again beat the team to the site. Standing by the entrance with his same three diggers, Peleg looked anxious to get started. He glanced at Larry and Shawn who were accidentally in matching outfits; only Shawn meant his tan polyester pants and cowboy cut button-down shirt as an ironic hipster statement.

Chris suspected that, after the teaser discovery of the large crystal, Peleg was as intrigued by the gutter as they were. Without knowing exactly where the items were buried, the entire length of the twenty-foot shaft needed to be excavated. Unknown to Peleg, Robo-Cam waited in the trunk on standby.

The drainage channel butted up next to the edge of the complex and then dropped off by a sloping cliff. The team had to straddle the outer wall to create plenty of room for the diggers to get the best angles. From where Jim stood, he could see part of Cave 4. First found by Bedouin in 1952, the man-made cave—which was really two caves—was littered with 15,000 fragments from hundreds of manuscripts. De Vaux and his band of archaeologists never noticed it while they were excavating the ruins, even though the Bedouin were siphoning off its contents in pieces to the highest bidders.

Initially, Peleg instructed the diggers to expose the exterior of the stone pipe, buried under sediment brought in by the desert winds. They then dug trenches two feet deep on the outer sides of the shaft. When the diggers came across a potsherd (piece of ancient pottery) they casually handed it to Peleg. Peleg organized them into two piles: flat or curved.

"Flat potsherds are nothing special. What I mostly care about are the curved ones," Peleg told me. I tried to coax him out of his shyness with questions. "Curved potsherds give better clues about what they were used for." Holding up two curved sherds, he went on, "These are both Herodian period. One was part of a bowl; the other was part of a cooking pot." Archaeologists like Peleg can instinctively recall arcane details about what differentiates one piece of pottery from the next. Finding an inscribed potsherd in the dirt is like spotting a double rainbow in the sky. The only inscribed potsherds at Qumran were found outside a boundary wall in 1996. One of the potsherds preserves eighteen lines from a deed of gift, possibly a witness to an Essene initiate donating his private assets which included his home, a slave, and trees.

Peleg apologized for his English; he was nimbler in Hebrew and Arabic. "I speak to you guys in English, the diggers in Arabic, and the whole time I'm thinking in Hebrew." He grasped his bald head demonstrating the headache of trilingualism. Working together for seventeen years, Peleg learned Arabic from bantering day in and day out with the same three Bedouin diggers. He learned English in school. Though he didn't like English, it played an important role in his professional life. He complained that any time an archaeologist in Israel received a permit to dig, they had to write an academic after-action report.

"Do you write it in Hebrew or English?" I asked.

"Gam v'gam," he said, meaning "both" in Hebrew. Smirking, he added, "But I have people to help edit my English."

In certain places, the stones were pieced crudely together with pockmarked brown cement. Peleg explained that when the Jordanians were in control of Qumran in the 1960s, they decided to make Qumran a tourist site. Wanting the site to live up to the fame of the Dead Sea Scrolls, the Jordan Department of Antiquities tried their hand at restoration, applying brown cement to rebuild walls and fill in holes.

When Qumran came under the control of the Israelis in 1967, the ideology changed. Peleg said, "We only excavate ruins, and we don't reconstruct them. We let them stay in their most authentic form." In rare cases, when the Israelis do need to reinforce parts of the ruins, they use an adhesive that blends better with the original mortar, a surface that has endured two millennia worth of sand abrasion.

As Peleg expounded on the divisive modern history of Qumran, he picked up an ax and hacked off a top capstone, cracking right through the Jordanian cement. He then had the diggers remove an additional capstone so that the once enclosed shaft had two top entry points to reach inside. After tediously tiptoeing around the complex to avoid harming the ruins, the team suppressed their gasps. Jim whispered to Chris, "Oh my goodness. He is serious."

Peleg instructed one digger to continue to create a trench along the outside of the gutter. The other two diggers worked, alternately, clearing the interior. Getting past cigarette butts and grocery bags to a first-century level took an hour. Despite Peleg's two new access points on the top, the diggers had trouble getting a good angle to reach down inside the shaft. They had to lie down across the rocks and stretch their arms down the pipe. Once they reached a level in the sediment that exposed no more potsherds, Peleg decided it was time to wind-up the gutter excavation.

Jim spoke up. "The Copper Scroll describes depths that are two cubits, or forty inches, below the original floor level," he said. "We haven't gotten close to that." Robo-Cam couldn't fit in the shaft without more debris cleared.

Peleg advised that the length of the shaft and the odd angling required them to return to it later with a metal detector. A scanner could perhaps pinpoint where along the twenty-foot tunnel the cache was buried, sparing them from excavating its entire length. After a mint tea and water break, Peleg recommended moving on to test a third site. Like the cave, Peleg promised that the gutter dig would be left open and not filled back in. The two capstones were laid to the side.

BROKEN PROTECTIVE WALL

As Jim looked over his report to identify the next test site, he heard a wailing siren, echoing off the cliff faces. Only once Peleg stood erect and folded his arms reverently, did the team realize that it was Holocaust Remembrance Day, *Yom HaShoah*. The siren blared from the loudspeaker at the nearby kibbutz. We quickly stepped up on the walkway next to Peleg, bowing our heads as a show of solidarity with him, and with the nation. Jim pushed up his fedora; Larry and Chris removed their baseball caps; and Todd unfastened his broad-brimmed hat. Oddly, Jews cover their heads to show respect, and Americans uncover them.

Every *Yom HaShoah*, the siren signals the whole country to observe two minutes of silence. Busy highways and bustling malls come to a complete standstill. Israel historian Tom Segev refers to the Holocaust as the civil religion of Israel. After the end of World War II, the Jewish nation was filled with Holocaust survivors trying to piece their lives back together. Among the elderly in Israel, the tattooed serial numbers of Auschwitz are often still visible on wrinkled forearms.

"What was that? Was that for Hitler?" the diggers asked.

Peleg evaded eye contact. He muttered, "It's to remember the Holocaust."

After the siren died away, Jim suggested digging at the fifth Copper Scroll location, where a hoard was buried at the shortest depth and in the smallest surface area: the *double entry pool.* Jim wanted to avoid repeating the same pattern as the first two dig sites which were not specific enough. Peleg, however, was hesitant to dig directly inside Qumran. Despite his willingness to knock off Jordanian cement at the shaft, he felt protective of the more iconic portions of the ruins.

Peleg preferred to stay on the outskirts of the complex for the test sites. Taking a copy of Jim's maps, Peleg pointed to a site at the edge of Qumran's outer wall. Jim was pleased that Peleg was familiar enough with the research to have a counter-location prepared. Though fearing the site would require a deeper penetration and longer width than Peleg would be willing to check, Jim simply nodded his approval in placation. As things stood, he aimed to sidestep any conflict with the archaeologist who held the keys to Qumran.

Location 45 and the first line of 46, according to McCarter, translates: *In a cavity, which is north of the entrance of the gorge of Beth-tamar, in the parched surface of some cracked plaster: everything that is in it is consecrated. In the sluice that is at the boundary.*[11] According to Jim's investigator's comparison, the text in column nine translates quite differently: *Brought here which was hidden on the other side pull up from the House of Hakkoz (still) erect with (narrow) entries is a wonderful fortune. All carried here was secluded and left in bags by the broken protective wall for water.* Jim identified Qumran's western boundary wall as the best match for the description of a *broken protective wall for water.* It was close to the House of Hakkoz (the watchtower) and ran parallel to Qumran's largest cistern.

At this location, the Copper Scroll leaves off the exact depth of the stash. Going by the average Copper Scroll entry, depths range from six to seven cubits—twelve to fourteen feet. The Copper Scroll does not specify where along the *broken protective wall* the stash was buried. To thoroughly excavate, they would have to dig a deep trench stretching the entire breadth of the wall. Peleg instructed the diggers to initiate a probe in the middle of the wall's perimeter and continue digging until he called them off. Jim held out hope that at their third test site the excavation would go to the proper levels.

The diggers looked irritated since their routine normally halted at virgin soil. Their backs still felt stiff from the awkward postures they held while hollowing out the drainage channel. Once they had a small three-foot-deep probe, they started murmuring to each other in Arabic. Mack was not content merely observing. "I wish I could get in there and do the digging myself," he told Jim.

Chris, inwardly praying, walked over to Casey. Wringing his hands, he vented, "We really need to find something. Otherwise, I don't see them still going."

Larry and Ken, noticeably hangdog, paced in the dirt. Shawn and Casey whiled away the time by frequenting the café for popsicles. Todd disappeared into the mountains to hunt for porcupine quills. I, seven weeks pregnant and still trying to keep it a secret, frequented the toilets to dry-heave. Jim stood in the sun reading through his research, hoping to find more clues that showed exactly where along the *broken protective wall* the bagged fortune was buried. Within a few hours, the diggers exhumed a hole three-feet-deep and four-feet-wide. During a tea break, Mack lowered himself into the cavity to measure its shallowness. The hole stopped short of Mack's mid-thighs.

Peleg sidelined Jim and told him, "It's time to halt the digging." Jim misunderstood Peleg to mean that the entire excavation was over. He tried to disguise his disappointment. He summoned the strength to extend his hand to Peleg and thank him for his efforts. Peleg reassured Jim, "We are done digging for *today*, I mean. We still have plenty to do. Archaeology requires patience, and I have a lot of it."

Peleg clarified that the three test sites would remain open. But he didn't want to waste any more days digging to ridiculous depths before he could scan the hideaways with a metal detector. First, Peleg had to get permission from his boss, Magen, to use a metal detector at Qumran. Once Magen signed off, they could go back to the *hill of Kokhlit*, gutter, and *broken protective wall* and scan each of the sites with the detector. Jim anticipated that once they had a metal detector they could also scan promising sites inside the ruins, like the *double entry pool*.

After witnessing the access issues of the three attempted test sites, Jim was convinced that the margin of error was large enough to justify the intervention of a metal detector. A metal detector revealing a positive read, Jim hoped, would spur the excavation on to the required depths. Without a powerful tool to scan the sites, they would have to dig dozens of probes twelve feet deep. Qumran would be left looking like a close-up shot of the moon.

KILLING TIME

Jim and Peleg agreed to meet back at Qumran in two days. Peleg needed the time to secure the metal detector and permission from Magen. Two days turned into a week. While Jim anxiously waited on a phone call from Peleg, the advance team padded around the house in Arad. With widely varying ages and backgrounds, we would have never kept company in the United States. Upon arrival, the only thing the motley crew had in common was a connection to Jim.

After a week of eating communal meals, staying up late, talking theology, joking, and galvanizing grievances about the dig progress, the group took on the camaraderie of cabin mates at summer camp. What the Qumran complex was to the Essenes, the Arad house was to the advance team—minus the ritual baths and white linen clothing. All cerebral people, we spent much of our downtime perusing Flynn's extensive library, which included a Hebrew/English edition of the *Zohar*, Judaism's foundational mystical text. Todd and Linda cooked elaborate low-budget meals. Casey, Shawn and I took advantage of the top-notch video equipment to produce scripted skits, unintelligible due to our hysteria, with Arad as our desert backdrop.

Despite the good times, the reason we blocked three weeks out of our regular lives and flew to Israel was to see the *Copper Scroll Project* through. The carrot that we kept chasing wasn't the Copper Scroll treasure; we chased after the experience, the chance to conclusively test Jim's research. Every day that we weren't excavating at Qumran felt like a missed opportunity. The longer we rested, the more anxious and fretful the group became.

Jim put on a patient appearance, but everyone knew he was addicted to the adrenaline rush of doing; the lack of progress was killing him internally. Plus, Jim had been using the down time to study the biblical legislations regarding the handling of holy items. He was burdened by the seriousness of the requirements. God struck down Uzzah the Levite for unlawfully propping up the Ark. Aaron's priestly sons were killed for bringing unauthorized fire into the Tabernacle. The *Copper Scroll Project* wasn't taking any chances.

On a weekday that we had hoped to hear from Peleg, Jim drove the group to Jerusalem. While most everyone was sightseeing, Jim paid a spontaneous visit to Gershon Salomon. Though Salomon had heard that the dig had commenced, Jim wanted to give him an update in person. In the meeting, Jim revealed no drop-off in his optimism despite the dig's slow start. Salomon, with his pink cheeks and silver hair, mirrored Jim's enthusiastic disposition.

"Gershon, we are out there digging," Jim began. "I know I sound like a lunatic, but on the off chance that we find something holy in that cave, I don't want any archaeologists, or a firefighter, making the mistake of handling the objects, or even being in their presence."

"Oh, no. It would have to be priests, the descendants of Aaron, the *Kohanim*," Salomon replied in a resonant voice.

"How would that work? Would Kohanim be able to get there if they were needed?" Jim asked.

"They'd be there in an hour," Salomon stated with infectious confidence.

"In Oklahoma, we call that lickety-split," Jim laughed with relief. "I've seen Indiana Jones. I don't want anyone getting fried as soon as the cave is opened."

Kohanim were the ancient Israelite tribe marked for Temple service. Long held family traditions combined with the scientific advances of genetic testing have allowed many of the Kohanim in Israel to be identified. In the months prior to the excavation, the Temple Institute announced that a caste of Kohanim from their registry, for the first time since the destruction of the Temple, were fitted for their priestly vestments. From the flaxen thread and elaborate embroidery to the expensive crimson dye, the vestments were prepared according to the blueprints provided in Exodus.

METAL DETECTOR

The next morning the whole team drove to Qumran to meet Peleg. As we got closer to the ruins, Jim brushed the knots out of his hair. Shawn sensed he was brushing his hair out of a nervous habit. Jim complained in a self-mockingly feminine voice, "I don't ever remember my long hair in high school getting so tangled. I think gray tangles easier."

As soon as the group arrived, they perceived a mood change in Peleg. He was alone, without his diggers. Normally laid back and friendly, he appeared rushed and tense. For the first time, he acted annoyed. He looked at Shawn and Casey, holding cameras by their side, and told Jim that no cameras could be around for the electronic scan. "Also, I need you to take my picture off your website," Peleg said. "Calls about it have come into the office."

Peleg's protest referred to a picture that Jim posted from his very first meeting with the ADCA. The picture showed Magen, Peleg, and Dorfman all sitting around a table at the Rockefeller Museum looking at Jim's research. Jim, who had included the picture in a blog update, apologized and guaranteed he would take it down immediately.

Peleg pulled a dirt-caked metal detector out of his truck. As a reservist, he was scheduled to participate later that day in ceremonies for *Yom HaZikaron*. "We have one hour to do this," he told Jim. "I have to be back in Jerusalem, on Mount Herzl, at ten."

Jim knew that one hour was a desperate attempt at best. Even though the metal detector was a good brand, it was designed to sense metals no deeper than three feet. "Okay," Jim said, feeling disheartened. "Let's see what we can do."

Peleg, Jim, and Chris darted off on their own to go over the test sites. The three walked in time and with heavy steps. At the *hill of Kokhlit*, the only time the detector beeped was when it touched Peleg's steel-toed shoe. The gutter ushered no recognition from the device. Jim figured as much since hidden gems would be impervious to a metal detector. Along the *broken protective wall*, the only thing the detector picked up was a gum wrapper.

The group could barely watch the pathetic attempts to buttress the research. The obvious shift in Peleg's demeanor struck Shawn as curious. He and Casey put the cameras in the van. Shawn knew his father was determined and didn't give up easily. Nervously scratching his goatee, he asked me, "What will Dad tell everyone back home if we have to quit already?"

Before Peleg hurried off to the ceremonies, he told Jim he would call him in five days. Jim tried to attribute the delay to the upcoming holiday and weekend, but everyone else took it for what it seemed: the end. The team piled into the van and Jim drove toward Arad. Jim, for the first time in two weeks, had a winced look. Only Shawn recognized the expression that often preceded his father's migraines.

During his army days, right after he finished basic training, Jim was hit by a pool stick. Needing to lock down the barracks, he told two soldiers to wrap up their midnight pool game. One of the guys refused to quit. "We exchanged a couple of harsh words. I thought we were doing a bit of chest bumping, and all the sudden I am laying in a pool of my own blood with the room spinning," Jim recalls. His skull was cracked close to the temple, an earlobe dangled by a thin piece of flesh and a shattered jaw sagged away from his skull. Jim's assailant was discharged from the army. Since that night, Jim suffered from occasional migraines and saw flashes of light that often make him unable to distinguish people's faces or read signs. The headaches were the reason he was medically grounded as a helicopter pilot. Afraid to drive, Jim pulled over; Chris took the wheel.

After a day cut short, a melancholy mood engulfed the van. Some of us were mentally calculating how we could move up our return flights. I had to get back home; my husband was deploying to Iraq in two months. Others were debating which Israeli city to visit next. All eyes were on the back of Jim's head, and he knew he couldn't succumb to the sense of siege that the botched dig created or let on to the pulsing pain in his skull. He tried to continue projecting ample resilience.

"This operation has been like having a huge bowl of your favorite ice cream placed in front of you," he said, "and only getting one lick." With that, he had Chris swerve into the next gas station. He sponsored *glida*, Hebrew for ice cream, for everyone.

A week passed with no call from Peleg. With all communication at a standstill, the group flew back home with no idea what had gone wrong or when the dig might resume. The team had expected to return either elated from a find, or disappointed from a dead end. Instead, we felt only uncertainty.

On their flight home, Shawn and Casey discussed what they should do with their small amount of footage. Ken and Larry clutched their bags of Israeli souvenirs. Linda and Todd traded recipes. Don analyzed Peleg's sudden mood change, suspicious of underhanded antics. Jim made notes in his research report. Chris prayed and thought about his dream with the desert holes and the hill. Anytime he was confronted by doubt about Jim's research, he reexamined the dream and the voice that told him Jim was ninety-five percent accurate. The dream was his faith anchor, a constant reminder that he believed the *Copper Scroll Project* was much more than a game of conjecture. Still, Chris felt that, even if Jim was correct about how to read the Copper Scroll locations, his dream didn't ensure that the stashes were still buried at Qumran.

Henry Wright Baker at the Manchester College of Science and Technology designs an elaborate, although crude-looking, device out of retired British army materials and other tools he borrowed from the school of dentistry. He successfully cuts the fragile scrolls without shattering them into pieces.

The Copper Scroll is cut into 23 strips and displayed at The Jordan Museum in Amman.

Jim as Fire Marshal at the Lawton Fire Department

Jim connects with Vendyl Jones for the first time at the veteran explorer's home in Grandview, Texas.

The *hill of Kokhlit* is the only description in the Copper Scroll which Jim places outside of the Qumran ruins. The rocky outcrop sits 300 yards northwest of the complex. According to Jim's research, the *hill of Kokhlit* is the hiding spot for the most significant of the Copper Scroll treasures, including another scroll.

Chris poses with Tamar Yonah, supporter of the *Copper Scroll Project* and hostess for Israel's most popular radio talk show in English.

Jim and Chris are invited to the Rockefeller Museum in East Jerusalem—the headquarters for the Israel Antiquities Authority—to present the research report to Shuka Dorfman, Yitzhak Magen, and Yuval Peleg.

Jim and Shelley video chat with Dr. Kenneth Hanson about nuances in the various Copper Scroll translations.

Chris and Peleg hold the thirteen-sided crystal that they fished out of Qumran's drainage channel.

Jim, Peleg, and three Bedouin workers set up a black mesh tarp at the *hill of Kokhlit*—the first test site in the April 2009 excavation. Shawn and Casey prepare the video cameras.

Jim and Peleg crouch under the tarp's shade and plan for the second test site.

The Copper Scroll advance team finds a non imposing perch, opposite from the tarp, to observe the Bedouin workers' progress.

Jim, Shelley, and Chris tour Qumran with Israeli archaeologist Oren Gutfeld.

Casey, Jim, and Shelley wait while digging preparation begins for the second test site. Peleg selects a twenty-foot-long stone pipe, or gutter, that sits on the edge of the Qumran complex. According to Jim's research, treasure is buried along the widest part of the pipe.

Peleg, preferring for the test sites to stay on the outskirts of the complex, takes a copy of Jim's maps and selects a site at the edge of Qumran's outer wall. However, the test is cut short because the location requires a deeper penetration and longer width than Peleg is willing to probe.

Jim befriends Eitan Campbell, the longtime director of Masada. Campbell arranges for Jim to present his theories to the Israel Nature and Parks Authority.

Knesset member Moshe Feiglin (middle) joins rank with the *Copper Scroll Project*. Feiglin, like other Temple Mount activists, is willing to assist Jim, hoping the Copper Scroll is an unconventional weapon in the fight for the Temple Mount.

Jim looks out on the Temple Mount with Rabbi Yehuda Glick. Glick, a year prior, was shot in the neck, chest, and stomach by a Palestinian terrorist.

Jim chips off a small sample of what looks like mortar from the cave entrance at the *hill of Kokhlit*. A research laboratory in Skokie, Illinois runs a petrographic analyst of the sample and determines that the mixture is most likely man-made mortar.

Shelley visits the Temple Mount after the UNESCO resolution.

Jim and Chris test the White's metal detector. Mack stands in the background.

CHAPTER 13

HAZING

A fter bodysurfing on an outburst of support all the way to Israel, Jim's friends and donors back home were anxious to hear the reasoning behind the dig's hasty end. The problem was that Jim was in the shadows too. His contacts at the IAA and ADCA were incommunicado. Jim phoned, sent emails, mailed letters; there was no response, not even from Dorfman or Peleg. Weeks turned into months. Drained and helpless, Jim felt like the tide had reversed, and now he was doggy paddling merely to keep the *Copper Scroll Project* above water.

Replaying the excavation events in his head, Jim wondered what triggered Peleg's transformation from initial enthusiast to silent dissenter: *Was it the picture of Peleg on the Copper Scroll Project's website? Did Peleg get into trouble with Magen, his boss, for breaking the rock covering of the gutter? Was Peleg bedeviled by the presence of such a large hodgepodge of American observers?*

Friends in Israel occasionally visited Qumran to check if any of the test sites were filled back in. As long as the probes remained open, Jim held out hope that any day Peleg would rematerialize, apologetic for his absence and ready to schedule the second phase of the excavation.

Despite Peleg's about-face, I never heard Jim mutter a negative word about the Israeli authorities. "I believe Peleg made a genuine effort, but he was operating on borrowed time," Jim told the team members, who felt less goodwill. "Magen, or someone else in authority, probably thought the excavation was a nuisance and vetoed its continuance."

In his final letter to Peleg, Jim wrote that he understood the need for "professional caution." He expressed his sincere gratitude, saying, "I will never be able to thank you enough." In closing, Jim wrote, "P.S. I apologize for any inconvenience and scrutiny you may have endured from the academic community." That correspondence, like all the rest before it, went unanswered. Only later did Jim find how closely his postscript expressed the truth.

MEDIA BATTLE

Until the dig stalled, Jim kept his research private, preferring the sites to be kept secret to avoid jeopardizing the excavation. After four months of no word from Israel, Jim reversed strategy and went public with the information. "I only want the items to be recovered," he answered when asked of his motives. He firmly believed that if average Israelis became familiar with his research, they would demand reactivating the dig. Israelis, like Americans, take pleasure in underdogs proving the experts wrong.

Running up to the April excavation, I published articles profiling Jim, but I was careful to stay quiet about the locations or specifics of the research. By August 2009, Jim was ready for full transparency, or nearly full. Nervous that I might ignite a gold rush, I hesitantly wrote a tell-all story naming Qumran as the potential home to all the Copper Scroll treasure. Published on the front page of *Jerusalem Post*'s weekly magazine, with a photo of the team at the Qumran cave, the article forced a response from the ADCA. Responding to the editor's questions, Magen stated, "We did tests and we didn't find anything. Nothing is there." The editors asked why the test sites remained open. Magen conceded that while the permit was technically active, Jim's research "did not hold up." That was the Staff Officer for Archaeology's official line. "For thirty years, each person has come with their own theory and they amount to nothing."[1] Peleg's continued silence, juxtaposed with Magen's scurrilous response, made Jim think that Peleg had to defer to his boss.

Shortly after the *Jerusalem Post* article, Jim was invited as a guest on his friend Tamar Yonah's Sunday morning radio show. Yonah—whom Jim describes as tenacious as a bulldog—made the introduction with her usual fanfare. "Can you imagine what would happen if in this secular world that we live in, a world where we're supposed to be so enlightened and religion is old fashioned and primitive, what would happen if, just if, the Bible was proven to be true?" Yonah continued, "What would happen if the Ark of the Covenant and holy vessels from the Temple were discovered?"

On the live program, Jim briefly explained his Qumran-centric theory. Wrangling over the details, Jim assured the listeners that Peleg's was the name on the permit and the person who oversaw the dig. Jim wanted to throw water on some fiery comments to my online *Jerusalem Post* article. A commenter accused the IAA of letting an amateur dig at Qumran. He iterated that his own role was determining where to dig and to what depth, which, given the way things played out, amounted to mere suggestions.

Mainly, Jim voiced his disillusionment with the level of effort shown in April, and his confusion as to why the excavation was torpedoed. "They stopped at a ridiculously shallow level," Jim said, following with explanations of the dramatic measurements given in the Copper Scroll.

To anyone listening, Jim made his call to action: "The only way we're ever going to know whether my research is true is if the agency continues with the archaeological dig that we started." Knowing the political sensibilities of Yonah's audience, Jim pleaded for urgency: "We have to get these items out of Qumran soon. With peace talks going on, it would be bad enough to give away the land of Israel, but for goodness sake, we can't let them give away the spiritual treasures belonging to Israel as well." Jim pegged her far-right listeners as the most likely Israelis to make phone calls to the IAA if they suspected foul play.

After outing his theory in Israel via print and radio, Jim was approached by contractors for the large television network, *Travel Channel*. They were producing a six-part television series titled "Secret Worlds," hosted by archaeologist Michael Arbuthnot. Each week, the mini-documentaries tackled archaeological wonders of the world, such as Angkor Wat in Cambodia and the monumental statues on Easter Island. The show's producer, Dan Jackson, wanted their final episode to star the Copper Scroll. In researching the scroll online, Jackson came across the *Copper Scroll Project*'s website. He hoped the inspirational firefighter's theory could be the climax of their story arc.

Jim traveled to Israel with the documentary crew to exhibit four of the Qumran sites that his research connected to the Copper Scroll. Jim stood by Qumran's watchtower as the host, Arbuthnot, walked up to meet Jim for the first time. Arbuthnot's look was ideal for television: clean smile, flawless complexion, and a crown of ebony hair. Jim wore a cream-colored oxford shirt and starched indigo jeans. It was his first experience with professional video production and Laurie had told him to dress neutral. Jim recounts, "As they filmed, Michael and I repeated the same conversations over and over, constantly redoing what we had recorded moments earlier."

With cameras and mikes circling around them, Arbuthnot and Jim strolled through the Qumran ruins, stopping at the *double entry pool* and walking up to the *hill of Kokhlit*. At each of the sites, Jim expounded on his theories. Leaning against the ruins and balancing his research report on one knee, Jim explained to Arbuthnot how the Essenes were anti-materialists. According to Pliny the Elder, the Essenes were committed ascetics. They lived utterly without money. Jim believed their commitment to poverty—on an individual level—made them the ideal acting treasurers for the surplus of Temple tithes.

"It's the same idea as getting a eunuch to guard your wife," Jim joked. "The Essenes were masters of self-denial." Both men tried to keep from mopping at the sweat stinging their eyes. While the cameramen changed batteries, Jim elaborated. "The Essenes had their own calendar system, priests, and rituals—apart from Jerusalem. Having an independent treasury was right in line with their mode of operation."

When the show finally aired in July 2010, the product was a comprehensive look at the Copper Scroll. Arbuthnot strung together the biggest questions surrounding the Copper Scroll: Who wrote it and how? To what bullion does it point? Where are the hoards buried? Scroll scholars—like Shimon Gibson and Danny Herman—were interviewed for the film to explain the background of the Dead Sea Scrolls and Qumran. In the last segment of the documentary, Jim was portrayed as the only standing hope for finding the Copper Scroll treasure. Answering Arbuthnot's questions on camera, Jim's chiseled tan face was softened by his irrepressible optimism.

Once Jim's story was laid bare to large audiences in both Israel and America, he crossed his fingers and hoped that public knowledge would demand bureaucratic movement. On his website, he posted a kindly-worded form letter, declaring endorsement for the *Copper Scroll Project*. He encouraged a grassroots level of followers to affix their name to the letter and send it to the IAA and ADCA. Unfortunately, he had no way to know how many people petitioned the government offices.

Online Adversaries

Grassroots excitement about Jim's research soon catalyzed raucous objections from the scholarly world. Correction: scholarly world is too broad of a term. The protests were specifically from three American professors with blogs: Robert Cargill, Eric H. Cline, and Jim West. The bibliobloggers, as they are known, compiled a short list of amateur explorers who they deemed triple threats. The first threat was to the public. Amateurs, according to the bibliobloggers, preyed on the naïve, abusing their trust, for their own fortune or fame. Second, amateurs had the potential to taint the reputation and preservation of archaeological sites with their religious zealotry and unsupported claims. Thirdly, but perhaps worst of all, the amateurs were taking over the airwaves, coming out of the realm of online conspiracy forums and self-published books, and into the light of mainstream media outlets. Jim Barfield was the newest rogue explorer to set off the bibliobloggers' threat radar.

Biblical archaeology is the glamorous science of digging up the Bible. Still, the highbrow language and nuanced theories of academics don't translate well for broader audiences. For that reason, television producers and reporters push scholars aside in favor of more relatable amateurs. Archaeologists worry that they are losing the information war to sensationalism.

The bibliobloggers' frustration with the media reached such a pitch by 2009 that the American Schools of Oriental Research (ASOR) organized a series of conferences to reform their media strategy. Eric H. Cline—a veteran archaeologist and professor at George Washington University—made it evident that he saw red when amateur enthusiasts practicing "junk science" were popularized by the media.[2]

Most of the attendees agreed that ASOR had to update its media strategy. Cline called for the creation of a war room, a media relations committee always on the offensive in contesting the latest claims coming from pseudoarchaeologists. Every time an erroneous report was published, committee members could swing into action with a timely rebuttal. Professor Robert Cargill suggested personal blogs as the best way to engage the public.

Cargill, an assistant professor of religious studies at the University of Iowa, is well-known among Dead Sea Scroll scholars for both his blog and his digital reconstructions of the archaeological remains at Qumran. His three-dimensional model—often turning up on television specials—piques the imagination by displaying the religious compound in its fully constructed form. As for the blog, Cargill's posts are sometimes personal and, at other times, professional. They consist of uploaded YouTube videos, university announcements, press releases, and satirical comments about conservative Christianity.

In the summer of 2009, Jim Barfield became Cargill's new pet subject. On the ASOR blog, Cargill introduced Jim to fellow members of the archaeological academy using the most cynical terms:

There is a scourge that has reemerged to plague professional archaeologists and biblical scholars, not to mention a gullible general public. It is powerful, seductive, ubiquitous, and quite media savvy. It is not confined to the realms of logic, sound judgment, peer review, and cogency, but rather exists in the sphere of circular reasoning and preys on the hearts and wallets of the religious, who want to believe the lies this deceiver is spouting.[3]

Cargill paid close attention to Jim's media appearances, even minor ones, and kept a sharp eye on Jim's website and Facebook page. Every time Jim made an online update or appeared as a guest on radio or television, Cargill blithely responded via blog. Within a year, Cargill published sixteen posts about the *Copper Scroll Project*.[4]

For a scholar, Cargill's posts seemed to go far beyond the bounds of propriety. Jim referred to Cargill privately as "the man who took the crown among the arrogant elite." Cargill's most stinging accusation was that Jim was using the project to merely feather his own nest. Jim's critics could hardly understand the amount of finances, energy, and sweat he sank into the *Copper Scroll Project*. On many occasions, Laurie was tempted to comment on Cargill's derisive posts, but she—as well as Jim and Chris—held their tongues and keyboards.

Cargill's main issue with Jim was his open admittance of his lack of credentials. In media interviews, Jim routinely confessed that he had a kindergarten level of Hebrew. Jim makes indulgent quips about his lack of formal education: "The only letters behind my name are DRREL, which certifies me to be a relief driver for the fire department." Jim never expected people to take him seriously based on his academic achievements, but rather his thorough analysis. Cargill wrote, "Only the uneducated don't realize they are uneducated."[5]

In January 2010, after my article in *Jerusalem Post* confirmed the ADCA's involvement with Jim, Cargill flew to Israel to meet with Peleg and investigate if his hypercriticism of the *Copper Scroll Project* was warranted.[6] Cargill's first question was if, in fact, Peleg allowed an amateur to lead an excavation at Qumran, a site for which few professional archaeologists can successfully attain permits. Peleg told Cargill that Jim and his team were mere observers. While Cargill surely knew that coordinating excavation dates with observers was an irregular practice, especially at no cost, he pushed Peleg no further. For his part, Peleg stayed quiet about how he went out of his way, in the months leading up to the dig, to consult Jim about test locations and to study Jim's investigative report.

Cargill proudly reported back to his readers that Peleg only tested Jim's theory in select areas that needed maintenance already. For example, Peleg excavated the gutter because clearing it was part of routine site management. Peleg left out the part about going to the extreme of breaking part of the gutter's covering to get a better angle inside. Peleg told Cargill that he picked the *broken protective wall* as a test probe from Jim's research because he wanted to check the area for a lower water channel. When the diggers hit untouched rock by the wall, Peleg halted the probe.

Cargill provided no direct quotes from Peleg in his post, a noticeable detour from his normal blog style and a curious omission considering he flew to Israel specifically for the interview. Jim couldn't be sure of Cargill's paraphrased account. Peleg was clearly trying to create distance from Jim, and Jim naturally felt the sting of that rejection. Still, reading between the lines of Cargill's post, Peleg was more self-protective than critical of Jim. What was left out of the interview was as important as what was said. For example, Peleg didn't mention a thing about digging for an entire day at the *hill of Kokhlit*. Since the rock heap sits well outside of the Qumran complex, digging at the *hill of Kokhlit* hardly qualified as routine maintenance of ruins.

Only once Cargill blogged about his meeting with Peleg did Jim realize the extent of pressure that Cargill, and perhaps other ASOR colleagues, were willing to put on Magen and Peleg. Cargill reported:

It seems that the Israel Antiquities Authority, who Barfield claims provided the permit for their excavation, has stopped returning their calls, and is no longer interested in working with them. Perhaps this is due to the fact that the *Copper Scroll Project* leaders have been making deliberately misleading claims about their role in the excavation. Or, perhaps it is due to a network of archaeologists, scholars, and bloggers working behind the scenes asking why the IAA would take money from posers like Barfield and the *Copper Scroll Project.*[7]

Cargill's hint about working behind the scenes to influence the IAA got my attention, especially considering the timing of a culminating ASOR conference at Duke University. In April 2009, Cargill, West, and Cline were among dozens of attendees at a conference entitled *Archaeology, Politics and the Media*. The conference provided a conclusive chance for ASOR academics to vent about their strained rapport with the media. Incidentally, the two-day conference began on Jim's third day of excavations at Qumran with Peleg.

The first two days of the excavation Peleg acted at ease. He was friendly with the team, unaltered by the presence of video cameras, and often thumbed through Jim's research. When victory was slow in coming, Peleg encouraged Jim, assuring him that the dig was hardly over and that although archaeology required Olympian patience, he had plenty of it. Peleg promised to meet back in a few days with a metal detector. A few days turned into a week. By the time the ASOR conference concluded and Peleg finally phoned Jim, he was terse and on edge as if something had happened that he wasn't willing to talk about.

Knowing nothing at the time about ASOR's enmity toward him, Jim assumed Peleg was pushed to stop by Magen. What he hadn't accounted for was a pressure campaign that had been applied to Magen. Judging from Cargill's posts, it seems logical that the loudest conference attendees lobbied the ADCA, indirectly or directly, to issue a stop order on the Qumran excavation and cut contact with Jim. Only two years prior, the ADCA had lost a lawsuit to Israeli researchers accusing them of withholding data. Magen surely felt vulnerable to another lawsuit, or at least an online smear campaign from American bibliobloggers.

TOTAL EXPOSURE

For every Cargill, hundreds more online voices jumped to the opposite conclusion. For Jim's followers, outside of the academic community, his solving the Copper Scroll riddle was an immutable truth. All Jim's backers needed to undergird their great hopes were the small revelations Jim gave about Qumran in the media, but most were still oblivious to the actual mechanics of his matching scroll locations with Qumran architecture.

Though he appreciated the vote of confidence, Jim wanted to earn it. He wanted to go further than their faith-filled instincts and appeal directly to their intellect. That meant telling them *how* he made his conclusions and showing them exactly *where* the treasure was concealed. After keeping his research report under lock and key for three years, the time had come to lift the veil and let the world in on the secret. Releasing the maps and explanations allowed every interested party, friend or enemy, to visualize, accurately and logically, how structures at Qumran matched the descriptions in the Copper Scroll.

Seeing, however, does not equal downloading or printing. Jim was prepared for people to view the report but having strangers study it anonymously made him ill at ease. To release his report, Jim used a fully automated viewer with a tracking and protection system. For a low fee, he offered a PDF of his report, an eBook essentially, accessible by password from his website. Since the digital product was locked down through the security system, the only way to view the report was by logging in. Jim, on the back end, could track who was viewing the report, when, and how many times. If he grew suspicious of a user, like multiple logins in a day, he refunded their payment and blocked their accessibility—a safety net which he only deployed once.

What Jim offered was more than his full report. He introduced the eBook by trying his hand at historical fiction. Writing in the third person narrative format, he told the intriguing story of Jeremiah's uncle and cousin visiting him in prison, in the year of Jubilee. After Jim's short narrative, the book launched into the meat of the disclosure: all 57 of his locations with corresponding graphics and explanations. Because the book was meant for online viewing, not expensive print, he was able to include full color satellite photos and Qumran maps. As for the April 2009 dig, he included a photo-documented essay showing exactly what was done and what remained to be done.

Within two weeks, 300 people downloaded the report—including several distinguished scholars, like García Martínez. When Robert Cargill logged on and perused the report's contents, Jim braced himself for the online hazing that he expected to soon follow. Instead, Cargill was silent. In the eight years since, Cargill has never blogged about Jim or the *Copper Scroll Project* again.[8]

In a blog post the year prior, Cargill had written, "Were Jimmy Barfield's conclusions the result of sound methodology and critical cross-examination, and found to be credible, I'd accept them whether he went to college or not. But he didn't."[9] Jim hoped that after Cargill read his scrupulous research and realized that he was not grabbing onto floating pieces of evidence, Cargill kept his promise to end the harassment. Or, perhaps Cargill was simply ready to move on to new vigils. Jim wasn't going to contact Cargill to find out the reason for the silence. He learned the hard way that scholarly territorialism was the most persistent threat to the project.

CHAPTER 14

PANTHEON

Though his first foray into the bizarre domain of biblical archaeology ended abruptly, Jim refused to join the pantheon of explorers who searched for the Copper Scroll's artifacts and failed. Before Jim, four men were on record for actively digging for Copper Scroll treasure: John Allegro, Vendyl Jones, Charles Robert Morgan, and Oren Gutfeld. All had fallen prey to the Copper Scroll's siren call.

JOHN ALLEGRO

From the instant he laid eyes on the contents of the Copper Scroll, after orchestrating its daring opening, John Allegro was seduced by its potential. He approximated that two dozen of the scroll's descriptions were in Jerusalem, even though the holy city is never named in the scroll directly. The rest of the locations, according to his provisional translation, were scattered throughout Israel.

From December 1959 to April 1960, Allegro made a highly publicized attempt to locate Copper Scroll artifacts. London's *Daily Mail* agreed to sponsor the exploration if they could have an on-site reporter sending regular dispatches to an anxiously awaiting British public. Never one to shy away from the camera, the handsome and lean Allegro was happy to pose for the tabloid's hero shots.

Though Jerusalem and the Dead Sea region were under Jordanian control at the time, Allegro established an amiable friendship with Jordan's King Hussein bin Talal. The King gave Allegro's team his full-fledged sponsorship. He provided expedition vehicles, water supply, generators, and a Jordanian security detail. During one of Allegro's later expeditions, the young monarch made a Christmas day visit by helicopter to deliver refreshments to Allegro's crew, especially the female college students.

Allegro's colleagues from the scrollery openly criticized him for his naïve ambitions. Copper Scroll editor Milik feared he was neglecting his editing duties. Yet Allegro was undeterred. He knew that if the overly cautious editors had their druthers, the Copper Scroll would still be rolled up in coils. Besides, he was working off of a different supposition. To them, the Copper Scroll's treasure was fictitious. To Allegro, the wealth was very real and awaiting recovery.

Allegro launched his hunt in the Kidron Valley among a strip of olive groves and funerary shrines that separate the Mount of Olives from the eastern wall of Jerusalem's Old City. Because all three monotheistic faiths attach eschatological meaning to the valley, the ancient cemetery is crowded with graves.[1]

According to Allegro's interpretation of the Copper Scroll, at least one cache was buried in or near the Kidron Valley's most iconic crypts: the tomb of Benei Hezir, Zechariah's tomb, and Absalom's Pillar. The three sepulchers of the Second Temple period, all lined in a row, are nobly distinguished from the valley's thousands of other grave markers.

The tomb of Benei Hezir has the appearance of being whittled directly out of the Mount of Olives. The motif of the burial marker is classic Greek architecture: two stout pillars reinforcing a sparsely decorated frieze. In some Christian traditions, the tomb was erroneously associated with James the brother of Jesus. A faint but legible inscription discovered in 1865 associates the burial complex with a priestly family, "the sons of Hezir." The edifice of Hezir's tomb made a sensible candidate for Allegro's location 52 in the Copper Scroll: *Below the Portico's southern corner, in the tomb of Zadok, under the platform of the exedra [porch]: vessels for tithe sweepings.*[2] The tomb's columned porch faces the Temple Mount's southern portico. Allegro believed that the "sons of Hezir" was synonymous with Zadok—the family name of a priestly caste going back to the era of King David.

Close by, a sixty-foot monument, surmounted with a conical roof, is named for Absalom, the unruly son of King David. For centuries, Jewish and Christian pilgrims assumed the freestanding shrine was the same one referenced in II Samuel 18:18: "Absalom had taken a pillar and erected it in the King's Valley as a monument to himself." Despite the anachronistic misnomer, a long-held tradition for Jewish fathers in Jerusalem was to bring their sons to throw rocks at the edifice. When the monument was first surveyed in the twentieth century, bushels of rocks were removed from its base.

According to Allegro's translation, the Copper Scroll's location 49 contained an early reference to Absalom's Pillar: *Under the monument of Absalom, on the western side, buried at twelve cubits: eighty talents.*[3] Although Absalom's Pillar has several interior vaults, Allegro looked to a cave south of Absalom's monument as an ideal hiding spot for treasure. Allegro's theory was invigorated by an anecdote about a Catholic school child who snuck around Absalom's Pillar during a picnic in 1900. When she reappeared, she was said to be carrying gold coins in her skirt.

Allegro's crew started at the tomb of Benei Hezir. They first scraped away dirt which had washed down off the mountain over centuries. They probed around the walls of the burial chambers and inspected the vertical shafts adjoining the cliff face. In the process, the survey extended out to Zechariah's tomb. A passage cut through the cliff connects the tomb of Benei Hezir to Zechariah's tomb, a monolithic cube with a pyramid shaped top, named for the prophet which legend held it entombed. On the western side of Zechariah's tomb, they hauled off rubble and moved a dozen modern Jewish graves, supposedly with permission from King Hussein. In the process of trying to find passage into the interior vault, they realized that Zechariah's "tomb," in fact, had no burial chamber.

The Kidron Valley showed no early signs of discovery. Allegro was on a tight schedule, splitting time between excavations and his editorial work. He made a judgment call to abandon the excavation around Absalom's Pillar and leave alone the rumor of the gold coins. In his report, he drily wrote that they achieved the primary goal: "corroboration of topographical references in the Copper Scroll."[4]

With the clock ticking, Allegro moved south from Jerusalem, pulling together a well-organized expedition to Hyrcania. Hyrcania is an isolated ruin three miles west of Qumran on the edge of Hyrcania Valley. King Herod—a ruler as famous for his elaborate construction plans as he was for his depraved mind—built a chain of hilltop strongholds, creating an elaborate defense system along the border of the Judean Desert. In the case of Hyrcania, Herod refortified a previously abandoned structure, first commissioned by the Hasmonean (i.e., Maccabean) King Yohanan Hyrcanus in the second century BCE.

King Herod supposed that if his rivals tried to usurp him, or the Jews rebelled against him, his kingdom could escape to the hilltops. If such a crisis arose, Herod made sure to it that his court would sacrifice no amount of comfort in the voluptuous interiors of his summit palaces. The hilltop ruins include swimming pools, mosaics, and bathhouses. Leisure and luxury need not be sacrificed for security. Unlike the Kidron Valley, Hyrcania was an unexplored ruin.[5] For Allegro, the sand-drifted ruins of Hyrcania had significant potential. It was exactly the kind of site for an academic to earn his excavation spurs.

Allegro linked Hyrcania to his translation of the first and second locations in the Copper Scroll: *In the fortress which is in the Valley of Achor, forty cubits under the steps entering to the east: a money chest and its contents, of a weight of seventeen talents. In the sepulcher monument, in the third course of stones: light bars of gold.*[6]

Though the ruins were concealed under mounds of debris, Allegro's volunteers eagerly pitched their tents and set to work. Over the course of several days, the dedicated volunteers combed the cisterns, climbed down a bat-filled shaft, and surveyed the remnants of halls and towers. Their daring efforts were documented by the *Daily Mail* photographer. Herodian pottery littered the undisturbed site. Allegro almost jumped out of his skin when they found what looked like a *sepulcher monument*. When he tried to scan the monument with a metal detector, the finest available at the time, the natural magnetism of the surrounding rock made the detector's positive clicks impossible to verify. The only way to check the *third course of stones* was to break through the monument's exterior. Even for the impulsive Allegro, the risk was too high, both for the ruins and his career.

In the process of surveying the rocky slopes at the base of Hyrcania's hill, the expedition discovered two mysterious passageways among the scree: a western tunnel and an eastern tunnel, 200 yards apart. The entrances, painstakingly cut into the limestone, stood at six feet high and three feet wide. Allegro was certain they had found location one's *steps entering to the east*. Clearing buckets full of sediment out of the western tunnel, they exposed a steep staircase which descended underground for at least a hundred feet. Unfortunately, the further they got down the tunnel, the more difficult exploring became, as light and oxygen dwindled. Clearing the staircases was a more mammoth task than Allegro had the will, or capability, to carry out.

While the volunteers labored at Hyrcania, Allegro worked simultaneously to attain permission to excavate under the surface of the Temple Mount. Allegro believed dozens of Copper Scroll fortunes were stockpiled in the labyrinth of chambers and passages below the plateau. Despite the Temple Mount being a clash point, Allegro felt positive that the required permission was forthcoming, particularly since he was on good terms with King Hussein. Allegro made no secret of his sympathy with the Arabs when it came to the conflict with Israel.

Allegro laid out his plans for the Muslim authorities in charge of the Temple Mount. The religious leaders first redirected him to the Minister of Education and then to the Jordanian military officials in charge of the site's security. Although Allegro had his doubts about involving the army, he gave an entourage of religious and military officials a walking tour of the sites he proposed to excavate. After the Brigadier General and head of the *Waqf* met privately about the matter, they denied Allegro permission to excavate, without explanation.[7]

Allegro's taskforce spent the least amount of time and effort surveying Qumran, despite the scholar's impression that a dozen of the burial locations were hidden in the Essene encampment. De Vaux's discovery, several years earlier, of coin-filled pots hidden underneath plastered flooring heightened Allegro's suspicions. When he first laid eyes on the Copper Scroll's message, he sent off an urgent message from Manchester to his boss Harding: "Somewhere in that pile down at Qumran there is, or was, 300 talents of gold buried, to say nothing of any number of deposits of silver." He instructed Harding, "Next time you're down at Qumran, take a spade and dig like mad!'"[8]

Like Jim's research, Allegro's translation pointed to the watchtower at Qumran being a favorite hiding spot. Even so, Allegro didn't dig at the watchtower, either because his time was up or because he felt the stinging critique of de Vaux who was certain Allegro was ignoring serious archaeological controls. Volunteers came across first-century pottery pieces, but little else. Harding cautioned Allegro that the floor levels in the watchtower were "dug into in strange ways," indicating that the treasure was looted in antiquity.[9]

In Allegro's final report, he recommended full-scale excavations to definitively test Hyrcania and the Temple Mount in the future. Allegro believed Hyrcania and her tunnels held immense promise. He also hoped the chambers below the Temple Mount would eventually be unsealed, letting the world discover Jerusalem's mysteries. Allegro's temperament was not one of a long-suffering, patiently-enduring archaeologist. In 1988, the maverick of the Dead Sea Scrolls died suddenly from an aortic aneurysm.

BOB MORGAN AND OREN GUTFELD

When a Continental Airlines pilot, Charles "Bob" Morgan, first read Allegro's account of *The Treasure of the Copper Scroll* in the 1980s, he was entranced. To the eccentric Baptist from Missouri, Allegro's book read like a mystery novel with no conclusion. Allegro had quit too early. The Hyrcania tunnels had yet to reveal their secrets. Going further in his leaps of logic than Allegro, Morgan connected Hyrcania to II Maccabees. II Maccabees places Jeremiah's secret cave near the mountain where "Moses looked down on the land which God had promised our people." Morgan wondered if Hyrcania's tunnels might lead simultaneously to the Ark of the Covenant and the long-lost tomb of Moses.

In 1986, Morgan flew to Israel. Though it was his first time in the country, he had zero interest in visiting the holy places or tourist sites. From the Tel Aviv airport, Morgan drove a rental car directly south, headed for Hyrcania. The closer he got to his destination, the thicker the dirt became on the roads, until it was impassable in a normal vehicle. Morgan abandoned the rental car and walked a mile through the dry riverbed, Wadi Secacah, before coming to the base of the isolated mountain. Exploring Hyrcania, he couldn't believe that despite its potential, no one had fully excavated the shadowy tunnels.

Resolving to finish what Allegro started, Morgan began a decade-long solo mission to clear out the western tunnel. From 1987 to 1999, flying to Israel twice a year, for a few weeks at a time, he clandestinely burrowed his way down the passage with a hand axe and flashlight. He had no access to electricity or water. Since the area serves as a firing zone for the IDF, Morgan's presence was illegal. Hiding inside the tunnels during the day, he stayed out of sight of Israeli tanks and artillery. On the weekends, when the IDF trainees returned home, Morgan hired local Bedouin to help form a bucket brigade.

While the Bedouin accelerated the pace of Morgan's venture, the pilot was still nowhere close to reaching the end of the passage. Also, the job was getting increasingly dangerous. Breathing at the deepest depth in the tunnel became so difficult that he risked suffocation. Finally, Morgan decided to let the Israeli authorities in on what he had been doing, figuring that they would either arrest him for antiquities violations or offer their support.

Morgan approached the Archaeological Institute at the Hebrew University to request the succor of a professional crew. A Vietnam veteran with wild eyes and an ill-fitting suit, Morgan made for a suspicious figure in the university offices. Though he managed to get an audience with the director, Amihai Mazar, Morgan dodged all questions about his intentions, only letting on that his site of interest was somewhere in the Judean Desert. The director pushed Morgan off on Oren Gutfeld, a young graduate student in archaeology with experience excavating Herodian fortresses. With a broad boyish face, barrel chest, and hair mowed close to his skull, Gutfeld was half Morgan's age and looked even younger.

At first glance, Gutfeld had a difficult time taking seriously the strange intruder with a forceful manner. He feared Morgan was one more victim of Jerusalem Syndrome. Gutfeld explains, "All kinds of people come to Jerusalem and are suddenly transfixed and transformed, infused with visions and apocalyptic pretensions."[10] Israel's health ministry records at least fifty patients a year are diagnosed with the madness. Since the institute at Hebrew University had experienced their share of millennial visitors ready to reveal messianic epiphanies, Gutfeld knew Morgan fit the profile. Still, Gutfeld was new to the field and curious about an ancient site that had been explored so little. He agreed to accompany Morgan to the desert.

At six o'clock on a Friday morning, Morgan showed up at the door of Gutfeld's home. They could only visit Hyrcania on a weekend, he gruffly explained, after the IDF soldiers went home for Sabbath. With Gutfeld riding passenger, Morgan drove his normal route, following tank treads through dirt roads before his rental utility vehicle threatened to give out. The two men hardly spoke as they went the rest of the way on foot. Neither man was the type to feel awkward with silence.

Seeing the stepped tunnel for the first time, Gutfeld was mesmerized. When he shone his flashlight down the shaft, he made out small niches in the wall, where oil lamps once illuminated the way. An academic, he didn't rush to equate the tunnels with the Copper Scroll. Still, the purpose of the ancient passage tantalized him, just as it had Allegro forty years before. Gutfeld recalled a legend he heard once from a Bedouin digger that Wadi Secacah had a gold-filled tunnel guarded by a genie.

Mostly, Gutfeld was impressed by Morgan's persistence under such harsh conditions. Allegro's team had cleared the first fifty steps of the tunnel. Crawling down the dangerous passage, Morgan managed to carve out an additional ninety feet with no access to water or electricity.

Morgan solicited Gutfeld to join him and make the excavation legal under the auspices of Hebrew University. Morgan pledged to raise the necessary donations from friends and co-opt his employer to sponsor a charter flight with volunteers and equipment to Israel. Gutfeld agreed, with a few conditions. They had to coordinate their efforts with the IDF's planned tank maneuvers— no more illegal digging in the dead of night. Also, if the ancient stairs were to be cleared properly, they would need real equipment: compressors to deliver oxygen to the shaft and a mechanical device that could assist in pulling out the debris. No more dangerous hacking.

With Gutfeld and Morgan committed to working collaboratively, they pooled their contacts to organize a band of volunteers. Morgan recruited American friends and fellow pilots. Gutfeld brought Hebrew University students and a Bedouin work team. The group worked as efficiently as possible, camping at night on a nearby plain. The further they got down the tunnel, the more dangerous the work became.

One day, as the volunteers were clearing debris in the deepest part of the tunnel, Morgan suddenly passed out. Another volunteer began complaining of pains in his heart. As a professional diver, Gutfeld felt lightheaded but he had just enough lung capacity, and wherewithal, to realize that he needed to call for help. Using baby monitors to communicate with workers at the surface, the three men were hauled out on a winch and resuscitated. After that, the crew used a leaf blower and aluminum duct to pipe fresh air into the tunnel. Still, the dig continued to have its share of setbacks.

At one point, the western tunnel came to a fork requiring double the work to clear the branches in both directions. They worked against the rainy season, when the spillover from wadis often flooded the area. One torrent washed into the tunnel as much debris as they had dug out, nullifying their efforts that entire year. Another time, roving Bedouin tried unsuccessfully to poach their generator, holding Morgan up at knifepoint. When the Al-Aqsa Intifada broke out in 2000, the IDF temporarily withdrew Gutfeld's permit to dig at Hyrcania. The area was under an escalated terror threat.[11]

Morgan, who went so far as to have his wedding ceremony conducted at the tunnel's entrance, eventually grew tired of the endless tunneling and faded out. He could no longer garner the finances to support the dig and soon stopped answering Gutfeld's phone calls. Gutfeld, proving himself to be a tenacious explorer, worked for another three seasons of excavation at Hyrcania without Morgan, but still with several of Morgan's volunteer recruits. With a new source of funding, Gutfeld pushed hard to reach the end of the two tunnels.

Before reaching the tunnels' end, Gutfeld was careful to avoid conjectures about their function, but he had a few ideas on their origins. Though the Essenes lived nearby at Qumran, Gutfeld believed they lacked the resources to have conducted such a construction effort themselves. He estimated that the tunnels were built under the direction of Herod. The chiseling of the limestone must have taken years of work by hundreds of men, without the modern luxuries of air compressors and generators. Josephus described Hyrcania as a notorious prison and execution site for Herod's enemies. That being the case, Gutfeld guessed that Herod forced his prisoners to carve stairs into the rock as compulsory labor.

As for the Copper Scroll, Gutfeld understood that the tunnels weren't carved solely to hide Temple vessels. The writing in the Copper Scroll indicated it was the product of a hasty operation; the tunnels were a slow and deliberate creation. Still, Gutfeld was open to the possibility that after the tunnel was carved, it served a secondary purpose, like harboring rescued Temple tithes. The ancient fortress of Hyrcania would be a fitting match for the Copper Scroll's opening line: *In the ruins which is in the Valley of Achor.*

In the spring of 2007, Gutfeld reached the end of the western tunnel and it's two branches. Where they had hoped to find relics, tombs, evidence of mining, or a water source, they found nothing but a wall of natural rock. Gutfeld and his colleagues were baffled as to the purpose of the 328-foot tunnel. No other tunnels had been found like it in all of Israel.

They thought perhaps the eastern tunnel would hold the answer and finished clearing it as well. The eastern tunnel stairs were carved into the limestone at a slightly sharper angle. And the tunnel had no fork. After discarding countless bags of debris, with the help of an electrical winch, the passage came to a similar abrupt end. Hiring American experts to electronically probe the rock walls with penetrating radar systems, Gutfeld hoped the right technology could detect cavities or hidden chambers. It did not. Gutfeld couldn't muster a spoken word for three days.

While digging, all they found in the tunnels were a human skeleton, an ibex skeleton, and an intact clay pot, clues that further confounded the tunnels' mysterious purpose. The skeleton of a middle-aged, first-century male was found 130 feet from the entrance of the eastern tunnel. Gutfeld guessed that the man had been swept to his death by floods. The ibex bones were found at the midpoint of the western tunnel. Strangely, the bones carbon dated to the fifth century BCE. Gutfeld had no explanation as to how ibex bones from the First Temple period found their way into the marrow of the Hyrcania Mountain. Morgan believed the ibex skeleton was evidence of the tunnel's sanctity, a former place for sacrifice. The empty clay pot, dating to the Hasmonean era (140–116 BCE), was possible evidence that the tunnels existed from Hyrcania's earliest phase of occupation. What was supposed to be Gutfeld's career-defining excavation turned out to be a literal dead end.

DIG CUT SHORT

A Christian pastor aiming to pry information from Jim about his research asked, "Jimmy D, out of all the other explorers who have looked for the holy vessels, who came the closest?"

Jim replied with perfect aplomb: "Jeremiah." He winked.

The pastor smiled and said, "I knew I liked you."

Though Jim was hardly the first Copper Scroll explorer, and not even the first to associate treasure with Qumran, he was the only one to try and pinpoint the exact hiding spots, recognize an organizing principle among the authors, build a full investigative report, and pursue an excavation in the Qumran ruins below the earliest level of habitation.

Most of the explorers who pursued the Copper Scroll's treasure came closer than Jim's "Jeremiah" quip indicated. Gutfeld's Hyrcania dig is a scant three miles from Qumran. Vendyl's *Cave of the Column* is easily visible from Jim's *hill of Kokhlit*. And Allegro, like Jim, thought parts of the Copper Scroll pointed to Qumran. The strength of Jim's thesis is not in its originality, but rather its simplicity; not in the break from his predecessors, but in his follow-through.

CHAPTER 15

SECRETS

Once his research was made available to the world in October 2009, Jim reached a point that he had to let go. No amount of publicity or public demand was prodding the Israeli authorities to action. Though his media rounds created a groundswell of interest in the *Copper Scroll Project*, the lack of communication from Peleg deflated the momentum. Website followers anxiously awaited updates, which grew further and further apart. Jim traversed the hellish mental landscape of uncertainty.

"Left totally in the dark, I had to pray that *Hashem*'s will be done, in his timing," Jim says. "But I made a vow that I wouldn't beg anymore. I would stop pushing and I would wait for the Israelis to come to me."

With the *Copper Scroll Project* at a standstill, Jim busied himself with neglected domestic duties, like shingling his roof. He started volunteering at the local Veterans Affairs office. Putting his investigative report writing skills to good use, he helped disabled veterans track down medical records and fill out mounds of paperwork for their compensation claims.

As for the advance team, they all moved on to new life phases. Shawn enrolled in film school. Chris ramped up tractor sales. Mack sold one of his ranches. Todd proposed to a woman he met in Israel. Linda donated a kidney to her son for a transplant. Ken went back to tinkering with robotics in his garage. I had my second child. Lawton's Society for Creative Anachronisms bought Jim's fringed medieval sukkah tent.

Even Vendyl neared the end of his career. On his last trip to Israel, Vendyl escorted a group of rabbis out to the *Cave of the Column*. Vendyl was determined to drill a deep shaft into a supposed compartment and drop down a remote camera to dramatically expose the contents to his witnesses. By that point, however, Vendyl was losing a battle with throat cancer. Due either to his failing memory or frail body, he couldn't find the rocky area to access the chamber. The elderly explorer fumbled around; the rabbis stood in the withering sun, diverting their eyes. Vendyl passed away shortly after, on December 27, 2010.

Vendyl had operated like a lone wolf. Since he never trained an apprentice, Jim was the closest thing he had to carrying on his legacy. Though Vendyl cast off Jim as a traitor for working with the Israeli authorities, Jim remained loyal. "He was pretty hard on me at the end, but I always respected him," Jim said. Jim and Laurie attended the funeral in Grandview, Texas and offered their condolences to his wife, Anita. "She was a precious lady, always kind to us," he recalled. Per his request, Vendyl's body was flown to Israel and buried in Kibbutz Migdal, above the Sea of Galilee.

Vendyl was not the only life snuffed out during Jim's extended season of waiting. For reasons that doctors did not understand, Jim's youngest son, Michael, and his wife, Violet, suffered the loss of a newborn child. A full term healthy pregnancy ended dramatically in stillbirth. In their moment of grief, Jim wanted to be by the side of his children and grandchildren. What that meant, however, was ending his Nazarite vow. According to the laws dictated in Numbers, if a Nazarite is bound by the vow, he must not encounter death. Death defiles ritual cleanliness.

The Nazarite vow is the singular way a layperson can attain the level of purity analogous to the biblical priesthood. Three years after taking the Nazarite vow, Jim's hair had grown to a thick curtain of grey. By chance, Jim's three-year anniversary fell on the same day that he met Peleg to scan Qumran with a metal detector. When it came to the timing of *Copper Scroll Project* events, Jim analyzed the importance of calendar dates like a gypsy reading tea leaves. He interpreted the three years as a symbol of his consecration, like the Essenes who required a three-year initiation process before pledges could become full members of the sect. To say Jim was hopeful on the day of the scan is an understatement. However, the pinnacle of his vow was a complete anticlimax.

The New Testament scarcely mentions the Nazarite vow, except in the case of the Apostle Paul. Acts 21 documents Paul accompanying four followers to the Jerusalem Temple to join them in their purification rites as they concluded their vows. Ending the vow required a series of burnt offerings and included shaving the Nazarite's head in the Temple courtyard. Paul may have been Nazarite himself at some point; Acts 18 briefly notes that Paul cut off his hair "because of a vow he had taken." Most rabbinical authorities regard the Nazarite vow as obsolete. There is no standing Temple where the vow can be completed as biblically prescribed.

"The rabbis have a fair point," said Jim. To be with his family during tragedy, he ended the vow with an unceremonious visit to the salon. "All I could do was ask the beautician chopping it off to put it in a Ziploc bag for me."

FATE OF THE ARK

While Jim maintained a lower profile, he fell into a period of serious self-examination. He couldn't stop wondering why things went wrong in the dig with Peleg. He worried that a misstep on his part had permanently stalled the excavation. Even worse, he was haunted by the idea that his own pride forced a divine hand. The Bible was replete with caveats. Moses, the central figure of the Exodus, ignored a seemingly trivial detail and died on the border of the Promised Land. David, the beloved king, gave into temptations of lust and ambition and had to forgo his blueprints for the First Temple. Jim and his project were not immune to punishment or tragic twists of fate.

During a Sukkot gathering at Lake Murray, Jim's depression was taken as fodder for debate by a hodgepodge of Messianic friends. Trying to cheer him up, they contended that the Temple treasures were not meant to be retrieved, not by Jim or anyone.

Though Jim was searching for any treasure listed in the Copper Scroll, his supporters and friends tended to focus on the most coveted prize: The Ark of the Covenant. He reminded them that the Copper Scroll does not name the Ark directly, but they knew enough about his research to remember that the last lines of the Copper Scroll contained a cryptic reference that hinted at the Ark. They also knew that Jim believed the scroll's *hill of Kokhlit* was the cave-dwelling where Jeremiah hid the holiest Temple furniture.

They brought up a conciliatory message in the book of Jeremiah, who speaking in the days of King Josiah, envisioned a future time when the missing Ark would be altogether forgotten: "'In those days, when your numbers have increased greatly in the land,' declares the Lord, people will no longer say, 'The Ark of the Covenant of the Lord.' It will never enter their minds or be remembered; it will not be missed, nor will another one be made." (Jeremiah 3:16) Jim believed his friends misunderstood the verse in Jeremiah. To him, the verse was more of a statement on the Ark's unknown whereabouts, than an oracle that applied to modern day.

Other perhaps less well-meaning acquaintances at Lake Murray tried to convince Jim that he was wasting his time; the Ark had been destroyed long ago. According to the biblical record, it seemed likely that the Babylonians successfully seized the Ark along with the rest of the Temple vessels and tithes. II Kings 20 recounts how King Hezekiah, during a brief period of cold peace with Israel's northern neighbors, toured ambassadors from Babylon around his palace, showing off all the riches in his treasuries. Isaiah, the biblical prophet contemporary to Hezekiah, was astonished by the King's lack of forward thinking. He warned Hezekiah that his boastful blunder would end with the Babylonians looting the royal palace and carting off his inheritance to Babylon.

In 597 BCE, the Babylonian army encircled Jerusalem, raiding the Temple's treasury and outer courts, just as Isaiah had predicted. Nebuchadnezzar had a low tolerance for rebellious vassal states behind on their payments of tribute. While it would be another ten years before the Babylonian army fully decimated the Temple, II Kings 25 gives a bleak account of this first phase of looting. Still, the Ark and its associated furnishings from the inner sanctums receive no mention:

> The Babylonians broke up the bronze pillars, the movable stands and the bronze Sea that were at the temple of the Lord and they carried the bronze to Babylon. They also took away the pots, shovels, wick trimmers, dishes and all the bronze articles used in the Temple service. The commander of the imperial guard took away the censers and sprinkling bowls—all that were made of pure gold or silver. The bronze from the two pillars, the Sea and the movable

stands, which Solomon had made for the Temple of the Lord, was more than could be weighed. (II Kings 25:13–16)

⌒⌒⌒

In the later biblical record, when the Jews return from Babylonian exile, after seventy years, to rebuild a Second Temple, nary a word is said about the missing Ark.[1] The Bible's silence is interpreted to mean that the Ark was absent from the Second Temple throughout its 420-year history. Though Ezra included a Holy of Holies in the original Second Temple design, the sacred chamber was deliberately left empty, and apparently stayed empty. With the absence of the Ark in the Second Temple, the intense spirituality of Jerusalem dwindled. Prophecy soon evaporated, and the priesthood grew corrupt. According to the Roman historian Tacitus, when General Pompey subdued Judaea in 63 BCE, barging into the Jews' Holy of Holies, he was shocked to find an eerily deserted sanctuary.

Jim and several of his self-educated Messianic friends were also well-versed in later Jewish traditions surrounding the Ark of the Covenant. The Talmud, Judaism's central collection of rabbinic writings, includes two contradictory opinions on the Ark's fate, leaving the debate at a draw. One tradition, promoted by Talmudic sages, states that the Ark was carried off into Babylon, permanently lost along with thousands of other Temple vessels. The other tradition holds that King Josiah and the Temple priests, years before the First Temple's destruction, stored away the Ark and the rest of its contents.

Medieval Jewish philosopher Moses Maimonides, in his famed *Mishneh Torah*, taught that King Solomon foresaw the Temple's future destruction. As a precaution, he cleared winding secret passages underneath the First Temple. Without citing the source of the tradition, Maimonides maintains that King Josiah, two decades before the Babylonian takeover, utilized Solomon's subterranean matrix to hide the Ark in a secret vault.

Josiah is one of the favorite ancient kings of the Bible. In addition to routing out foreign cults, he concentrated worship in Jerusalem. The last biblical coordinate given for the Ark is in II Chronicles 35:3. When King Josiah commanded the Levites to return the Ark to the Holy of Holies. Why the Ark was removed from the Temple in the first place is left unsaid, but it has often been suggested that the Ark was sequestered during the abominable reign of Josiah's grandfather, King Manasseh. Manasseh was the first king in the Davidic dynasty who dared to import foreign worship and pagan images into the interior of the Temple. Does the chronicler insinuate that priests had a habit of hiding the Ark during intervals which threatened the Temple's purity?

Rabbi Nachman bar Isaac, a rabbi of the Talmudic period living in second-century Babylonia, passed on the story of a Temple priest who was working in a room near the base of the Temple where the priests stored firewood. As the priest was deep in thought, he happened to notice a few stones on the floor that protruded differently than the others. Certain that he discovered the Ark's hiding place, he ran to tell another priest. He died en route. The disciples of Rabbi Ishmael ben Elisha, a rabbi of the Mishnah, follow on with this tradition. They record that two unclean priests were once examining firewood for the altar. When one of them accidentally dropped his axe, a flame came up and consumed him. The combined lesson: even if the time to reveal the Ark's secret location is prolonged, the waiting vessel retains its power and purpose.

Since the Bible is silent on the Ark's fate and the rabbinic writings are contradictory, Jim looked for traces of the Ark in the apocryphal books. Jim believed those texts preserved the remnants of an oral tradition about the Temple rescue operation. By association, he tried to restring the antique beads of a Temple legend necklace, hoping to find the pearl of truth.

For example, he was intrigued by an Ark tradition from the *Syriac Apocalypse of Baruch*. In the introduction, the two-part book purports to be authored by Baruch ben Neriah, the close confidant and scribe of Jeremiah. Some of the text is formatted as an epistle to the Jewish exiles in Babylon five years after the Babylonians burned Jerusalem. Scholars place the *Syriac Apocalypse of Baruch* within the Jewish pseudepigrapha—a collection of writings spuriously attributed to famous biblical characters, mostly penned between 200 BCE and 200 CE. Unlike the other pseudepigrapha, Baruch makes a blatant assertion of authority; he was an eyewitness to the events. Whatever the actual context, Baruch provides a fascinating read. In addition to cautioning the people to repent and patiently submit to foreign rule in anticipation of redemption, Baruch tries to come to terms with the suffering of his people. After Jerusalem is reduced to ashes, Baruch gazes upon his beloved city and has a heavenly vision:

And it came to pass on the morrow that, lo! The army of the Chaldees surrounded the city, and at the time of the evening, I, Baruch, left the people, and I went forth and stood by the oak. And I was grieving over Zion, and lamenting over the captivity which had come upon the people. And lo! Suddenly a strong spirit raised me, and bore me aloft over the wall of Jerusalem. And I beheld, and lo! Four angels standing at the four corners of the city, each of them holding a torch of fire in his hands. And another angel began to descend from heaven. And said unto them: "Hold your lamps, and do not light them till I tell you. For I am first sent to speak a word to the earth, and to place in it what the Lord the Most High has commanded me." And I saw him descend into the Holy of Holies, and take from there the veil, and holy ark, and the mercy seat, and the two tables, and the holy raiment of the priests, and the altar of incense, and the forty-eight precious stones, wherewith the priest was adorned and all the holy vessels of the Tabernacle. And he spoke to the earth with a loud voice: Earth, earth, earth, hear the word of the mighty God. Receive what I commit to you, and guard them until the last times. So that, when you are ordered, you may restore them. So that strangers may not get possession of them. For the time comes when Jerusalem also will be delivered for a time. Until it is said, that it is again restored forever. And the earth opened its mouth and swallowed them up.[2]

According to the *Treatise of the Temple Vessels*, Baruch the Scribe assisted Shimmur the Levite in hiding Temple items. For this reason, Jim deemed the account, supposedly redacted by the same scribe, worthy of consideration. Jim thought perhaps the *Syriac Apocalypse of Baruch* was a mystical rendition of the startling events which surrounded the Copper Scroll. The four angels in Baruch's vision, Jim surmised, could be an emblematic rendering of the four men under Shimmur who led the Temple rescue operation. The earth "opening its mouth" sounded like a description of Jeremiah's cave. Like the *Treatise* and II Maccabees predictions, the Baruch oracle promised the Temple vessels would stay hidden "until the last times."

Fourth Baruch is another text alleged to have emerged from the pen of Jeremiah's scribe. Dated to around the second century CE, the pseudepigraphal work was canonized by the Ethiopian Orthodox church and is alternatively titled *Things Omitted from the Book of Jeremiah*. Like II Maccabees, the author records the tradition that the prophet Jeremiah hid the Temple furnishings. With less pomp than the *Apocalypse of Baruch*, *Fourth Baruch* describes Jeremiah hiding the vessels under divine order.

And the Lord said: "Speak, my chosen one Jeremiah." And Jeremiah said: "Behold, Lord, now we know that you are delivering the city into the hands of its enemies, and they will take the people away to Babylon. What do you want me to do with the holy vessels of the temple service?" And the Lord said to him: "Take them and consign them to the earth, saying: 'Hear, Earth, the voice of your creator who formed you in the abundance of waters, who sealed you with seven seals for seven epochs, and after this you will receive your ornaments. Guard the vessels of the temple service until the gathering of the beloved!'"[3]

The *Treatise of the Temple Vessels* infers that only a natural event, at the end of time, can bring back the revered objects and the Ark that, according to the apocryphal books, were swallowed by the earth. After the Israelites are gathered from the four ends of the earth back to the land, the *Treatise* writes, "A great river will issue forth from the Holy of Holies of the Temple. Its name is Gihon, and it will flow to the great and dreadful desert and become mixed with the Euphrates River. Immediately, all the vessels will float up and be revealed."[4] The idea of living water flowing out from Jerusalem is also found in Ezekiel 47 and Zechariah 14. Ezekiel paints a glittering eschatological image of the Dead Sea waters suddenly blooming with life.

While rivers of floating vessels invoke a fantastical legend, Qumran does in fact sit at the base of a geological fault line, the Great Rift Valley. Earthquakes are common in this area. The Dead Sea lowers a little more each year because of the constant shifting of the plates. Some geoscientists have predicted that due to increasing tectonic tension, a large earthquake is expected soon. The Dead Sea region would be its epicenter.

Qumran has already experienced one large earthquake in antiquity. Its principal mikvah still shows a diagonal crack.[5] Archaeologists believe that the natural disaster, which even Josephus mentions in his annals, forced Qumran's occupants to temporarily abandon the site.

Could another natural disaster disgorge hidden treasure? Could the cave under the *hill of Kokhlit* be opened by shifting tectonic plates? Jim didn't want to wait around to find out, but just in case, he kept an occasional eye on reports of seismic activity in Israel.

If the Ark was indeed meant to be found, whether a firefighter was destined to help in the process was the question on many people's minds, including Jim's. Not even Jim's full measure of charisma and conviction could hide the deep fear that the answer might be negative. As time passed, Jim felt like the trail to the Temple vessels was growing cold. Digging up little known apocryphal traditions with Temple rescue plots was one way to keep hope alive.

METALLURGY

With no dig date on the horizon, Jim needed other projects to fill the void left in his mental and spiritual life by the Copper Scroll. Proving his addiction to industriousness, he found himself tinkering in metalwork.

When the *Travel Channel* ran the episode of "Secret Worlds" featuring the Copper Scroll, he was intrigued by the show's tutorial on the inscription process. The video crew filmed scholar Sherry Whitstone demonstrating the tediousness of banging out the letters of the Copper Scroll. To make the metal more pliable, Whitstone believes they used a heating process called annealing. Whitstone showed how the scroll's raised letters could be replicated by hammering into pliable copper with a series of sharp metal punches. A piece of wood lay underneath the copper as a soft base. Some of the letters' awkward formations and curvatures indicated that the copyist lacked the range of metal punch shapes necessary to chisel the Hebrew script properly. For example, the smallest Hebrew letter *yud* was indistinguishable from the more elongated straight letter *vav*. He likely only had one straight chisel and two curved. Certain lines of the scroll crowded up, and other words were misspelled, evidence to the unforgiving standards of metal inscription.

The exceptionality of the material of the Copper Scroll, aside from its astonishing content, cannot be overstated. Among Israeli cuneiforms (objects covered in ancient script), embossed letters are much rarer than engravings. Out of the Dead Sea Scroll corpus, the Copper Scroll was the only document not penned on papyrus or animal skin.

The Copper Scroll is one of the longest ancient inscriptions ever discovered on a metal medium. The closest parallel to the Copper Scroll was found by archaeologists at Medinet Habu, the mortuary temple of Ramses III near Luxor, Egypt. Oddly, the Medinet Habu inscription is a copper plaque cataloguing Egyptian temple fortunes. The inscription was laid out in columns very much like the Copper Scroll. Dating to the first century BCE, Egypt's Roman period, the Egyptian document hints at a rare, but multi-cultural practice of using copper for documents of extreme importance.

Jim had his own idea for making a Copper Scroll reproduction. He printed out a paper facsimile of the scroll to match the copper plates' actual size. By heating a thin copper sheet and laying it on a rubber mat, he used a stylus pen to trace the backwards letters from the overlaid paper copy onto the metal. Considering that he got his supplies from a local craft store, the final product was quite impressive. After studying the document for two years, he had almost memorized the ancient handwriting style.

Jim constructed the reproduction so that he could reference it when he was checking his research. He relished it as a self-produced piece of art. "I am looking for the right frame for it," he told me. When he did speaking engagements, he started bringing his replica with him and holding it up for display when explaining features of the historic document. Jim used a picture of his Copper Scroll replica to create a customized decal for his Harley Davidson motorcycle. Every biker in Lawton became familiar with the Copper Scroll script.

QUMRUSALEM

Although the report was completed in its final draft form at the time of the April 2009 dig, Jim occasionally tweaked his research when he came across new information about Qumran or the Essenes. Research mode was his default position. Every time we talked he had something new he was considering.

One morning in his home office, Jim was surfing the internet for old maps of Jerusalem. He came upon a website called Bible Lands and Cities that hosted a collection of maps from ancient Israel. One series of maps showed the evolving structural adjustments to the walls of Jerusalem from the time of the Davidic dynasty to King Herod. The maps used the archaeological evidence on the ground and the clues preserved in biblical and historical documents. Browsing through the series, Jim paused at the second map down on the page. He felt a strong sense of *déjà vu*.

Though the map was described as Jerusalem in Jeremiah's time, the outline looked strikingly like the layout of Qumran, a sketch frozen in his head. The way the city walls jutted out, the placement of the watchtowers, and the locations of several portals all looked the same—like an ink stamp of each would have left matching blotches. The primary difference was the orientation and size. Qumran was clearly a smaller and more compact version of Jerusalem. Qumran's east was Jerusalem's west and its south Jerusalem's north.

Besides their oddly similar layout, a dozen of the buildings and major structures marked on the Jerusalem map matched Jim's map of Qumran, according to his Copper Scroll translation. What Jim identified as Qumran's *women's house, sheep's pen, Zadok's residence,* and *watchtower* all paralleled naturally what was labeled on the Jerusalem map as the *women's gate, sheep's gate, Temple,* and *watchtower.* While the wording slightly differed, the function of the buildings was the same.[6]

Jim noticed that the positioning of purification pools at Qumran eerily overlaid those of Jerusalem. The Copper Scroll, according to Jim's translation, referred to the double entry pool on the northwest edge of the complex as the *atonement mikvah.* From studying the sectarian scrolls and the observations of Josephus, Jim believed that the Qumranites performed ritual purifications each morning. After emerging from the *atonement mikvah,* they conducted their communal prayers in a courtyard. On a map of pre-exile Jerusalem, the Pool of Siloam stood at the southwestern end of the capital, on the slopes of Mount Zion.[7] The faithful were required to immerse themselves at the Pool of Siloam, their atonement mikvah, before ascending to the Temple precincts, their courtyard.

Once again, Jim was left sitting in his office so engrossed in maps that he forgot to eat breakfast or lunch. His appetite was often numbed by new discoveries. Wondering what scholars had made the connection between Qumran's ruins and First Temple Jerusalem, he and I both dove into the abyss of academic literature. Scroll experts were in the business of analyzing every line in the inscriptional materials and every record in the archaeological inventory to extract the most arcane details about the Qumranites' daily life and sectarian laws. Surely, we thought, someone had noted the parallel.

In de Vaux's initial excavations, he studied Qumran's water system. He observed how Qumran's unusual stepped pools with partitions were like immersion baths excavated in Jerusalem. Yet de Vaux merely thought it worthy of note. In his documentation, he did not flesh out the meaning of the architectural similarity any further.

Jodi Magness noticed that the disposition of space at Qumran followed the same rabbinic regulations that applied to Jerusalem. Without knowing the exact usage of all Qumran's rooms, Magness observed that the compound was designed with an intent to guard purity's boundaries, like the walled city of Jerusalem. The western half of the settlement contained "the rooms with the greatest degree of purity," including the dining rooms, meeting room, and scriptorium. The eastern half of the camp housed service rooms with lesser degrees of purity: storerooms, workshops, and a toilet.[8] For both Jerusalem and Qumran, the most impure place, the cemetery, lay furthest east, outside the city walls.

A theory from Barbara Thiering coupled nicely with Jim's observations. A controversial historian, Thiering is often discredited by her peers for her views on the Dead Sea Scrolls and the origins of Christianity. In analyzing the architecture of Qumran, however, Thiering points out that a rectangular room near the large Iron Age cistern at Qumran measures as a half-scale reproduction of the Solomonic Temple, thirty by ten cubits.[9] The upper third of the sanctuary room had a dividing line of stones running across. Thiering believed the small enclosure marked off the Holy of Holies. She also observed that Qumran's miniature Temple structure boasted side rooms that corresponded to the priestly chambers in Jerusalem.

Jean-Baptist Humbert, a French archaeologist responsible for publishing de Vaux's excavation notes, was intrigued by the same building as Thiering.

According to his view, the rectangular room was modeled off of Jerusalem's long-room Temple. Humbert pointed to the well-finished interior of the room. He thought the small enclosure looked mysteriously like the Holy of Holies.[10] Humbert theorized that the community boycotted the sacrificial system at the Temple, instead using Qumran to fulfill the injunctions for ritual sacrifice.

Though no remains of an altar or sacrificial vessels were discovered at Qumran, archaeologists unearthed mysterious bone deposits from at least 200 kosher animals. Buried at shallow depths at fixed points along the perimeter of buildings, the bone deposits were usually contained in jars with lids. In one case, a bone pile was simply covered by a plate. Scholars found no evidence that the bones were the remains of animal sacrifice. If the bones were left over from communal meals, the significance of burying the bones remains unknown. Peleg and Magen guessed that the residents of Qumran had to bury the carcasses from their dinners to avoid attracting wild animals. Yet bone deposits haven't been found at any other ruins. And Qumran's animal bones were buried with such ritualism that they seem to have more significance than mere waste management.

According to Magness' theory, the bones are evidence that the sectarians—whom she thinks were disaffected Temple priests—viewed Qumran as a substitute Jerusalem, "with each full member living his everyday life as if he were a priest."[11] In Jerusalem, priests had designated areas where they buried the bones from animal sacrifices. Preserving the Temple's purity was of the utmost importance. Magness contends that the Qumranites treated their communal meals with the same sense of ritual and purity as the Temple's sacrificial system. The *Community Rule* elevated meals to a near messianic status: "Together they shall eat; together they shall bless; and together they shall take counsel." The head priest extended his blessings during meals, and the seating order was arranged according to the hierarchy of the adherents. Adherents were thought to transfer the importance of ritual sacrifice in Jerusalem to the liturgy of meal time at Qumran.

Jim was encouraged to see that several scholars had promoted a Qumran-Jerusalem connection. Nevertheless, Jim had a bonus tool in his analytical belt that the experts lacked. Juxtaposing his multi-colored site map of Qumran with the First Temple Jerusalem map from the internet, Jim created a striking graphic which he labeled Qumrusalem. He added a new chapter to his research report explaining his logic about Qumrusalem. Jim had to condition his theory by explaining his method for identifying Qumran's buildings based off the descriptions he culled from his particular Copper Scroll translation.

Jim's understanding of the Copper Scroll offered important clues in a puzzle that scroll scholars had been building for decades: What was the connection between Qumran and Jerusalem? Even if the Essenes did build Qumran to model First Temple Jerusalem, why did the renegades leave Jerusalem in the first place? Were they ousted from the city or did they choose their desert seclusion? Did they view their sanctuary as permanent or did they long to return to the eternal capital? The Dead Sea Scrolls provide insight, albeit no straightforward resolutions or single explanation.

JERUSALEM AND THE SCROLLS

The sectarian Dead Sea Scrolls read like a first-century soap opera, pitting the truly virtuous against evil pretenders in an elaborate plotline. The authors of the scrolls identify themselves cryptically as the Yahad, Sons of Zadok, or Sons of Light. The leader of the Yahad was called the Teacher of Righteousness. Under the enlightened and even infallible direction of the Teacher of Righteousness, the Yahad maintained a divine standard.

The *Community Rule* infers that the sect separated itself from Temple Judaism and opted for self-banishment. They battened down their hatches in Qumran, studying and composing their scrolls and practicing what they interpreted as the purest form of the ancient faith. Just as the Jews' stint in Babylon proved to be a time of purification and consolidation, the sect's wilderness seclusion was meant to play a role in their communal growth and virtue. According to their worldview, they were the elect, the remnant, the wise teachers which Daniel prophesized would "instruct many" during the "time of the end."[12]

By going to the Dead Sea region, the splinter group saw themselves as fulfilling the messianic prophecy from Isaiah 40:3: "In the desert, clear the road of the Lord; straighten in the wilderness a highway for our God." If Qumran was God's highway, the Yahad believed the standards of ritual purity that once applied to Jerusalem and the Temple were transferred to their alternative society. Going to great lengths to maintain the sanctity of the complex and Qumran's denizens, purity standards were far more rigorous for the zealots than normative Judaism.

The scrolls indicate that the Yahad used Qumran as a stand-in for Jerusalem. However, they had an inherent paradox in their theology. As faithful Jews, the Jerusalem Temple continued to hold the utmost importance in their messianic hopes, even if it was temporarily defiled. Famous for their strong messianic notions, the nonconformists felt they were living in the End of Days, waiting in expectation for the day that Jerusalem would be purified, the established priesthood dismantled, and the city's exalted status restored. In the interim, Qumran had to be a close second to Jerusalem, imbuing the Yahad with a sense of place.[13]

If Jim's belief that Temple ritual objects were buried all over Qumran proved correct, then the Essenes' strict standards for purity made even more sense, both for themselves and their compound. Either they were maintaining purity for the sake of the hidden vessels, or Qumran made an ideal endpoint for a Temple rescue operation because it was already undefiled. Surely the priests hiding the items identified Qumran as the only place, outside of Jerusalem, that held a high enough standard to preserve the sanctity of the caches.[14]

While studying the Dead Sea Scroll corpus to understand the Essenes position toward Jerusalem, Jim paid a visit to his friend Joseph Good, an expert in materials associated with the Temple sacrificial system. In Good's opinion, Jim's research hinted that Qumran was the ultimate genizah, storage unit for unserviceable documents. Secluded, abundant in dry air and lightless hard-to-reach caves, the area made an ideal repository for an accumulation of retired Temple objects. Good explained that Jewish law not only forbids throwing away writings bearing the holy name, it also commands major precautions to be made for the retirement of consecrated Temple vessels and priestly garments. Many scholars already viewed Qumran's caves as scroll repositories—much like the Old Cairo genizah—but perhaps Qumran was also a hiding ground for consecrated vessels and vestments.

Between the apocryphal books, the Qumrusalem maps, and the genizah concept, Jim's belief that he had solved the Copper Scroll riddle was growing bone-deep. Despite his friends' questioning the fate of the Ark, and despite the personal attacks of the bibliobloggers, Jim was more impervious than ever to second-guessing his research. If he was working off his own line of logic, however, authorities in Israel were unlikely to give him a real chance. He learned that much in 2009 with Yuval Peleg. Archaeologists were well trained in the art of tearing down other scholarly assertions to advance their own theories. To get the project moving again, Jim needed more than theories, spirituality, or gut feelings. Apparently, he even needed more than a well-composed and thoroughly argued research report. He needed indisputable scientific proof, a smoking gun. He also wanted for allies in high places.

CHAPTER 16
FALSE STARTS

In the spring of 2011, exactly two years after the inconclusive Qumran excavation with Peleg, Jim had his first brush with the illicit world of black market antiquities. One afternoon, Jim was talking with the regulars at his favorite coffee shop when he received a phone call from a Jordanian man named Neal. Neal learned of Jim when he came across the *Copper Scroll Project* website. "Mr. Barfield, I have something you might want," Neal said. "I have in my possession another ancient copper scroll."

Jim's curiosity piqued. He tucked his things under his arms and walked outside into the sunlight to hear the rest of what the mysterious man had to say. "The tiny scroll was given to me by my father who found it decades ago along the Jordanian side of the Dead Sea," Neal explained. "My father kept it in a tiny jar which he occasionally brought out for display. We have held it in the family all this time. But I am 54 and have been out of work for seven months. I want to sell it."

Antiquities thieves often treated their collections like investment portfolios, waiting for the right time and the most interested buyer before making a deal. Jim was not going to be that buyer, but he was willing to try to steer the man in the right direction, in case he was holding onto an important artifact. "Have you tried to contact the Israel Antiquities Authority?" Jim asked. "If it's authentic, they might make you an offer."

"I don't want my name known in Israel. I have family there and visit the country often," Neal explained. "I don't want anything to happen that will bar me from getting in."

Neal's paranoia was justified. If Israel caught him in outright antiquities dealing, they could block his entry. Though globally Israel was unique for legalizing the buying and selling of antiquities, they closely monitored the trade. Antiquarians were only allowed to sell artifacts unearthed before 1978, before Israel enacted its patrimony law. Anything found after 1978 was considered property of the state.

In practice, the law is difficult to enact. Shop owners selling antiquities to tourists, like oil lamps and Roman coins, argue that their inventory is legal because it predated 1978. The truth is that archaeological sites in Israel get fleeced regularly. Unprovenanced finds steadily stream into the black markets. Tourists—the ones creating the demand for Holy Land antiquities—unknowingly participate in the trade, blissfully unaware of its adverse consequences.

The IAA employs their own Theft Prevention Unit, charged with the task of protecting Israel's 30,000 archaeological sites from looters. Journalist Nina Burleigh wrote an enthralling book, *Unholy Business*, documenting the unit's mammoth responsibility:

> Amateur, nonacademic digging, treasure hunting, or looting is a common enterprise in the Holy Land, and even a profession for some Palestinians. These excavators form the bottom tier of the antiquities trade, digging up objects that increase hundredfold and thousand-fold in value as they move farther away from their origins. It is not uncommon for some collectors and licensed dealers to step across a military checkpoint, go no farther than a few hundred meters into Palestinian territory, cut a deal with a digger or more likely a middleman, then bring back into Israel an object whose provenance is utterly unverifiable by Israel law.[1]

Jim knew that if he handled the situation the wrong way, Neal would be scared off and the artifact lost forever—perhaps to a private collector's library. But Jim also understood that besides looted artifacts, the antiquities market pulsated with counterfeit antiquities. What Neal said was a first-century scroll could have been forged in his basement to tempt the gullible.

Jim found out that when Neal wasn't in Jordan, he resided in a largely Muslim area of Pittsburgh. Jim called Chris and asked if he was up for a road trip to Pennsylvania. "Yeah," Chris said, "Let's take my new hybrid. I want to test the gas mileage." Despite being a tractor salesman, Chris was an early adaptor to fuel efficient vehicles. Jim happily agreed. Since he had long stopped fundraising, Copper Scroll ventures were mostly financed out of his own pocket.

They broke the trip up into two days. The only part of a road trip that Chris didn't care for was fast food or gas station snacks. He had become increasingly more of a health nut when he entered his forties. "I spent the first half of my life putting poison in my body," he rationalized. "I'm trying to spend the second half reversing that." In lieu of alcohol or drugs, he bought only organic produce. He ditched coffee and sodas in favor of powdered wheat grass and herbal supplements. Chris's Whole Foods bag reclined next to Jim's chips and beef jerky in the backseat.

"You are like a modern-day Essene: celibate, disciplined, and studious," Jim half-joked, eyeballing Chris's snacks.

The two agreed that they would proceed with caution when meeting Neal. In the best-case scenario, the artifact would provide some clue to the Copper Scroll—a slim possibility, but a topic that fueled more than one hopeful conversation during the long trip. Alternatively, Jim cautioned, "If the guy strikes us as shady, we are backing out fast. The black market for antiquities has bad *juju*, and I don't want that on us."

Jim and Chris arrived at their Pennsylvania hotel in the mid-afternoon. The neighborhood was made up of a string of sleepy pawn shops, nail salons, and Chinese buffets. They spied Neal, sitting in an old clunker in the parking lot. With a stubble chin and wide black brows, wearing a chestnut turtleneck and baggy leather jacket, Neal got out of his car and strode over to them. Jim thought he looked the part of a genial Arab shop owner in the Muslim Quarter of Jerusalem.

After introductions, Neal quickly pulled the artifact out of his pants pocket, displaying in his palm a corroded copper tube in a Ziploc bag. It appeared a little wider than a cigarette and only half as long. Jim and Chris were shocked by the size of the miniature. "It's hard to imagine that this could roll out to be a scroll," Jim noted. "This thing could fit inside a ballpoint pen."

Still, Jim had been a student of biblical archaeology long enough to know that luck and chance played an oversized role with many of Israel's most significant finds. The tiny copper tube reminded Jim of a similarly sized silver amulet found in a mortuary outside the Old City of Jerusalem in 1979. The microscopic inscription is the oldest version of the priestly blessing.

Haunted by "What if?" questions, Jim felt duty-bound to ensure that the Jordanian's unopened copper amulet was presented properly to those in the know. They checked into the hotel to investigate the artifact further.

In the hotel room, Chris unpacked Shawn's high-quality camera and Jim's table-mounted magnifying glass. Chris asked Neal to pose for the camera while holding the artifact. In case Jim and Chris were ever questioned about involvement in what looked like an illegal trade deal, they wanted a picture to identify the owner. Opening the dusty hotel windows to let in natural light, Jim strained to analyze the amulet under the magnifying glass. The sky was so gray from smog that the light made little difference. The letters protruding from the outer layer were too miniscule to be distinguishable. Chris set up a makeshift studio to take photos of the amulet from every angle with micrometer measurements.

While Chris photographed the amulet, Neal chattered in the background about his travails in trying to sell the artifact. With an ingratiating tone, he told Jim, "If I let the Israelis get hold of this, they will take it from me and say it belongs to them."

Jim pressed Neal more on the origins of the copper piece, trying to understand the context in which it was discovered. Something seemed off-key as Neal tripped over his answers, contradicting the original story he told on the phone about his father. As Jim found out later, alleging an artifact had a long family history was a standard tactic to protect antiquities' owners from prosecution and confiscation.

"I have a big collection of ancient coins," Neal boasted. "I regularly sell them to a buyer in California, but unfortunately he's not in the market for amulets."

Jim understood that Neal was prodding him to determine if he was a potential buyer.

"Tell me more about these coins," Jim prodded back.

Ducking the issue of the coins' provenance, Neal went into detail about the inventory in his collection of antiquities. Though Jim was not intimate with the many layers of the antiquities trade, he took Neal for being a courier—a middleman who buys relics from looters in Israel and sells them to the highest international bidder.

Sensing that Jim was opposed to treating precious relics as commodities, Neal tried to make a deal that passed Jim's sniff test: "If you help me sell the amulet to the Israel Museum," Neal said, "I'll give you a percentage."

Neal's offer to split the profit and a shiny spot on the amulet were all the red flags Jim needed. He still wanted Neal to pursue opening and authenticating the amulet, but he refused to get intimately involved with the antiquities trade. Jim told Neal that he would send him a composite of the photos they had taken and advised him to consult an expert paleographer who could better decipher the markings. Jim also gave Neal the phone number for a metallurgist in England who could date the artifact. Other than that, Jim made it clear he did not want to be involved.

On the way back to Oklahoma, Jim and Chris stopped for a tour of Gettysburg National Military Park. Walking through amber wheat fields, Jim pondered the forward march of history, the importance of turning points, and the invaluable contributions of leaders like Lincoln. Jim was on constant guard for a pivotal moment in the *Copper Scroll Project*. After experiencing his share of false starts, he felt he needed the wisdom of Abe to inspire history, and to nudge it.

A year later, Jim got a short email from Neal saying that the English metallurgist had dated the small artifact to Israel's Byzantine chapter (330–638 CE). Neal sold the unopened amulet for thirteen thousand dollars. To whom did he sell it? Neal didn't say. Jim didn't ask.

Throughout Jim's time pursuing the Copper Scroll treasures, he had one working credo: "Walk through every door and take every chance." That philosophy encouraged him to return telephone calls from strangers; to befriend an aging black-listed explorer; to track down leaders in the Temple Mount movement; to fly to Israel for one-off meetings; and to listen patiently to the unsolicited advice of strangers. Though he never knew what was around the corner, in some cases, he got a peek and had to make a quick retreat.

IRON DOOR

Jim continued to be on watch for the antidote to his impasse. For four years, he had looked to the ancient past for clues. He successfully identified the echoes of a tradition purporting that Temple vessels were hidden in the Judean Desert. The IAA had no patience for echoes, however; they demanded a gong. In the meantime, new possibilities were unfolding in the world of technology.

During the first excavation, Peleg made clear that the Copper Scroll depths were far too deep to dig blindly. If Jim hoped to reconnect with the Israeli archaeologist and have him agree to dig ten-foot probes in sacred ruins, he needed more confirmation than his theory could provide, and he needed exact pinpoints. To get that standard of data, he had to secure a high-quality, deep-penetrating metal detector—something seriously scaled up from the dinky one that Peleg used over the test sites.

As a child, Jim's father was a strong believer in the promise of technology solving age-old riddles. Though the family income was limited, his father collected and sold aluminum to save up for his first metal detector. In the evenings, Jim's father would sit outside, with his metal detector laid across his lap. Swatting at flies, he spellbound his four children with stories about a legendary iron door in the Wichita Mountains, a few miles from Lawton. Behind the rust-stained door, his father said, lie hordes of Spanish plunder. Rumors circulated, as rumors do, that a group of Comanche Native Americans in the late 1800s attacked a caravan of Spanish conquistadors on their return from burying gold. Treasure hunters had been scavenging around the boulders and granite knobs ever since. Jim's father once told him, "Jimmy, if I ever find that gold, I'm going to use the reward money to buy a private helicopter that we can land in our front yard."

From the time of his father's daydreams, metal detectors had grown more advanced, and more expensive. Still, one morning on a whim, Jim called White's Metal Detecting Company to ask them for a quote on their deepest penetrating equipment.

The secretary at the home office in Oregon answered his call. She sounded like she had been interrupted in the middle of a busy morning of multitasking. Jim asked, "Excuse me, ma'am. I'm looking for something that could detect large quantities of gold and silver buried as far deep as twenty feet."

On the other line, Jim heard a sudden halt to the clatter of typing on a keyboard. Whether she recognized his voice or his description of treasure, the secretary asked point blank, "Are you Jim Barfield?"

"Yes," Jim replied, startled.

"Can you hold on just one minute?" she said. "Don't go anywhere."

The secretary handed the phone to her boss, Melissa Wise. As it turned out, Wise saw Jim on the *Travel Channel*; she had been an avid follower of the project ever since. Jim explained how he hoped that one day the excavation would get moving again, and this time he wanted the highest caliber of equipment.

Wise told Jim, "I'll give you our best detector, the TM-808, if you'll wear a company shirt with our logo on it during the excavation."

"You give it to me," Jim replied, "and I'll wear your company underwear."

The TM-808 detector was designed to electronically penetrate soil up to twenty feet deep in search of metal. Another important feature was its ability to adjust for variables in the soil's mineral content, critical in the Dead Sea region. Allegro first aborted his hunt for Copper Scroll treasure because the detectors fifty years ago had no way to dismiss the area's natural magnetism. An electrical engineer named Tim Williams also gave Jim a specialized computer of his own design to attach to the detector; he called it the Arc Geo Logger. The sound output from the detector is logged and downloaded onto the computer to produce a grid of the metal objects sensed under the surface. The computer images are to scale, estimating the size of the objects and their depth.

Chris and Jim began practicing with the free equipment right away. Walking side by side in the backyard, Jim held the detector at his side, and Chris walked next to him with the Arc Geo Logger. For two hours, they worked on matching their stride to the same tempo. When they got it right, the signals digitized the findings in real time. "Looks like you're doing the waltz," Laurie teased them from the kitchen window. "Now let's hope someone in charge at Qumran decides to let you use it."

ASHER LEVY

Self-aggrandizers and conspiracy theorists fluttered to Jim like moths to a flame. Jim's email inbox regularly hosted messages from strangers eager to see his theory tested—many of them claiming to have political connections in Israel. "Every random cold caller tells me that they are best buddies with some distant cousin or nephew of Benjamin Netanyahu," Jim said.

Jim sympathized with people's earnest desire to be involved, as well as their impatience for action. Even so, he had to vet strangers requesting to represent the *Copper Scroll Project*. He had learned that hard lesson when he got wrapped up with the two Texas con artists, an opportunist prophetess, and a crooked Israeli tour guide. All it would take is one person, overtaken by the Copper Scroll's infectious hope, to make a wrong move and land Jim on the IAA's blacklist.

Asher Levy, an Israeli and an active member of the Temple Mount pressure groups, was the most persistent of the strangers who tracked Jim down. Asher was certain he could use his connections to get the excavation moving again. Starting in August 2012, he emailed Jim, commented regularly on the *Copper Scroll Project's* website, and called Jim's cell and home phone repeatedly. At first, Jim didn't respond, but then Asher started leaving messages for Laurie on her personal Facebook page. Asher's messages were always presented as urgent and typed in all caps, the electronic form of yelling. Laurie tolerated the sporadic messages at first, until Asher threatened in his telltale form: IF JIM DOESN'T RESPOND, I'M GOING TO THE ADCA MYSELF.

Jim emailed Asher: WHAT CAN I DO FOR YOU?

As it turned out, Asher had good news to deliver. Yitzhak Magen, Peleg's boss, had finally retired from his lifetime term as Staff Officer for Archaeology at the ADCA. Jim long suspected Magen of leashing Peleg during the April 2009 dig. Only with a new Staff Officer could Jim get a fresh start with the ADCA.

Asher informed Jim that Magen's successor, Hananya Hizmi, was said to be reforming much of the way the antiquities authorities formerly operated, particularly their lack of transparency. Part of the reforms included opening the permit process. Asher asked if he could visit Hizmi on Jim's behalf. Jim doubted Asher had the influence to get past the ADCA's brick walls of communication, but he thought the suggestion was a good first challenge to test what this stranger, Asher, could achieve.

Asher managed to get the ADCA's first official response as to why the Copper Scroll excavation was suspended, something Jim had desired for two years. A short letter from Hizmi, written in Hebrew, was addressed to the IAA head Shuka Dorfman, but delivered to Asher, who then showed it to Jim. The letter stated that the 2009 dig was stopped at the potential cave, or *hill of*

Kokhlit, after Peleg observed a natural rock layer. The letter explained that the other test sites—the interior of the gutter and along the *broken protective wall*—were halted once the diggers reached virgin dirt. Without any corroborating archaeological evidence, Hizmi wrote, "The excavation was complete with no need to do further testing."

No doubt, the ADCA's long overdue explanation irritated Jim. He vented to Asher, "How can they say the dig was conclusive when we barely did anything? And the first part is not true. We never reached a natural rock layer at the *hill of Kokhlit*." Hizmi's absoluteness came off as strange, considering he received all his information secondhand from Peleg.

Like many on the religious right in Israel, Asher's trust in the archaeological authorities was as shallow as the Dead Sea shoreline. "If they perpetrate this crime against us again, and on all the people of Israel, and upon every Jew," Asher sneered, "then things will definitely be different this time in how we respond." Even though Jim was frustrated too, he paid close attention to the overly volatile comments of his new ally.

Asher assured Jim that he had close access to political leaders in Israel who might be willing to help. Jim inquired about the source of Asher's connections, but he had a difficult time understanding Asher's English on the phone. All Jim knew was that Asher had an unimpressive fundraising website where he solicited donations for "outreach activities" in preparation for the Third Temple. From what Jim observed, Asher was an extremely passionate and gregarious man who considered it his solemn duty, as an Israeli and religious Jew, to follow the Copper Scroll dig through to the end.

Jim talked the exhaustingly assertive Asher down from treating Hizmi's letter as an act of war. Instead, Jim asked Asher to try and arrange a meeting with Hizmi for Jim to personally present his theory. Unless Peleg or Magen had shown Hizmi a copy of Jim's research, the busy Staff Officer needed a chance to make his own judgments about the theory. Jim never doubted the persuasive power of his research report. He assumed that those who rejected it simply hadn't read it.

Asher apparently ran in the highest echelons of Israel's religious circles, and promised Jim, "If you can get to Israel, I'll make sure you get a meeting with Hizmi and the Sanhedrin."

Jim cleared his throat. "*The* Sanhedrin?" he asked. He nervously picked at a stray thread on his jeans.

"I know the rabbis will be curious to hear what you have to say," Asher responded.

The Sanhedrin, during the Second Temple period, had been the supreme religious tribunal, adjudicating Jewish law from Jerusalem that applied to Jews in Israel and in the Diaspora. After the Temple's destruction, a modified Sanhedrin continued to meet in northern Israel for four centuries, until finally the institution disbanded. After a hiatus of nearly 1,600 years, a group of 71 rabbis and Judaic scholars in Israel revived the Sanhedrin in 2004.

Asher was hardly the first stranger wanting to make political connections for Jim, but he was the first who vowed to gather the Sanhedrin, a move that pulled on Jim's heartstrings. Jim gulped. "If you can arrange that," he said, "I can get there by September."

On previous trips, Jim met with Temple Mount movement leaders to try and rally them around the cause of the *Copper Scroll Project*. He envisioned them putting aside any rivalry to work in tandem once the ancient Temple items were located. Though the new Sanhedrin was impotent in terms of power in Israel, it was the only coalition of rabbis ready to provide quick judgments on religiously significant events.

While Asher organized the meetings with Hizmi and the Sanhedrin, Jim completed a few tasks of his own. He asked two friends to clear their schedules so they could come with him and Chris to Israel: Mack the cattle rancher and Mike Winger, a long-time friend of Jim's.

Mike had a gruff exterior combined with a good-ol'-boy manner. He owned a successful dent-repair business which chased hail storms; the family business motto was "Hail Yeah!" Like Chris, Mike had led a wild life as a young man. In his late twenties, he was arrested in a drug raid and thrown in jail where he heard the Christian gospel for the first time. His newfound faith eventually led him into a Messianic congregation. Though Mike had been an avid fan of the *Copper Scroll Project* and fully supportive of Jim's quest, Jim had not brought Mike along on previous trips.

Jim wondered if visiting Israel for the first time might overly fuel Mike's desire to get the research tested. His irrepressible excitement sometimes blurred his better judgment. Jim could not risk anyone spiriting away from the house in Arad to pitch a protest tent at Qumran or launch a hunger strike in the IAA's parking lot.

At the last minute, Jim decided to take his downloadable research report off the website. If things were heating back up, he didn't want to take any chances. Other than discreetly breaking the website link to his report, he kept quiet. Jim's family and the Copper Scroll team were the only ones who knew about his upcoming meetings in Israel. Jim told Chris, "I can't risk anyone raising a big stink again." In case the meetings went swimmingly, Jim packed his new metal detector.

Chapter 17

SANHEDRIN

While Jim was waiting in baggage claim at the Tel Aviv airport, he got a call from Asher. Just as Asher promised, he had succeeded in setting up meetings with Hizmi and the Sanhedrin. Jim guessed that either Asher had substantial influence in Israel or his persistence made him impossible to refuse. Either way, Jim felt reassured that Asher was no Barney.

"After listening to Asher talk a blue streak, maybe some people were disoriented enough that they didn't know what they agreed to," Jim told Mack. "Either way, so far so good." Israeli security didn't hold up the metal detector. Mike's only breach of etiquette during the plane ride was getting into a friendly discussion about the gospels with two Orthodox Jewish men.

The meeting with the Sanhedrin was scheduled for the first Sunday after the group arrived in Israel. Like usual, they were staying at Flynn's house in Arad, driving the two-hour commute to the important meetings. On the morning of the meeting, Chris drove a rental car through Jerusalem's stop-and-go traffic while Jim leaned out of the passenger side window. Asher had given Jim the address over the phone, but the GPS that came with the rental car wasn't working. He shaded his eyes, squinting into the sun's glare while he read street names. They were looking for an apartment on a narrow side road south of King George Street.

Outside of Jerusalem's Old City walls is a mixture of dilapidated Soviet-style apartment buildings and towering luxury hotels. Up ahead, Jim spotted the elegantly designed Great Synagogue. He knew they must be getting close. This was the unofficial border where Old Jerusalem ended and New Jerusalem began. Anxious about the traffic, Jim bounded out of the car to find the address on foot while Chris hunted for parking.

Though Jim and Asher had yet to meet in person, Asher recognized Jim from pictures and came charging over to him on the sidewalk. "Shalom! Welcome, my friend. *Baruch Hashem*," Asher said, pointing upwards to acknowledge his thanks to God. Jim recognized the booming voice. "You cut your long hair?" Asher asked. Jim nodded but instinctively grabbed for his missing ponytail.

Wearing a white satin *kippa* that somehow clung to his gleaming bald head, Asher kept his tzitzit tucked in under his wrinkled white button-down shirt. He had a large barrel chest and towered over Jim as they stood next to each other waiting for Chris, Mike, and Mack. Asher talked excitedly. He told Jim that he had his own metal detector and was doing some scans at various sites in Israel. He was thrilled to hear that Jim brought his equipment. Once Jim's companions caught up to them, Asher led them through a couple of narrow side streets and up a flight of stairs to a one-bedroom apartment.

"You'd think the Great Sanhedrin would meet in the King David Hotel or some illustrious banquet hall, not a storage room in a back alley," Mike mumbled to Chris.

Though he'd fretted about being late, Jim was among the first to arrive. Sanhedrin members soon piled in. They took their seats around a table stacked high with prayer books. Their heavy breathing from the trip up a short flight of stairs exhibited the effects of the rabbis' under-exercised and uber-studious lifestyles. Judging from their dress, the rabbis—or sages, as the Sanhedrin members were known in Temple times—represented many streams of Israel's Orthodox communities. Jim had acclimatized to Israel's eclectic religious landscape but sitting in the stuffy room he couldn't help but chuckle, observing how Israel's supreme judicial body made for quite the gaggle.

Orthodox Jews have stylistic ways of marking their religious communities. The most obvious are the fabric and color of their headwear, the length of their beards, and the presentation of their sideburns. Many members at the meeting sported black velvet *kippot* and long beards. A few went for alternative head coverings, like straw fedoras and oversized knitted *kippot*. Several had closely trimmed beards and short sideburns.

One of the members had yet to remove his tefillin from that morning's prayer ritual. Tefillin boxes contain small parchment pieces inscribed with scripture. The practice comes from Deuteronomy 11:18: "Fix these words of mine in your hearts and minds; tie them as symbols on your hands and bind them on your foreheads." The oldest known tefillin were found near Qumran in Cave 4, proving the long continuity of a tradition central to Jewish prayer life.

To start off the presentation, Asher made a long ad-lib introduction in Hebrew, explaining the background of the *Copper Scroll Project*. Though Jim couldn't understand Asher's exact words, he knew when Asher touched on the importance of the buried treasures by the number of times his eyes rolled back in his head.

Before Jim began his PowerPoint, Rabbi Hillel Weiss, a literature professor from Bar-Ilan University near Tel Aviv and the spokesman of the Sanhedrin, got straight to the point. "We are accustomed to the work of Vendyl," Weiss said. "Vendyl met with our group many times."

Indeed, Vendyl Jones had been an active proponent of the Sanhedrin since its inception. He strongly believed that once he recovered the Copper Scroll treasures, the secular and democratic government of Israel would dissolve, and the Sanhedrin would take its rightful governing place. Vendyl also believed that if he followed the Copper Scroll's clues to the ashes of the red heifer, the Levitical priesthood could reestablish the sacrificial system. At one point Vendyl said, "Whoever gets these ashes will rule the world."[1]

Professor Weiss asked, "What are you presenting that is new, beyond what Vendyl showed us?"

"My research goes far beyond," Jim said firmly. He wrung his nose which was tickling him from the aggravation of layered dust in the room.

"Okay, let's hear it," Weiss summoned.

The first slide Jim put up on the projector was a modern outline of Jerusalem's Old City walls. "I'm going to start off by asking you three questions," Jim said. "First, do you recognize this city?"

The rabbis quickly answered, "Jerusalem."

Jim then projected the ancient outline of Jerusalem's walls, from the time of Jeremiah.

The members chimed in, "Jerusalem, again."

Jim then put up a map of the Qumran compound and asked, apparently rhetorically, "And where is this?"

Someone sitting closest to the screen replied, "Jerusalem, from a different era."

"This is actually the outline of Qumran's ruins as they still look today," Jim said. "What I'm about to show you will demonstrate a direct link between the Qumran settlement and Jerusalem."

Jim had their attention. Rabbis nudged each other and mumbled knowingly about Qumran's potential. Then the whole room went quiet at once. The founding head of the Temple Institute, Rabbi Yisrael Ariel, walked in late. When the mild-mannered rabbi was 28, during the Six Day War, his paratrooper unit directed the advance on the Temple Mount. His life mission has since been intertwined with the fulfillment of the Jewish prayer, recited daily, for the Holy Temple to be "rebuilt speedily in our days." Jim waited as Ariel circled the room, with members kissing his right hand in turn: an uncommon display of respect in Judaism.

Since Vendyl had already familiarized the Sanhedrin members with his interpretation on the background of the Copper Scroll, Jim skipped the patchwork history lesson. Instead, he used his maps, calculations, and translations to explain his logic locating all the Copper Scroll treasures in or near Qumran. Heads nodded approvingly at the preciseness of the details.

Normally in Israel, Jim was careful to filter out religious references when briefing secular authorities on his research. In a room full of rabbis, however, he spoke candidly about the treasure's spiritual significance. Jim emphasized the need to restore the implements for use in a Third Temple. In any other setting, speaking of a Third Temple in practical terms was completely taboo, but not with this crowd.

Putting more emphasis on the Sanhedrin's prestige than perhaps the Sanhedrin members themselves, Jim assured, "I came to Israel to meet with you all because I believe that if the Copper Scroll treasures are found, they should be handed over to the Sanhedrin so they can be treated according to Torah law." Jim continued, "I've been consistent on this point since the start of the project. I suggested this to the archaeologist we first worked with, and I'll tell it to the next one." With satisfied looks on their faces, the members sat up straight in their chairs.

The man wearing the phylacteries spoke up, "You said it yourself. The Israeli government should not be in control, but they will be." He went on, "If these things are found, they will put them in a museum, and prevent their restoration. If we know that will happen, maybe now is the wrong time to go looking."

Jim winced. When speaking in Christian churches and Messianic congregations, someone usually cautioned Jim to wait for the Messiah. Few things made Jim as irritated as calls for inaction mixed with eager fatalism, especially on his tenth trip to Israel. Spreading his fingers out on the table, he leaned in and said, "You gentlemen pray for the restoration of the Temple seven times a day. Now is the time to take what belongs to you. I really believe *Hashem* has kept these things secret and hidden for all these centuries. And now he let a firefighter from Oklahoma figure it out. Something is either very wrong with this picture, or something is very wonderful."

Heads nodded in agreement—saying *ken, ken* (Hebrew for *yes, yes*). The pre-eminent Rabbi Ariel didn't utter a word of endorsement, or disapproval, throughout the entire roundtable. If Rabbi Ariel was convinced of the Copper Scroll's potential, Jim was confident that the leader would have no problem jumping into action once he deemed it beneficial for his cause.

In fact, during Jim's trip the newspapers announced that the Temple Institute was constructing an altar and its attached ramp. The architects adhered to the respected opinion of Maimonides to create a biblically permissible, yet functioning, altar of the smallest dimensions. According to Exodus 20:22, the stones for the altar of burnt offering had to be unwrought: never touched by iron tools. Rabbinic tradition even passed on the specific recipe for the mortar so that it could sustain high temperatures. The altar is modular by design, so it may be easily disassembled and reassembled. After its completion, the Temple Institute announced that the completed altar was ready for the renewal of the divine service on the Temple Mount, "should the historic opportunity arise." In the meantime, they showcased the altar at the Temple Institute, stowed under a twentieth-century fire alarm.

A man sitting opposite Jim questioned, "But why would the *Beit ha-Mikdash* [Temple] treasures be hidden at Qumran? And why would they design Qumran to look like Jerusalem? I always heard that the Essenes were on bad terms with the priestly leadership in Jerusalem."

Before Jim could answer, a rabbi with a sparse red beard and thick side curls, raised his hand. "Go ahead," Jim said. "We have some here from the tribe of Benjamin."

Looking pleased, he tucked his side curls behind his ears. "The Essenes and Hasmoneans were enemies. But during the war with Rome, a rebel priesthood wrested control over Temple services. The men of Qumran could have been in good standing with the last priests."

Jim assured the group that if Temple treasures materialized at the renegade settlement, scholars would be left reconsidering Qumran's connection to the Temple, prophets, and priests.

Getting back to the core of his presentation, Jim projected the image of one of Qumran's prominent ritual baths onto the wall. According to Jim's translation of the Copper Scroll, location 29 describes the mikvah: *Enter the square space where the consecrated are anointed, go one cubit, there are 400 talents.* "Just think," Jim extolled the members, "Some of the later prophets could have been baptized right here. Oops. I mean *mikvahed*."

Snickers erupted in the room as a red-faced Jim let out an apology for his semantic mistake. He worried they would start spitting at him, like the Temple Institute rabbi when he first misunderstood Jim on a point. Thankfully, the members weren't offended; they blew it off. Jim backpedaled by briefly mentioning how the immersion pools at Qumran testify to the long continuity of Jewish ritual objects' form and function.

Feeling spurred by hopeful thoughts of restoring long lost ritual objects, the rabbis spontaneously started an internal debate about whether *am ha'aretz* was ready for the Third Temple. *Am ha'aretz* was a biblical term for "the people of the land," which in modern parlance referred to secular Israelis.

"If *am ha'aretz* wanted the Temple restored, they would have done it already," one rabbi said. "The Temple was designed to last forever, but when the Jews broke Torah and ignored the prophets, *Hashem* allowed for it to be destroyed. Now, they object to its modern restoration."

Chris was quiet and unobtrusive for the whole of the presentation. When it came to secular Israeli society, he had a knee-jerk response that broke his silence. Everyone looked to the back of the room where Chris was standing. "When these things come out of the cave at Qumran," he said, "there could be a spiritual awakening in Israel. They will be tangible reminders for *all* the people of Israel about her God-given covenant."

Professor Weiss agreed, "True. We know from the prophets that through the Mishkan [Tabernacle], *Hashem* revealed Himself clearly to the people. Miracles rest on the Mishkan." A smile spread across Jim's face. Rarely was he in such like-minded company.

At the close of Jim's presentation, he challenged all the members present: "I'll be meeting with the ADCA this week. If for some crazy reason they allow me to do an electronic survey of the locations, and these items are finally found, you all need to establish custodial rights of the artifacts."

Jim understood that few rabbis in the room had ever encountered officials at the IAA or ADCA, or even understood the archaeological permit process. These weren't the men that were going to help Jim get access to Qumran; they were the ones he wanted on hand when he glimpsed the first sacred vessel gleaming through the dirt.

Before the meeting was adjourned, the cantor in the room led the rabbis in the *Shema Israel*, the anthem said twice daily by observant Jews. Translated the text begins with the declaration from Deuteronomy 6: "Hear O Israel, the Lord is our God, the Lord is One. Love the Lord your God with all your heart and with all your soul and with all your strength." The *Shema* is the first prayer taught to Jewish children and, ideally, the last words to leave one's lips before dying. Hearing *Shema Israel* ethereally echoing off the room's cement walls, Jim fidgeted with the top button on his shirt, gulping down the lump taking shape in his throat. Mike, on the other hand, dropped his chin to his chest and let the tears fall freely.

The members collected their books and filtered out of the room, wishing Jim luck and promising to revisit Qumran's ruins with new eyes. Professor Weiss approached Jim. As a rabbi, Weiss offered Jim his blessing to succeed.

Jim gave Weiss a copy of his full research report to keep. Weiss said, "Please add your signature to it. I know you will be famous one day."

"I really am touched by your support," Jim replied, still trying to hold back any overt signs of emotion.

Weiss's brow furrowed as he looked at Jim intently, grabbing his shoulders. Jim recognized the look in his eyes. Weiss had succumbed to the infectious fever of hope regularly incited by the Copper Scroll. "Forget about religion right now. Forget about the Sanhedrin," Weiss instructed. "When you go to the archaeological authorities, in their eyes, religion will be a negative thing playing against you. Right now, you need to get them to let you dig."

MEETING WITH HIZMI

The next day, Asher scheduled a meeting with Hananya Hizmi. The ADCA's center of operations is in Ma'aleh Adumim, a large Jewish settlement in the West Bank, popular for its cheap real estate in comparison to nearby Jerusalem. Jim and Chris first visited the settlement in 2008 to make dig plans with Peleg. They wondered if they would run into their old friend at the meeting or if he would continue to avoid them.

The ADCA compound stands in stark contrast to the IAA's inspiringly designed, historically rich offices in Jerusalem's Rockefeller Museum. A six-foot fence surrounds the ADCA office complex, and a steel gate guards the entry. Several prefabricated office trailers, encircling a small lawn, house a staff of forty administrators, academic specialists, and field workers—all coming and going. Most of the employees are Israeli, but the ADCA made a point of retaining a handful of Palestinians, as well. "The offices here look more like a well-kept construction yard than a government facility," Jim said as they waited for the security guard to give them clearance to enter.

In the lobby, Hizmi's secretary—a kind, older woman named Mrs. Avraham—offered the guests Turkish coffee in small glasses before directing them into Hizmi's office. Jim took a sip prematurely and got a mouthful of grinds. Hizmi sat hunched over paperwork behind his desk, frowning in concentration. With dark skin leathered by the sun and oversized calloused hands, Hizmi looked out of place in a cramped office with fluorescent lighting. Like Peleg, he preferred working in the field, getting dirty. His appointment as Staff Officer required him to assume the role of a no-nonsense bureaucrat.

Catching sight of Jim's laptop, Hizmi escorted them out of his small office and into a conference room with a screen. The halls smelled of fresh paint. Along the way, Hizmi pointed out a few artifacts from Qumran displayed in their vitrines. Hizmi turned to Jim, looking him dead in the eyes, and said, "I know Qumran very well."

Jim matched Hizmi's serious tone and rejoined, "If you know Qumran, then you, especially, will understand what I am about to show you."

As Jim powered up his computer, Mike, uncomfortable with silence, asked Hizmi, "Sir, have you ever heard the phrase 'the proof is in the pudding'?" Mike couldn't resist the urge to honey most conversations with colloquialisms.

Before the Staff Officer could respond, Chris gave Mike a little kick under the table, and Jim pulled up his first Qumran map.

Jim had no idea what Hizmi already knew of the *Copper Scroll Project,* but he was acutely aware that this would be his only chance to set a first impression. "I believe I have figured out the Copper Scroll," he said with a slight quiver in his voice. "A lot of other people believe it too." Loud construction carried on outside the compound. Jim had to adjust his volume to be heard over the rumble.

Hizmi replied, "Other people have looked for those Copper Scroll instructions. They haven't found them yet. You already looked in 2009. *Nu?*" (*Nu* is the Hebrew equivalent of "Well?"—used ad nauseam by many Israelis).

"Not exactly," Jim explained. "To dig according to the Copper Scroll directions, we should have gone at least ten feet deep, but the deepest we went at any of the test sites was three feet. I don't know what happened, but a stop order was enforced on the dig. This is your country. I'm playing in your backyard."

"So, you must play by the rules," Hizmi retorted.

"And, therefore, I'm here to see you," Jim replied.

Jim wanted Hizmi to know he was extremely respectful of his time. He expected to have Hizmi's attention for only twenty minutes. In that time, he planned on presenting to him the first three and last five Copper Scroll locations. Once Jim got started, Hizmi's disposition softened. He listened closely and asked engaging questions, making no indication that he wanted Jim to cut the discussion short. Hizmi was most curious about the *hill of Kokhlit.*

"When you dug at the cave with Peleg, did they fill back in the dirt?" Hizmi asked.

"No. The dirt was never put back," Jim explained. "I've been out there since. It looks like the waters that washed into the area during the last couple of rainy seasons did their part to deepen the trench six inches more than how we left it."

Jim was surprised Hizmi knew so little about what happened during the first excavation. Jim wondered why he issued a definitive letter to Dorfman, repeating the ritual intonation that the Copper Scroll excavation was "complete with no need to do further testing." Jim almost brought up the letter, but his intuition told him to play ignorant of it. Sensing Hizmi was growing increasingly more fascinated with the three-tiered connection between Qumran, Jerusalem, and the Copper Scroll, Jim didn't want to ruin it by putting Hizmi on the defensive. This meeting was meant to make a fresh start between Jim and the ADCA.

Unlike his speech to the Sanhedrin, Jim stayed away from the religious ramifications of the potential artifacts. He only highlighted the academic and historical breakthroughs that could transpire if Qumran proved to be a burial spot for Temple treasures. Still, Hizmi cautioned, "Sometimes it's better to leave things as they are already; let it rest." Jim knew it was going to take a lot more than stirring his curiosity to convince the Staff Officer, the vigilant gatekeeper of Qumran, to disrupt precious ruins.

Jim looked up at his last map projected on the wall with 57 marked locations in the Qumran ruins. He understood that it was daunting to grant an unlimited excavation of Qumran. Treading cautiously, Jim explained the abilities of his advanced metal detector to Hizmi, highlighting the unobtrusive nature of electronic surveys. Jim promised, "With your permission, all I want to do is scan the site and give you the results. It's up to you what to do with the information."

"If you find something—if you get a positive read—you are going to want to test it," Hizmi replied.

"If I'm wrong, I will go home," Jim said with his best poker face. "If I'm right, I leave it up to you."

The men walked back to Hizmi's office. Hizmi had Jim print out the map of Qumran, highlighting the exact locations Jim thought most pertinent to scan. He then asked Jim to prepare a report about the abbreviated 2009 dig, recapping exactly what happened. With the report, Hizmi wanted Jim's technical proposal for a permit to scan, including details about the functionality of the TM-808 metal detector.

"We have the metal detector in the car, if you want to see it," Chris said. "The detector's main box was broken when security at the airport went through my bag with a fine-tooth comb. Jim and I spent yesterday soldering it back together and reconnecting the battery assembly."

"Unnecessary," Hizmi said, "I'm not a specialist in metal detectors."

Jim was hesitant to leave the offices before he had some assurance that an electronic survey was possible. He didn't want to write a proposal that would collect dust in the ADCA's pile of permit requests.

"What will you do with the report?" Jim asked.

"I'll show it to the Archaeology Advisory Committee to check if your idea holds," Hizmi explained. "Every quarter, the committee screens the permit applications, and we evaluate our obligations and make our budgets. Right now, we don't have the resources for any new digs."

Asher, who had been quiet thus far, countered, "You don't need funding to let him walk around Qumran with a metal detector."

"Look," Hizmi said, restraining his voice. "The entire world—well, at least Christians and Jews—is looking for Qumran to be something important for their faith. I'll say it again: We have to be careful what we go looking for."

As they walked out the door, Hizmi mentioned a significant technicality: Jim needed a bona fide archaeologist to sign onto the permit and guarantee a university sponsorship. According to antiquities laws, only university-backed archaeologists, with at least a master's degree in archaeology, can apply for excavation permits. The rule also applies to conducting electronic surveys.

FRESH START

Jim and Chris, accustomed to the mysterious workings of the antiquities authorities, left the meeting contented. Though Hizmi's mood was icy at the start, he quickly thawed. Jim felt confident that when the Archaeology Advisory Committee convened, the members would realize that a noninvasive free scan of Qumran was harmless, even beneficiary. Hizmi was just doing his job by trying to muzzle their expectations.

Asher and Mike, on the other hand, walked out of the office with their heads hung low. Jim believed Hizmi was merely putting up red tape; Asher and Mike perceived it as tripwire. On his first trip to Israel, Mike expected to behold the world's most important archaeological excavation. During the meeting with the Sanhedrin, he could hardly contain his excitement. By the time they met with Hizmi, he was writhing in anticipation. As Mike realized that Hizmi felt zero sense of urgency, his greatest hopes faded into total despair.

For Asher's part, he smelled treachery, not slogging. "The ADCA doesn't want anything of spiritual importance to be found. They never have and never will," Asher vented. According to Asher's view, Hizmi was using budgetary excuses as a pretext for dodging the world changing repercussions of unearthing Temple artifacts.

On the car ride back to Arad, Jim quietly listened to Asher and Mike brainstorming ideas for sidestepping the ADCA. Asher ticked off the potential capabilities of his various political connections. As if he were moving chess pieces, he named ministers of government, their religious status, and their areas of responsibility—analyzing which contact was most likely to put the ADCA in checkmate. Jim interrupted when he felt it necessary to temper Asher's interventions. He was averse to Asher commandeering the *Copper Scroll Project*.

"Asher, please don't contact any politicians, yet," Jim said with a look of heavy-lidded exasperation. He pointed the air conditioning fan away from him. "I only want you stepping in if Hizmi and the advisory committee deny the permit. If Hizmi starts backpedaling, then we can go another route, respectfully. Until then, let's play nice and honor their application process and guidelines."

"I'll hold off, for now," Asher replied. "But I know these guys at the ADCA want you to disappear."

"I'm confused by what you mean by 'disappear,'" Jim said, "but I hope it's not in the literal sense." Jim changed the subject. "We need to focus on how I'm going to get an archaeologist with university backing in Israel."

Jim asked Asher to contact Professor Weiss from the Sanhedrin for help. Weiss seemed supportive, and he likely knew a few archaeologists from his home university that would be willing to get involved. Getting Asher to channel his vexation onto restricted tasks was the easiest way to distract him from unwarranted interventions elsewhere.

AN ARCHAEOLOGIST

Jim spent the next week in Israel busily meeting with various credentialed Israeli archaeologists—including Gabriel Barkay. Barkay is well known for his exhaustive work sifting through earthen debris illegally cleared by the *Waqf* in 1999. The *Waqf*'s declared intent was to build an emergency exit for a newly built prayer hall. The reality was an archaeological crime: 400 truckloads of artifact-laden landfill were discarded with zero oversight. After waiting for a permit from the Israeli authorities for five years, Barkay finally got a green light to launch a massive sifting project. The ongoing work, conducted by thousands of short-term volunteers, has unveiled a host of precious artifacts from the First and Second Temple: coins, clothing, jewelry, figurines, arrowheads, pottery, tiles, and even a stone seal from the time of King Solomon.

Weiss arranged for Barkay to meet Jim at Asher's home. The seventy-year-old archaeologist's form of greeting was to vent about the inflating price of cab fares. Barkay sat down unceremoniously in Asher's office. After taking off his signature newsboy cap and adjusting his spectacles, he picked up Jim's research report and started flipping through it. His fingernails were impacted with dirt.

Jim inquired about the progress of the sifting project. "Discoveries are being made daily," Barkay said. "However, people still ask me why there is no physical remnant from the Temples. The Muslim authorities prohibit excavations on the Temple Mount and then accuse us of not having enough proof for the Jewish Temples. They can't hold the rope at both ends."

Although Barkay was an expert on excavations in Jerusalem and a frequent guest on archaeology documentaries, he had spent little time at Qumran. During their short meeting, Barkay made it clear that he was uninterested in getting involved with an excavation based on the Copper Scroll. Still, he was a practical man; he gave Jim names of other archaeologists who he believed best fit Jim's quest and mode of thinking. Jim insisted on giving the famous archaeologist money for the cab ride home.

Weiss and Asher worked quickly to put Jim in touch with the archaeologists recommended by Barkay. Jim and Chris drove back and forth from Arad to Jerusalem, giving rapid-fire presentations of the Copper Scroll theory to anyone who could affix their name to a permit application. Mike and Mack spent their last days in Israel hanging back in Arad, hiking in the desert and reading at the house. One night, over dinner at *Muza's*—one of the few restaurants in Arad—Jim vented about the lack of progress in finding an archaeologist. After an appetizer of pita and baba ghanoush, Mike began to press Jim to let him sneak into Qumran. He had been dreaming up ways he could discreetly test the locations without detection.

Chris was unequivocal: "If the Israelis catch you poking around their ruins with a metal detector, you will find yourself in jail."

Jim added, "I'll be the one to bail you out, and then no one will ever let me back into this country."

Mike refused to relent. "Forget I ever asked," Mike said. "If I'm caught, I'll say I was operating on my own. No one will find out that I know you."

The next morning, Jim and Chris drove to Tel Aviv for one last meeting with an archaeologist from Bar-Ilan University. Mike killed time in Arad by poking around Flynn's storage rooms. To his luck, he came across a pointed metal probe, six feet long and a half inch thick: a push rod normally used by plumbers to find the direction of underground pipes. As Mike stared at the T-shaped tool, he got an idea. He fitted white pipe over it and draped the pipe with fabric curtains. The result looked like a crude Byzantine relic, a holyish cross.

Mike thought if he was going to get past Qumran's front entrance with his pipe cross, he needed to imitate a local monk, or at least an eccentric tourist. He scanned Flynn's closet for biblical era clothing, routinely worn at Israel's holy sites by large tourist groups. He had to settle on wrapping himself up in a tan bed sheet, toga-style.

When Jim got home, Mike greeted him at the door, holding his cross with a toga tied over his t-shirt and jeans. In his slow country drawl, Mike asked, "Well, Jimbo, what d'ya think?"

Jim had to pull up a chair to steady his knees buckling under him from laughter. He stared at the portly build which gave comic shape to the sheet. "You look like a defrocked Armenian monk!" Jim howled between convulsions.

Chris, also guffawing, buried his face on the kitchen table, shaking his head "No, no, no!" Once they could finally look Mike in the eye, they heard out his scheme.

Mike knew that, because Peleg cut short the dig at the Copper Scroll's *hill of Kokhlit*, Jim never got to find out if the sloping dirt mound was blocking a cave entrance. If Mike could get into Qumran as an oddball tourist, he could march to the *hill of Kokhlit* and use his cross to probe for cavities. The probe wouldn't disturb the site, but it could provide Jim with extra insight into the structure of the rock formation.

Much to Jim's dismay, he didn't hate the idea. With a return flight fast approaching, he was feeling particularly desperate. The archaeologists Weiss had introduced to him so far were intrigued by his research. Still, none of them agreed to apply for a permit to electronically scan the site. Jim wrote to Peleg twice. After apologizing for his naïve mistakes in 2009, he asked that Peleg please consider working with him again. This time, he promised, they wouldn't have to blindly probe. Peleg never responded. Jim felt the lack of an available and willing archaeologist acutely.

Ignoring the alarm bells sounding in his conscience, Jim gave Mike a green light. He had visited Qumran enough times to know that mystics, clergy and hippies toured the ruins daily, dressed in more eccentric getup than Mike. Getting past the pay booth was easy enough. Jim also knew that he had casually walked up from the ruins to the *hill of Kokhlit* dozens of times; not once was Jim questioned on his purposes.

"Sit down," Jim said, still wiping tears of laughter from his eyes. "I have to draw out the area along the *hill of Kokhlit* that you will need to test with your probe. I mean cross." He added, "But you have one mission: testing the potential cave. Don't wander into any other part of the complex."

"Deal!" Mike exclaimed.

The next morning, Jim, Chris, and Mack drove Mike to Qumran. They dropped him off at the entrance and parked on the far side of the lot to be sure he got past the ticket counter. Smiling proudly with cross in hand, Mike paid his admission fee. Eager to play the part of a monk, he motioned the sign of the cross as he passed the watchtower; Jim saw him touch his hand to his head and both shoulders but noticed he forgot the chest. "What a knucklehead," Jim said. Mike walked through the ruins and scampered directly up to the *hill of Kokhlit*. He completely ignored the nonchalant approach Jim had mapped out for him beforehand.

A walkie-talkie was hidden underneath Mike's sheet toga. Once he was tucked behind the rock's natural structure, he radioed to his friends that he was set to probe. Chris drove their getaway car a half mile down the road where they had full view of the *hill of Kokhlit*. If security followed Mike's path up the hill, they could send him an early warning.

On the first test, the pipe cross penetrated the dirt straight down, proving there was at least six feet of soil. Mike transmitted the information to the van by walkie-talkie. The hairs on the back of Jim's neck prickled. "Stay right along the face of the rock," Jim instructed. "You can probe all along the trench where we excavated before."

Mike pushed the pipe into the dirt again. They could hear him chuckling as he held the walkie-talkie with his chin. On the second test, the pipe hit solid rock, only one foot underneath the surface. He continued to test at three more points along the trench; each time he hit the same shallow rock surface. As he probed, he reported the results back to Jim. Within fifteen minutes, Mike was finished. He mopped sweat from his forehead with the bedsheet.

"We shouldn't gamble going back to the parking lot to pick him up," Chris told Jim. They weren't certain who at the Qumran complex noticed the fake monk's detour. They directed him to hike over from the cave, through the wadi, toward the waiting vehicle.

Mike's adrenaline was pumping hard as he slung open the door and threw off his toga. The armpits of his undershirt were stained with moisture. Still, he wore a look of distress. He didn't feel like he'd provided Jim with any significant revelation.

Jim assured Mike, "Don't worry. You got perfect results. Your lumbering around helped me to realize why there might be solid rock right where I had expected a cave entry. In II Maccabees, after Jeremiah hid the most valuable of the Temple treasures, the prophet sealed up the entrance. I bet the rock is a manufactured false wall that extends over the entry to the underground cave."

Mike sighed with relief. However, if Mike had only found dirt all the way down, Jim would likely have given perfunctory interpretations of those results as well. As the years waned on, Jim sought a silver lining for every darkened cloud. Maintaining his indomitable optimism at such a pitch was a relentless impulse, the source to keeping his sanity. Self-doubt may have occasionally crept into his thought life, but he never gave it a moment to fester. The only evidence Jim would consider conclusive was an actual find. Until then, no excavation at Qumran would be deep enough. No metal detector was strong enough. No crude pipe cross was thorough enough.

CHAPTER 18

CONSPIRACY

$\frown$

B ack in Oklahoma, Jim started putting together the permit request for Hizmi. At the same time, he continued his hunt for a certified Israeli archaeologist with university backing. Dr. Oren Gutfeld stood out from all of the recommendations as one of the few professionals to have searched for Copper Scroll treasure. Gutfeld had three other prominent things going for him: familiarity with Qumran, a long history with the ADCA, and a position at Hebrew University. Jim had never met Gutfeld, but he knew of his work from documentaries. He thought of him as a person of like mind. Both believed the Judean Desert had yet to divulge all of its long-held secrets.

Gutfeld taught classical archaeology and regularly served as an excavation director on behalf of Hebrew University. The Hebrew University connection was critical since permit requests required the sponsorship of an academic institution's archaeology department. Among his peers, Gutfeld had a reputation for tenacity, owed to his multiple dig seasons enduring the harsh conditions at Hyrcania. In addition, Gutfeld had a penchant for working with noncredentialled explorers. If he took a chance on the eccentric Bob Morgan, then Jim would be a soft gamble by comparison.

For eight seasons, Gutfeld operated as the assistant dig director with Randall Price—director of the Center for Judaic studies at Liberty University in Virginia, and an outspoken supporter of Israel, author, and explorer. Gutfeld's role was to provide in-depth assistance to Price's excavations on Qumran's southern plateau, like obtaining the necessary permits, building a base camp, securing equipment, and arranging for the processing and storage of finds. The two had some success together. In addition to finding numerous animal bone deposits, the excavation located a large, intact, sealed storage jar—much like the jars that encased the Dead Sea Scrolls. The jar contained a deposit of gypsum, a mineral used to make plaster. They also discovered the plateau had a subterranean storage complex.

Most importantly, the years Gutfeld spent clearing the Hyrcania tunnels as a graduate student weighed fresh in his mind. He was still waiting for an explanation as to why the tunnels ended abruptly, deep in the crux of the mountain. In the hundreds of bags of silt cleared from the shafts, Gutfeld found no hint of their purpose and no trail of treasure. The endeavor also appealed to Gutfeld's sense of adventure. A professional scuba diver, he was at his happiest when hiking desert gorges and taking plunges in the Red Sea.

After he recovered from the letdown at Hyrcania, Gutfeld conducted a foot survey of the Judean Desert with local Bedouin to try and locate any similar tunnels. Amazingly, he found entrances to two ancient tunnels, with the same descending steps and nooks for oil lamps. Though he didn't yet have the funding or time to excavate, Gutfeld's new tunnels were within sight of Qumran.

After Jim's first phone conversation with Gutfeld, he sent him a link to a password protected copy of his research report. He invited Gutfeld to decide for himself if the Copper Scroll connection to Qumran was worth pursuing. Jim could tell from the tracking metrics that Gutfeld logged in to read and review the report several times. Soon after, Jim received an email from Gutfeld stating, "From my viewpoint, this research looks incredible, and I would be honored to take part." Thrilled with the unreserved nature of the response, Jim called Gutfeld's office right away.

On the phone, Gutfeld treated Jim with the respect that most academics reserve for their own. He had even read the history related portions of Jim's report and studied Jim's First Temple theories.

"You know you aren't totally alone in your thinking," Gutfeld started. "My friend Hanan Eshel also thought the Copper Scroll was referencing First Temple vessels. The Essenes maybe wanted to be seen as keepers of the secret knowledge of the hiding places."

"Really, I didn't know that," Jim replied.

"I want you to know that I am not a treasure hunter," Gutfeld stated. "But I do take the Copper Scroll very seriously."

"Nor am I," Jim replied. "But I am a firefighter with an idea. I need your expertise to help the project get out of this logjam."

"Don't be too humble," Gutfeld said. "I am aware that you are an award-winning investigator. But I think that I'm missing something. You want to scan the same spots that you already tested with Yuval Peleg?"

"That's right," Jim said.

"Yuval was a good friend and a serious archaeologist," Gutfeld told Jim. "I am sure Yuval had good reason for stopping." Before Jim could protest, Gutfeld conceded, "In my experience, however, excavating in the Judean Desert is always worth the effort. They say the area has been totally explored, but it hasn't. There is still work to do. Much has been overlooked."

With Gutfeld's signature, the permit request for a scan was complete. In the list of demands Hizmi ticked off in their first meeting, Jim met all of them. Attached to the standard permit request, Jim included an analysis of the brief excavation with Peleg, the details of the new scanning equipment, and the logic behind his Copper Scroll theory. On New Year's Eve 2012, Jim flew to Israel to hand deliver the paperwork to Hizmi's office. Asher and Chris accompanied him.

"Here is the report. I believe I have adhered to all of the ADCA's policies," Jim told Hizmi, laying the bound file on his cluttered desk. "If my research is correct, you will notice on the attached map that there are many overlapping locations in each area. Several locations can be covered in a single scan."

Asher chimed in, "All Jim is asking for is a simple walk across Qumran with a detector capable of taking underground pictures. As soon as he gets the graphs printed out, he'll hand them over to you." Asher added with nervous energy, "We can expect a permit will be coming soon, *nu?*"

"I'll let you know when the committee has made their decision," Hizmi responded. "I'll meet with Oren Gutfeld about this soon as well." Hizmi then switched to a lecturing tone. "But whatever you do, don't go out there and do an unauthorized scan."

Jim nodded, hoping his expression didn't give away the sudden guilt of remembering Mike traipsing through Qumran as a faux monk.

CAMPBELL

Gratified to have the permit request in Hizmi's hands, as well as the signature of a respected archaeologist, Jim and Chris went back to Arad and had dinner at *Muza's* to celebrate. Located in a gas station complex, *Muza's* interior feels like a New England pub but with a Mediterranean menu. Mahogany wood and polished brass line the bar. International soccer banners sown together create a quilt-like wallpaper covering the restaurant from floor to ceiling. The sight of the decor always made Jim nervous since the banners were such an obvious fire hazard. "One small fire in the corner, and the whole place would be aflame in seconds," Jim pointed out to Chris.

Jim and Chris walked into a robust greeting from the wait staff. Several of the long-time workers at *Muza's* had been following the *Copper Scroll Project*'s progress for four years. In the beginning, they took the two for eccentric Americans. Gradually, Jim and Chris became regular clientele. The staff anticipated their Copper Scroll updates and often pitched their own ideas for next steps. Emmie, their favorite waitress, sat down next to them to translate several emails that Asher forwarded to Jim from archaeologists and bureaucrats. Emmie is a single mother. Her nine-year-old son scooted his chair close to Jim. He knew very little English, but he too felt familiar with the American man and his dusty boots and tilted fedora. Emmie jotted down her translations. Jim and the boy shared a bowl of complimentary almonds.

Something about Jim made many Israelis want to root for him. The story was so unorthodox that it fit nicely into the larger Jewish narrative: A man with extreme stage fright guides a colossal band of slaves out of Egypt; A God-fearing prostitute plays an instrumental role in the capture of Jericho; A ruddy shepherd boy is anointed king; A Jewish orphan in Persia thwarts a plan to annihilate her people. And now, a retired firefighter, an *Okie* with no formal education, inadvertently solved a mystery from the most shadowy of the Dead Sea Scrolls.

With a soccer match playing on the televisions, the bartender motioned Jim over. "The other night I was telling my wife about you guys. She works at Masada," he explained as he poured Jim and Chris a glass of water. Thick glass shelves behind him showcased *Muza's* selection of liquor bottles. "My wife thinks you should meet Eitan Campbell, the director of Masada. He's

American. Well kind of, but he's a cool guy. Maybe he could pull some strings for you."

By coincidence, Campbell swaggered into the restaurant at that moment. He came for a quick drink and to check in on the restaurant owner, a friend. As he draped his khaki Parks Authority jacket over the back of a bar stool, the bartender tilted his head toward Campbell and pointed with his eyebrows "That's him!" he whispered to Jim.

Campbell's gruff charm was undeniable: thick forearms, wild brown hair, and a cleft chin so prominent that he looked like a caricature drawing. When he ordered a Goldstar beer, he spoke Hebrew like a native Israeli, punctuating the request with chutzpah.

In 1968, Campbell's parents, both Christian Zionists, abruptly quit their jobs and sold everything to move their family from Delaware to Arad. The Israeli military victory in 1967 impressed them as the dawn of the new millennium. Establishing residence in Israel was a grandiose gesture to show solidarity with the embattled but thriving state. At twelve, Campbell was enrolled in Israeli public schools while his parents scrambled for work. At seventeen, he applied for a maintenance job at Masada. The director of Masada at the time thought Campbell was too small for the heavy lifting that the position required. However, the director's daughter was one of Campbell's classmates. She encouraged her father to take a chance on the scrawny Delaware boy.

Over the next thirty years, Campbell worked his way up through the ranks, occupying every menial post Masada had to offer: janitor, ticket collector, and emergency medic. After holding the post of director for thirteen years, it is a gross understatement to say that Campbell knew the site like the back of his own hand; no one knows their hands that well. Though he worked at Masada his entire career, his passion for the ancient man-made wonder never dimmed. When speaking about Masada's backstory, which is as bravura as the view from the mountain top ruins, Campbell always gets emotional.

The site of the last stand for Jewish zealots hopelessly combating the mighty Roman army, Masada ranks high among Israel's national symbols. Rather than submit to slavery under Roman masters, the zealots participated in a mass suicide. On any given day, a tourist is as likely to witness a bar mitzvah celebration as they are to run into a group of eighteen-year-old Israeli soldiers, M16's slung over their shoulders. The IDF has their annual swearing-in ceremony on the mountain's peak with the war cry, "Masada shall not fall again!"

Jim scooted over three seats and plopped right next to Campbell. The bartender made introductions, offering Campbell his surprisingly comprehensive view of how Jim and Chris had come to be Arad's most celebrated explorers. Having a heart for underdogs, Campbell was immediately intrigued by their story. Without the aid of his research report, Jim relayed to Campbell the telescoped version of his research. Campbell, for his part, absorbed the details of Qumran and the Copper Scroll's connections like an excitable youth.

The thought of unearthing the mother lode of biblical history tantalized him. Campbell had spent his life in the service of preserving Israel's national history. Though he personally identified neither with Judaism nor Christianity, he was tender toward both—as the son of Episcopalians and a patriot of the Jewish state. By the end of the night, he was convinced that Jim had solved the Copper Scroll riddle and that Qumran was far more significant than he had imagined.

When *Muza's* closed, Campbell invited Jim and Chris over to his house which, by happenstance, was located a few streets down from Flynn's home. Shivering in the parking lot from the winter desert winds, but feeling too cheery for the night to end, they caravanned over to Campbell's together. Even in the winter, the Negev's brightly lit desert sky has a way of fooling a person into forgetting the late hour, like a windowless casino.

Propped next to Campbell's front door was a surfboard someone scrawled with graffiti: "Dead Sea Surf Club." Twice divorced with four grown children, Campbell's bachelor pad was filled with music albums and collectible instruments. If Campbell's first love was Masada, music came in as a close second. He brought out his favorite guitar, launching into his playlist of classic rock. Jim and Chris, never opposed to a sing-along, belted out familiar ballads in a brotherhood of tone-deaf harmony.

Before Jim and Chris retired back to Flynn's house, Campbell assured them they had found an ally. For years, Campbell had asked the ADCA to excavate fully around the remains of the Roman ramp at Masada's base, to no avail. Campbell also mentioned how he and Shuka Dorfman bumped heads over the permanent display of Masada's most important archaeological finds. Dorfman believed they belonged in the Israel Museum in Jerusalem; Campbell wanted the originals to remain at Masada's onsite museum. Campbell won that dispute, but he was careful to avoid initiating any more. "I'm afraid that I'm zero help to you when it comes to the archaeological authorities," Campbell said. He leaned back and laced his fingers over his stomach. "But there may be another avenue."

As director of Masada, Campbell's position fell under the Israel Nature and Parks Authority (INPA). "I think the parks guys could be useful to you," Campbell mused. "Much of their jurisdiction overlaps with Hizmi's. The guys at the INPA are flexible. I'm going to work it out so that you can meet them and tell them what you've figured out."

"I appreciate all the help I can get," Jim said. "I'm really honored by your support."

"Destiny," Campbell replied with a smirk.

Parks Guys

Campbell was quick to deliver on his promise. Within a week of their introduction at *Muza's*, he pulled together a meeting with the most relevant players that worked for the Parks Authority. Most importantly, Campbell briefed the park director of Qumran and the principal archaeologist for the INPA beforehand. Both men were bothered that they had never heard of the *Copper Scroll Project*. The park director somehow missed the *Jerusalem Post* articles and televised documentary filmed at his site. The head INPA archaeologist even had to sign off on Peleg's excavation at the *hill of Kokhlit* in 2009, but Peleg didn't provide any details about why he wanted to excavate around an odd rock formation.

On such short notice, the only day all the participants could get together happened to be the same day Jim and Chris were scheduled to fly back to the United States. Qumran's director agreed to host the meeting at his office in a temporary metal building that stood east of the Qumran complex.

On the morning of the meeting, they pulled up to the parking lot with their suitcases packed in the trunk of their rental car. "Chris, don't let me get carried away talking and lose track of time," Jim said.

Ash-colored storm clouds gathered over Qumran, teasing the desert fauna with the rare promise of rain. "In this weather," Chris noted, "there's a chance our flight will be postponed anyways." As Jim trawled through the backseat for chewing gum, a drizzle quickly evolved into a downpour. They made a run for it.

Shaking off his wet fedora at the entryway, Jim spotted Campbell running through the rain behind them. Campbell darted into the room and pulled his soaked parka over his head, right as a flash of lightning careened across the sky.

Campbell put the weight of his large hand on Jim's shoulder and spoke quietly: "I know these are my friends and colleagues, but regardless, this room is overflowing with ego. Be ready." Jim, a social chameleon, always felt ready. He had a knack for adjusting to the taste and temperature of his audience. Whether it was a group sober Christian Zionists or swashbuckling Israeli outdoorsmen, Jim changed his lexicon to suit his listeners without ever having to alter his goal. Behind Campbell, he watched two men approach, both wearing the Parks Authority khaki uniform, as they side-stepped ruts already brimming with rainwater.

The director of Qumran, Yaakov Dahan, was the first to slap Campbell on the back, a command signal to commence introductions. Campbell and Dahan looked genuinely happy to see each other. "Jim, this is Yaakov. He and I go way back," Campbell told Jim. The truth was that Campbell went way back with every park director, none of whom came close to Campbell's record-holding stint working at one site. Wearing a velvet *kippa* and white dress shirt, Dahan was in his late sixties and the first Orthodox government official Jim had ever met. The dryness of his manner made it difficult to tell whether he was joking or serious.

Pointing a finger at Chris, Dahan said with a pensive look, "Now, I'm sure I've seen this guy before."

"Me? Really?" Chris replied.

"And you also look very familiar," Dahan noted, turning to face Jim.

"Well, I don't think we've ever met formally, but we have come to Qumran many times," Jim understated. He hoped the director was oblivious to most of his maneuverings at Qumran.

"Mr. Barfield, you are an Oklahoma man?" Dahan asked.

"You bet. I'm from a sleepy little town there." Jim was happy to steer the introductions in a different direction.

"I once dated a woman from Oklahoma."

"Oh really, what was her name?"

"Karen Cohen."

"No kidding! That's my mother." Jim chewed slyly on his gum. "I'm just messing with you!" he exclaimed.

Campbell erupted in laughter. The more quizzical Dahan grinned sideways at Jim, a sign of appreciation for his ease of humor which somehow never came off as forced.

Campbell directly addressed Dahan. "You are due for a visit to Masada. You haven't come since all the renovations."

Dahan pressed his finger to his lip as if telling Jim and Chris a secret no one should overhear. "I think Masada is too much fuss." He followed up his jab at Campbell with a wink.

Now it was Jim and Chris's turn to laugh. When the two site directors spoke of Qumran and Masada, it was like the jockeying of college football fans, complimenting the other's team without betraying any loyalty to their own side. Prejudices poked through every sentence.

Campbell ushered Jim to the conference table and introduced him to the rest of his colleagues. Tsvika Tsuk, the Director of Archaeology for INPA, gave Jim a firm handshake. He spoke in a baritone voice and had an imposing presence. Tsuk was known as one of the foremost experts on Israel's ancient water systems. To join the meeting, Tsuk had to step away from his primary role excavating a rock-hewn water tunnel in the ancient Canaanite settlement of Gezer.

Also sitting at the table was a young man, Eran, INPA's head of education. Eran had a notebook in one hand and gripped a pen with the other. His eagerness was a telltale sign that he was new on the job—or at least more comfortable scribbling notes than small-talking.

The room was adorned with little more than a coffee bar and conference table on concrete flooring. Campbell opened the meeting by explaining the broad mission of the Israel Nature and Parks Authority to Jim and Chris: "Our job is to protect nature and preserve the heritage sites, but within that role we believe our heritage sites are a public asset meant to be enjoyed by all." What

Campbell didn't say is that the access roads, bathrooms, information signs, and shade pavilions are also the products of INPA. Without them, visiting Israel's historic sites would be much less comfortable. Campbell waited, signaling the floor was Jim's.

Chris hooked the room's projector up to Jim's laptop. His new computer cover sported a custom decal of a wolf howling at the moon. Jim pulled out a hard copy of his research report. It landed on the table with a thud. Eyeballing the thickness of the report, Dahan said, "It must be good to be retired." He smirked at his own joke. Jim smirked back but cleared his throat—an indicator of a rare twinge of insecurity.

Over the course of an hour, Jim discussed the most convincing sites in his usual conversational style. He explained the theories behind the location matches and his translation. Jim had given the exact talk so many times that his cadence, comedic timing, and dramatic pauses appeared set to an internal metronome. Little broke his rhythm.

While he spoke, Eran wrote vigorous notes; Dahan nodded his head in approval; Tsuk offered proactive commentary. At the start, Tsuk appeared skeptical, asking in a bombastic tone: "If they have dug all over Qumran for decades, why have they never found these items?" Jim patiently explained that they had never dug below virgin soil. As Jim continued with the details of his research, Tsuk's doubts were placated and he transitioned to planning mode. He gave practical advice, estimating how certain locations could be accessed and at what angles. The meeting was time-saving since most of the men present were familiar with the most mundane details of Qumran's layout.

Jim had to keep a check on his own sanguinity, even though their boys' club enthusiasm created an atmosphere akin to a pre-excavation brainstorming session. No matter how much the INPA appreciated his research, they lacked the authority to act alone. According to the rules of excavation in Israel, Hizmi had to approve the permit request before Tsuk could add his stamp of approval. INPA was the cart, but the ADCA was still the horse.

"I came to Israel to submit a new permit request to the ADCA to do a scan of the site with a deep penetrating metal detector," Jim announced by way of conclusion. Tsuk started to call his secretary to have her fax the ADCA paperwork. Jim interrupted him to clarify his point. "The technical report is turned in already. Oren Gutfeld, the archaeologist, is waiting on the committee's response," Jim said. Tsuk and Dahan looked impressed, realizing he was further along in the process than they had expected.

"If the permit goes through, I want the ADCA and the Parks Authority to be in on this working together, both fully informed," Jim said. "I'm not here to step on Hizmi's toes or start a contest between you guys and them."

Aware that an outsider called them on their complex inter-agency power dynamics, shoulders shook with repressed chuckles. Everyone in the room agreed that they had no desire to offend Hizmi, who was still new to the job. After reviewing the legitimacy of Jim's research, they felt optimistic that the permit request for a simple scan would be approved, especially with Gutfeld's name on the paperwork.

"After I do the scan, assuming I get the permit, Gutfeld and I will hand over the results to you all and the ADCA," Jim said, speaking loudly to compensate for the noise of beating rain. "I do wonder, though, if something is found, how Israel will handle the political repercussions with her neighbors."

Dahan spoke before anyone else had the chance. He waved off the concern. "There are always impediments from our neighbors, no matter what we do." He spoke like someone who knew this fact intimately and was undaunted by it: Dahan lived in the West Bank.

Jim left the meeting with assurances to keep in touch. Eran asked Jim to update them on the permit's progress. Jim saved Tsuk's email to send him a digital copy of the research in its entirety. The "parks guys," as Campbell referred to them, seemed sincerely hopeful that Jim's research had a chance to be tested, come what may. They were true to their mission to keep the sites alive in the national consciousness.

Miraculously, Jim and Chris made it to Tel Aviv in time to catch their overnight flight to the United States. Once they were in the air, the drone of the plane and the site of the stretching horizon put Jim and Chris both to sleep. Suddenly, the pilot announced that they were about to encounter weather-related turbulence. For what felt like an hour, but was actually only fifteen minutes, the plane lurched from side to side. Panels in the cabin vibrated violently as loose bags slid across the floor. Children cried. Even adult passengers failed to repress their yelps.

Jim glanced at Chris, gripping the armrest so tightly that his knuckles were pale white. A water bottle on a leather strap swung from his armrest. Jim wondered how many more times he would need to fly to Israel before he could see the excavation through. He prayed the same prayer that he had been reciting since he first made the discovery: "May your will be done, but please let this happen in my lifetime."

PATIENCE VERSUS SUSPICION

Jim anticipated that he would hear from Hizmi by the end of the month. However, he understood the glacial tempo of bureaucracy and wanted to give the committee members the time they needed. Counting from the moment that he first made the discovery in his study, he had played the waiting game for six years, rolling with every punch.

After the first month came and went, with no word on the permit request, Asher started pestering Jim daily. The more time that passed, the more suspicious Asher became that the ADCA was hiding something. Jim wanted to give the committee the benefit of the doubt. Asher suggested overtaking Hizmi's office, or worse, going to the press with a vociferous open letter—in the spirit of *J'accuse!*

Jim understood that Asher lacked any sense of proportional response. Still, once someone was part of the *Copper Scroll Project*, they rarely got booted out. Grateful for what Asher had orchestrated thus far, Jim kept him clued-in, but made sure to sound glowingly positive when they spoke. "If I fuel his fires of suspicion, it will be like releasing a wild mustang," Jim told Laurie. "Asher will be kicking down doors everywhere, running amuck in the Knesset." Instead, Jim gave Asher small tasks with the aim of keeping him too busy to pester Hizmi.

What Jim didn't voice aloud to Asher, however, was that he was beginning to feel heavy in his spirit. Every few weeks, Jim started contacting the ADCA, inquiring into the status of his permit request. At first, Hizmi claimed the committee meeting was postponed. Then he cited budgetary restrictions. Eventually, Hizmi stopped responding to Jim's overtures altogether.

As the radio silence from Hizmi droned on for months, Jim's patience began to unravel and, for the first time, he allowed himself to entertain thoughts of actors plotting against him. On some days, he told Laurie that he refused to be melodramatic about the situation. On other days, he would ask Laurie, "Is it possible that the authorities don't want anything to be found because of the political fallout? Are they trying to stop these things from coming above ground?"

As conspiracy theories pulsed through Jim's bloodstream, he got a call from Gutfeld. "The archaeological department at Hebrew University said they won't support our permit request to scan at Qumran," Gutfeld said. As a member of the faculty, he usually received easy approval—especially for simple scans. Though he was as bewildered as Jim, Gutfeld maintained an uncomplaining professional face. His time at Hyrcania had proven his long-enduring temperament—a ripe feature in the greats of archaeology.

On the other end of the line, Jim went quiet, his mind foggy from disappointment. All he could hear was the ticking clock in his office. Jim finally asked, "Why do you think everyone is stonewalling? I feel like I'm being played for a fool." He felt the genesis of a migraine stretching up his neck and over the back of his skull.

Gutfeld said, "I don't know. This has never happened before." He mumbled a few bromides about things opening up in the future, and they hung up.

Up against the wall, Jim called Asher. For months Jim had worked to turn all of Asher's mountains back into molehills, but now he felt he had to inform him of the direness of the situation. They were back to square one with no university backing or credentialed archaeologist. "Looks like we're going to have to take an alternative course," Jim wrote to Asher.

Asher responded to Jim in an email: GOOD, LOADING GUNS. Jim was sitting next to Laurie in bed when he got Asher's message. "Laurie, I pray he is using a figure of speech," Jim said.

From the second Asher had Jim's marching orders, he set to work. First, he charged into Hizmi's office, demanding an explanation. He assumed Hebrew University only withdrew their sponsorship of Gutfeld's permit request because the ADCA intervened. Asher wanted a formal letter from Hizmi stating the logic behind the permit's denial. Hizmi resisted Asher's muscling. He knew Asher was trying to gather evidence for legal recourse. Sitting at his desk, stationary as a statue, Hizmi told Asher, "For professional reasons, we must protect the ruins. That is all."

"It's a simple scan," Asher hissed, hot with anger. "How could it possibly damage the ruins?" Hizmi remained pensive, content to forfeit the last word.

Asher paid a same-day visit to Gutfeld to pry for more information. Gutfeld had no intention of collaborating with Asher against the ADCA. He offered no hints, rightfully so. The last thing Gutfeld wanted was Asher storming through Hebrew University and demanding answers from his mentors. It was bad enough that Asher included Gutfeld in angry emails to Israel's Minister of Culture and the Minister of National Infrastructure.

Gutfeld sent Jim a message: "Asher isn't being helpful over here." The news came as no surprise. Though it wasn't Jim's intention, Asher and he were enmeshed in a good cop, bad cop routine.

Jim dreaded the phone call, but he had to quiet Asher. "Asher, it's time to call off the dogs on this war path. We've knocked on the right doors and let our situation be heard. Now we need to wait and see," Jim instructed.

Asher agreed on a short-term truce, after going off about his nemesis: "The ADCA will pay for this scandal! They have betrayed the people of Israel. I can't believe Israelis pay taxes toward the salaries of these imposters!"

Jim felt desperate for a more rational cure to the deadlock. Valuing the friendship, Jim had resisted asking Campbell for any more help, but he reached the point where he had no other recourse. Ever since the evening at *Muza's,* Jim and Campbell had kept in touch. Their sporadic correspondence was warm, with Campbell regularly offering Jim and Chris his well wishes.

When Jim called Campbell to update him on the permit request, Campbell didn't seem surprised. He disclosed a rumor that the advisory committee wanted to block any further excavations at Qumran for at least a year or more. The committee wanted to give the site "a chance to rest." Jim's jaw clenched at the idea. The window of opportunity had closed in on him.

Jim solicited Campbell to see if a collegial intervention from the guys at the INPA was possible. They seemed so optimistic and proactive in their meeting with Jim. Surely, they could encourage Hizmi to allow one last survey of Qumran. Campbell backed down. "Everyone in our field is nervous about a confrontation," he said. "Sorry, my friend. I wish I had another way. As trying as it may seem at times, I truly believe your efforts will be rewarded."

Jim understood. He told Campbell, in non-Jewish terminology, "At this point, I need a Hail Mary."

Before Gutfeld was denied the permit, Jim was inclined to believe that Hizmi and Peleg were at best too protective of Qumran, and at worst too lazy to excavate so deep. Jim's permit drama hardly equaled *The Da Vinci Code*'s high-speed chases through European back alleys and cathedrals. However, the events of 2013 allowed for Jim's misgivings to gain the upper hand. For the second time he was suddenly, and without explanation, stripped of a permit and an archaeologist.

CHAPTER 19

RACE

66 "Jim, this is Hillel Weiss. I caught word of Qumran's closure." The rabbi phoned Jim at home. It had been months since they last talked.

"Hizmi is saying a year, but I bet it could be even longer," Jim responded.

"I am going to ask the Sanhedrin to address what I suspect is the suppression of archaeology in the interest of politics," Weiss informed him.

Jim was pleased that Weiss also intuited a possible smoke screen. He deeply valued the rabbi's enthusiasm for his research and his ability to bring all of the Temple Mount movement leaders together. Weiss had an aching sense, common among religious Israelis, that archaeology held out a promise to reconnect his compatriots, the People of the Book, to the Land of the Book. From their first encounter at the Sanhedrin meeting, Jim saw Weiss as a kind grandfather—someone who jingled change and peppermints in his pocket. Jim trusted him instinctively.

The grandfather characterization would have come as a surprise to anyone who witnessed Weiss's sharp tongue in action at political rallies. In his forty years of activism, Weiss lost track of the number of times Israeli police removed him from the Temple Mount. His name made the press most often for his fiery statements about public officials.

SUBCULTURE TO MAINSTREAM

When Weiss first championed the Temple Mount, he stood on the fringes of Israeli society. Temple Mount movement organizers—like Gershon Salomon and Yisrael Ariel—were considered far-right radicals. The microculture of Temple Mount advocates embarrassed secular Israelis who suppressed Temple talk. They feared that Israel—already treated as an international pariah—would be perceived as a backward theocracy. Religious Israelis had their own reasons for sidelining the Temple Mount movement. According to the Chief Rabbinate of Israel, Jews were absolutely forbidden from visiting the sacred site. Temple Mount groups were in violation of Jewish law.

The tradition of Jews physically avoiding the Temple Mount evolved over centuries of foreign rule in Jerusalem. Christian and Muslim overlords varied in their levels of tolerance toward Jewish pilgrims. In 1166, Maimonides journeyed from North Africa to Jerusalem. He risked being arrested by Crusaders, arguably the most possessive occupiers of Mount Moriah. In his *Mishneh Torah*, Maimonides describes his visit to the Temple Mount as a pinnacle moment in his spiritual life. He cautioned Jews to ascend the plateau with the utmost reverence. Over time, rabbinic thought came to emphasize the cautions of Maimonides over his inspiration. Exalting the Temple Mount while also avoiding the Temple Mount created a perpetual tension.

By the time Jerusalem changed hands to the Ottomans, a series of religious rulings prohibited Jews from entering the Temple Mount. Jews generally complied with the prohibition and prayed at the Western Wall, even though local Muslims treated the area as a refuse dump in order to humiliate Jewish worshipers. In the fifteenth century, Sultan Suleiman ordered the clearing of piles of garbage from the Western Wall, but Jews were still forbidden from bringing chairs or a partition to the wall.

In 1948, during Israel's War of Independence, Jordan's Arab Legion captured the Old City. Jewish residents were immediately expelled. Jordanian troops vandalized ancient synagogues and desecrated Jewish graves. The Jordanian *Waqf* cemented their control over the Temple Mount and Western Wall. For nineteen years, not a single Jewish person was granted rite of passage. On holidays, Israelis gazed at the Old City walls through barbed wire.

After the Six Day War, a surge of messianism pulsated throughout the country. Israelis could hardly believe the reversal of their fate. However, the Chief Rabbinate of Israel quickly threw cold water on any dreams of reviving pilgrimage to the Temple Mount. A warning was issued over the radio, hours after the Temple Mount's liberation, for Israelis to avoid the sacred enclosure and instead worship at the Western Wall.

Most Jews jumped at the chance to openly worship anywhere in the Old City so there was little protest. Six days after the ceasefire, a quarter of a million euphoric Jews congregated at the Western Wall to celebrate Shavuot. A few ignored the warnings and ascended the Temple Mount. A status quo developed where the Western Wall was reserved for Jews and the Temple Mount for Muslims.

While the Israeli government permitted Jews to enter the Temple compound after 1967, Jews have never been allowed to pray atop the Mount. During the Al-Aqsa Intifada (September 2000 to November 2003), the Temple Mount was completely closed to Jews. The reign of terror was incentivized by the rumor—endemic among Palestinians—that Israel was intent on destroying Al-Aqsa Mosque. Since the Temple Mount's reopening, Jews are again allowed to visit, albeit on a restricted basis, and the ban on non-Muslim prayer holds.

Over the last several years, many Israelis have expressed a desire to reconnect with the preeminent site of their religion. In cafés from Tel Aviv to Jerusalem, Jews are revisiting the debates of 1967 and discussing topics that were once taboo: Is the Temple Mount likely to be transferred to a new Palestinian state in final status negotiations? If the Temple Mount is the preeminent holy site for Jews, why is their worship restricted to one of its retaining walls? Why are Israelis disenfranchised at the site? Since Israel captured the complex in 1967, shouldn't the state exercise that sovereignty, rather than relinquish it?

The Israeli shift of public opinion is partly due to intensifying fear of complete loss of the sacred site in permanent status negotiations and partly due to the modification of the Temple Mount activists' message. Rather than emphasizing construction of a Third Temple, a seemingly impossible task, they are now advocating for a less eschatological cause: unrestricted Jewish access to the Mount and the right to worship. Rabbi Yehuda Glick—the founder of the umbrella group, Temple Mount Heritage Foundation—said his priority was for "Jews to become part of the scenery at the Temple Mount."[1] By reframing the issue and making a concerted effort to push more peaceable and short-range goals, the call for Jewish *civil rights* on the Temple Mount is inching toward the mainstream.

Many Orthodox rabbis feel that the proliferation of Temple Mount pressure groups is an aberration; restoring Temple Mount pilgrimage is akin to preempting the Messiah. However, in 1996, the Council of Yesha Rabbis—an Orthodox group from Judea and Samaria—made a milestone decision to lift the prohibition and encourage their congregants to ascend the Temple Mount. For the same reasons that many Orthodox Jews avoid the platform, others are drawn to the site: the belief that a unique potency of the *Shekinah* rests on Mount Moriah's high point. A swelling number of rabbis are leading groups on visits to the Temple Mount,[2] while attending to the restrictions of Jewish law. They stick to a defined path on the tree-lined esplanade which stays outside the presumed borders of the former Temple area.

Religious nationalist Israelis are only a portion of the Jews visiting the Temple Mount. According to police statistics, the number of Jewish visitors nearly doubled from 2009 to 2014. A new tradition is developing for Israeli brides and grooms, across the religious spectrum, to visit the holy precinct before their nuptials. The Mount has been added as a popular destination for Diaspora Jews on tours of Israel. A mobile app tracks Jewish visits on the Temple Mount in real-time.

Although 11,000 annual Jewish visits to the Temple Mount trumps the previous two millennia, it still pales in comparison to the eleven million visits each year to the Western Wall. Israel has developed an ongoing schizophrenia regarding the Temple Mount, induced by conflicting rabbinic opinions.

The holiest place in the Jewish religion, regrettably, is a hostile environment for Jewish people. On the best of days, non-Muslims are restricted to a two-hour window in the morning and one hour in the afternoon to visit the site. They can access the holy plateau through only one gate while Muslims choose from ten gates. The *Waqf* criminalizes non-Muslims for praying, prostrating, dancing, kneeling, or visibly mourning. Torah scrolls or Jewish prayer books are confiscated at the entrance. Even if a Jewish person's lips move silently, or they shield their eyes or raise their hands, they risk arrest for public disturbance. Decorum forbids Jews from eating or drinking on the Temple Mount to avoid the accompanying blessing. If visitors look overtly Jewish, such as wearing a *kippa* or menorah necklace, they require an Israeli police escort. The official position of the Israeli government has never wavered from the status quo, allowing for Jewish visits to the Temple Mount, but outlawing Jewish worship.

News reports of riots against Jews on the Temple Mount pushed many Israelis to consider a reverse course. In 2013, the Maagor Mochot Research Institute conducted a poll to quantify the opinion shift. To the question of whether the Temple Mount should be divided between Jews and Muslims, around sixty percent of Israelis said "yes."[3] When asked how to fight for greater religious freedom on the Temple Mount, a majority thought it was time for legislative measures. Suddenly, the issue of legalizing Jewish prayer on the Mount moved from the religious sphere to the political. Just as the Temple Mount hot potato was tossed into the Knesset's hands, a new politician arrived ready to catch it: Moshe Feiglin.

Feiglin was the first Israeli politician to join ranks with the *Copper Scroll Project*'s diverse cadre of allies: Gershon Salomon, Hillel Weiss, Asher Levy, and the Sanhedrin; Tamar Yonah; Eitan Campbell; Oren Gutfeld; Oklahoma state senators; Comanche and Kiowa Native Americans; and an executive at White's Metal Detecting Company. Add to that the groundswell of support from American Messianics, Evangelical Christians, and Orthodox Israelis. Of course, over the years long course of the *Copper Scroll Project*, some friendships grew cold like with Vendyl Jones. Some relationships rightfully turned sour like with Barney Eaton and Blake Foster. And some connections went silent as was the case with Yuval Peleg and Shuka Dorfman. In general, however, Jim maintained his network by keeping them informed and never taking for granted their advice, support, endorsements, or efforts. The *Copper Scroll Project*'s progression relied on the people who surreptitiously got swept up in its orbit.

MOSHE FEIGLIN

Moshe Feiglin won a seat in Israel's Knesset during the 2013 election cycle. Israel's left-wing parties lampooned the unconventional politician as a fascist. Religious Zionists lionized Feiglin as their new poster child. He saw himself as the man to bring God to the Likud—the largest of the right-wing political parties.

Feiglin, an Orthodox Jew, made a name for himself in Israel by his loud opposition to Palestinian territorial demands. In a stormy protest to the Oslo Accords in 1993, he spearheaded massive acts of civil disobedience. He organized 100,000 demonstrators and successfully blocked eighty of Israel's busiest intersections. As a resident of the West Bank, he wanted Israel to annex the Palestinian territories; he fought against their partition. "This is our land," was his movement's mantra. Police took him into custody and slapped him with the charge of sedition against the state—catalyzing his political personality.

To the chagrin of Feiglin's Knesset colleagues on the Left, his domestic platform was as combative as his opposition to Oslo. He thought Israeli officials should be elected based on their commitment to the Torah. He longed for the laws and institutions of the state of Israel to reflect Torah values. He opposed homosexual marriage and abortion. He advocated for a free market economy balanced by a charitable society. When Israeli police destroyed an unauthorized Jewish outpost in the West Bank, Feiglin helped them replant their vineyards. In all things, Feiglin advocated the long view. In his opinion, Israel's most pressing crisis was beyond the conflict with her Arab neighbors: *am ha'aretz* suffered from a widespread loss of Jewish identity.

Most significantly, Feiglin aligned with the Temple Mount devotees. He made monthly visits to the Temple Mount for his own spiritual vitality and as a statement of Israel's ownership over the sacred esplanade. Feiglin was unsparing in his call to action: "We must encourage Jews to ascend *Har Habayit* after the proper halakhic preparations, and to actualize their sovereignty over the beating heart of the Jewish Nation."[4] He was twice arrested during his visits.

Though Prime Minister Netanyahu and Feiglin both belonged to the Likud, Netanyahu viewed Feiglin through the jaundiced eyes of politics. They were rivals within the same ruling party. Rather than start his own party, Feiglin chose to infiltrate Likud and bring his supporters with him. Feiglin's faction, *Manhigut Yehudit* ("Jewish Leadership"), was the largest faction and the furthest to the right of the Likud Central Committee. Feiglin planned to gradually grow his movement as he worked within the parliamentary system to promote religious Zionist values.

Buzz spread on the Arab street that Feiglin's election was part of a sinister Jewish scheme to infiltrate the Temple Mount; Muslims were hardly oblivious to the growing encroachment of Jews onto the monumental platform. For fear of a provocation, Netanyahu temporarily banned Feiglin from his routine visits to the Mount and made other small overtures towards peace with the Palestinians.

Netanyahu possessed no interest in moving the Temple Mount—Israel's tinderbox—into the spotlight of political theater. Feiglin had every interest. On August 7, 2013, Feiglin called for a massive rally at the Mughrabi Gate to protest the mistreatment of Jews on the Temple Mount. For the whole of Ramadan, the wooden access bridge was closed to non-Muslims, even when it overlapped with the Jewish holiday of Tisha B'Av. The police said the closure was out of concern for public safety—meaning zealous Muslims were likely to assail Jewish visitors. Feiglin accused Netanyahu of relinquishing all sovereignty over the sacred compound. If Muslims harass Jews on the Temple Mount, the standard procedure for the patrolling Israeli police is to clear the area of non-Muslim visitors. Their priority is to preserve order and protect public safety, but the consequences are disproportionately shouldered by Jewish worshipers.

Though the rally at Mughrabi Gate was sparsely attended, a portion of the press unexpectedly empathized with the protestors' sentiment. Press coverage of the rally examined the developing pattern on the Temple Mount where Muslim aggression spurred Jewish expulsion. The strategy was obviously self-defeating. Banners at the rally read: "Why are Jews being punished for Muslim violence?" and "Why do Muslim holy days trump Jewish ones?" The Israeli police directed the protestors, including Rabbi Weiss, to furl their banners.

During his term in the Knesset, Feiglin initiated the first impassioned debate in the Knesset on the issue of Jewish religious freedom on the Temple Mount. Calling for the implementation of Israel's sovereignty over the Temple Mount, Feiglin addressed his colleagues: "The Temple Mount is the heart and organs of the country. Whoever rules *Har Habayit* rules the Land." Pandemonium followed. Members of the Knesset from the Left clamored to indict Feiglin for derailing Israel's peace process with the Palestinians. They feared he and his backers—who they deride as "Feiglinites"—would ignite the fury of the Muslim world. Palestinians responded to the news of the Knesset discussion by rioting on the Temple Mount. In Jordan, members of parliament signed a petition that threatened to rescind the peace treaty with Israel.

TEMPLE DENIAL

When Professor Weiss called Jim about Qumran's closure in July 2013, the two men agreed that the timing was ripe for the Copper Scroll's promise to be realized. Talk of Jewish rights to the Temple Mount was popularizing in Israeli society. Feiglin's election gave the Temple Mount devotees political cover. All the Sanhedrin lacked was a smoking gun, tangible evidence that proved to their neighboring enemies that they held the deed to Jerusalem and the Temple Mount.

Weiss spoke to Jim in a prophetic spirit: "The giving up of any symbol belonging to Jerusalem or the Israeli nation is now unfashionable. The movement is too strong to deny. I am hopeful you will soon get permission to search for the Temple's treasury."

During the Israeli-Palestinian negotiations at Camp David in 2000, Yasser Arafat famously denied that a so-called Temple in Jerusalem ever existed, much to President Bill Clinton's amazement. Though the negotiations collapsed, a new mantra in Palestinian propaganda was born. As part of the Palestinian Authority's effort to expunge Israel's historical claims to Jerusalem, Arafat soon forbade Palestinian historians from referring to a Jewish Temple in Jerusalem. Palestinian textbooks, television programs, and mosque sermons omit any mention of an ancient Jewish tie to Jerusalem. The head of the Supreme Muslim Council, Ekrima Sabri, dismissed Solomon's Temple as an "unproven allegation."[5]

A favorite talking point among Palestinian leaders pedaling Temple Denial is the lack of archaeological evidence from the Jewish Temples. President Abbas, speaking at an Arab League conference in 2012, stated, "Despite all the enormous capabilities that the occupation authorities made available to the extremists who engage in never-ending digging [and] threaten to make Al-Aqsa Mosque look less significant and vindicate the Israeli narrative, they have failed miserably."[6] Abbas ignored the Muslim *Waqf*'s ban on professional excavations under the Temple Mount.

Such historical reconstruction is unwarranted considering the retaining wall from King Herod's Temple still stands. Even without a physical trace from the First Temple, scholars do not debate whether a Jewish Temple once topped the Temple Mount. Too many historical sources, outside of the Bible, give witness to the existence of the Temples.

In fact, Temple Denial contradicts the belief of Muslim historians who, over the preceding centuries and because of their Abrahamic faith, insisted on the historicity of Solomon's Temple. As early as the ninth century Muslims referred to the Dome of the Rock as "the rock of the Bayt al-Maqdis," which translates "The Holy Temple." In the tenth century, the Muslim historian Al-Muqaddasi wrote that the foundations of the Al-Aqsa Mosque "were laid by David." Up until 1948, it was a point of Islamic pride that the Dome of the Rock was a successor to the Jewish Temples. Even the Waqf's official guide book stated that the Temple Mount's identity as the former site of Solomon's Temple was "beyond dispute."[7] Only after 1967 did the revamped Palestinian narrative manage to trump prior understandings and take root in Muslim society. The new narrative says that Jews have no proof of an ancient presence in the land; that Jerusalem was and is an Islamic city; that there was never a Jewish Temple.

Admittedly, Palestinian historians are correct that archaeologists have no artifacts from the interior of either Temple. For holy buildings that were remembered for their immeasurable wealth and luxury, their surviving archaeological footprint is miniscule. After centuries of Jerusalem's cyclical destruction by Romans, Byzantines, Muslims, and Crusaders, the Old City lacks the grandiose ruins one might expect. King Herod's building frenzy submerged much of the pre-Roman structures. During subsequent occupations, fragments from Jerusalem's oldest buildings were quarried to construct newer buildings. Scattered stones and broken walls in the City of David represent the little left from the united monarchy.

In the nineteenth century, French archaeologist Clermont-Ganneau found rare physical evidence from the Second Temple complex. He recovered a limestone signpost, once embedded in the fence around Herod's Temple. The sign's Greek inscription warned gentiles not to enter the Temple's inner court: "Whoever is caught, will have himself to blame for his death which will follow." The equivalent of an ancient "No Trespassing" placard, the sign is now housed in the Istanbul Archaeological Museum.

In 1968, Israeli historian Benjamin Mazar discovered a first-century basalt stone at the base of the Temple Mount's southwestern corner. The broken stone bears an incomplete Hebrew inscription which reads, "To the place of trumpeting." It is believed to be a directional placard for the exact spot where Temple priests once stood to announce the Sabbath and holidays by blowing the shofar. A reconstruction of the full inscription is in the Jerusalem Archaeological Park.

In 1981, the Israel Museum paid half a million dollars for a thumb-sized ivory pomegranate believed to be an ornament placed on the scepter of the high priest. A restored inscription on the pomegranate reads, "Belonging to the Tem[ple of Yahwe]h, holy to the priests." Because the scepter was held as the lone surviving evidence of the First Temple, enormous crowds flowed through the Israel Museum on opening night to get a closer look at the miniature. The museum had to extend its hours until midnight. In 2004, the IAA's Theft Prevention Unit determined that the pomegranate was part of an elaborate forgery scheme and the Israel Museum took the pomegranate off display.[8]

In Israel, archaeology reaps global fascination when a new find illustrates the reliability of the Bible, like an ancient seal impression from King Hezekiah. On the local level, consequences of exciting biblical finds have a multilayered effect. Antiquities that display the land's long Jewish heritage galvanize the zeal of religious Zionists. Palestinian Muslims denounce archaeologists for digging illegally or forging artifacts in a plot to fortify Jerusalem as Israel's united capital.

Simon Sebag Montefiore, in his biography *Jerusalem*, explains the difficulty in unpacking the city's history from the filters of religious passion. "Archaeology is itself a historical force," Montefiore writes. "Archaeologists have at times wielded as much power as soldiers, recruited to appropriate the past for the present."[9] Montefiore's analysis rings especially true on the Temple Mount, a cauldron of conflict due to clashing Jewish and Palestinian entitlements. Jews claim precedent on the Temple Mount. Muslims tout their prolonged dominance of the site. So, it goes, whichever stakeholder wins the pitched battle over the historical narrative has a better chance in securing religious rights at the holy places.

The Temple Mount movement understands Temple Denial to be a tenet of biblical prophecy. Zechariah foresaw the day when Jerusalem would be a "very heavy stone for all peoples" and the nations would rise against it (Zechariah 12:2). Never short on will or strategy, Temple Mount movement leaders commissioned Jim to the frontlines in their battle to definitively prove that Jewish roots penetrated Jerusalem soil at the deepest level. For his part, Jim was drawn to an alliance of like minds and energized by their urge for action. Accordingly, Jim's project became embedded in the Temple Mount movement.

If Jim led the Temple Mount devotees to even one of the lost Temple treasures, they would have an ideal banner under which to march. Unearthing a startling relic would not only eclipse Islam's exclusive title to the Temple Mount, it had the potential to awaken the faith of all unbelieving Israelis. Past archaeologists were weaponized with trowels and spades. Times had changed. In the carriage of modern archaeology, Jim told Weiss, "I've got a White's metal detector, and I'm not afraid to use it."

CHAPTER 20
BREAKTHROUGH

Fighting the ADCA to allow Jim to search for Temple vessels was easily grafted into Feiglin's platform of grievances. When Feiglin learned of the *Copper Scroll Project*, the Knesset member had his scheduler allow for a private meeting with Jim during his trip to New York City in May 2014. Jim and Mack made their first pilgrimage to the Big Apple, and I met them there by train.

Each spring, *Manhigut Yehudit* organized a banquet in New York for the faction's top American donors and allies. The banquet was a pep rally and fundraiser. At the 2014 rally, attendees were steadfast in their belief that Feiglin would one day be the Prime Minister of Israel. Unlike American politicians' tendency to publicly dither about their presidential aspirations, Feiglin was forthright.

In the afternoon before the banquet, a *Manhigut Yehudit* supporter picked Jim, Mack, and myself up from a Holiday Inn near LaGuardia Airport and drove us an hour to a Jewish neighborhood in Long Island. Rather than hotels, Feiglin preferred staying in the homes of friends and donors. Keeping Sabbath and eating kosher was far easier that way.

Feiglin had spent the morning in Manhattan with Minnesota Congresswoman Michelle Bachman, the banquet's keynote speaker. The conversation with Bachman went longer than expected. Rarely did Feiglin meet a foreign legislator who so thoroughly agreed with his controversial views, including his fight for the Temple Mount. Since Feiglin was running behind, we were the first to arrive to the Long Island home. The host ushered Jim to the kitchen table to prepare his laptop and projector for the presentation. Mack plunked his cowboy hat down on an end table. The host eyed Mack's calloused farm hands and size thirteen Tony Lama boots with wonder.

"I have some pizzas being delivered for lunch," the host explained. "My wife will kill me if I don't do this first." He spread out a disposable plastic cover over his wife's Pepto-Bismol pink tablecloth. The walls were crowded with family portraits and paintings with distinctly Jewish themes. To clear a space for Jim's PowerPoint slides, the host had to take down an oversized picture of the Old City of Jerusalem.

Feiglin walked into the house unceremoniously with a few of his closest political companions. In his early fifties, Feiglin's narrow face was framed by a closely trimmed beard. He wore a pair of thin wire eyeglasses. He was lean and fit with no residual symptoms of a recent mountain biking accident that broke his collarbone.

Though Feiglin was Israeli-born, his aides were mostly American Jews who became citizens of Israel in adulthood. Shmuel Sackett, originally from New York, cofounded *Manhigut Yehudit* with Feiglin in 1998. He was far more outgoing and approachable than Feiglin. If Feiglin ever won Prime Minister, Sackett was presumed to be his choice for Foreign Minister.

Sackett was the first to introduce himself to Jim and Mack. Boisterous, with wild grey hair and an untrimmed beard, Sackett had a warm persona and get-it-done attitude. Rob Muchnick, the U.S. director of *Manhigut Yehudit,* was next in line to shake Jim's hand. Muchnik had a successful real estate career which freed him up to volunteer full-time for the faction. Mack nodded. He understood full well how the blessing of funds and an independent profession allowed for following your passions.

Muchnik said, "Nice to meet you, Professor Jones." It was not the first time Jim shook off a reference to the fictitious Indiana Jones.

"Seriously," Muchnick added in an unreserved tone, "if we could help you bring up the Ark, it would change the world for the better. It would change everything!"

Feiglin was the quietest one in the group and the only one to speak English with an Israeli accent. His eyes looked tired. Blinking around the room, he apologized to no one in particular, "I'm sorry. I'm not good at this jetlag thing."

"I totally understand," Jim said. He continued with his rehearsed introduction. "I look forward to having a trusted government source who can direct my steps and help me fight through the political obstacles in Israel."

Everyone sat down at the table and snacked on cashew nuts and sipped cream soda while they waited for the pizza delivery. Sackett's phone continually buzzed. The banquet was mere hours away, but supporters called to ask for last minute tickets.

Before Jim began his presentation, he asked Feiglin what he already knew about the Copper Scroll. Feiglin admitted that he knew very little about the scroll or Qumranology. Speaking quickly, Jim presented his analytical overview of the Copper Scroll's finding, opening, and unusual content. From the perplexed look on Feiglin's face, Jim could tell that his hurried explanation hardly did the Copper Scroll justice. He wished he had brought his Copper Scroll replica for effect. Still, Jim didn't want to dawdle on information which Feiglin could easily research on his own. Jim had come to New York to show him *his* research.

Jim explained the Copper Scroll's first five and last five location matches inside Qumran. He also showed his Qumrusalem maps. Feiglin perked up at the site of the Jerusalem maps. Jim explained his First Temple history for the Copper Scroll and his belief that the treasure was connected to the story of Jeremiah from II Maccabees. He didn't have time to go into the complicated puzzle of the *Treatise of the Temple Vessels*. As Jim took his first pause for breath, the pizza delivery man arrived.

They got up and went to the kitchen for the ritual hand washing prayer. Mack stood in the kitchen holding himself oddly. His back was hunched slightly, and his hands were in his pockets almost as if he was trying to diminish his size, self-conscious of his height in comparison to his hosts. Mack and Jim had become such close companions over the years that when Chris was unavailable, Mack happily stepped in as Jim's aide-de-camp. Also, Mack's wife Shirleen had succumbed to a long battle with cancer the year prior. Trips with Jim were a welcome distraction from his gnawing grief.

As everyone served himself a pizza slice on disposable plates, Feiglin mused, "If I were the one hiding these Temple items, I don't think I would put the treasure map right next to the site where the treasure was buried." Folding his pizza in half like a taco, he continued, "Wouldn't that make it too obvious, too easy to find?"

Jim had never heard that specific inquiry and had to consider it for a moment. I realized that when he presented his condensed version of the Copper Scroll history, he created the impression that the copper coils were found out in the open. I clarified, "the Copper Scroll was hidden behind a collapsed wall, separated from Cave 3's other manuscripts, and therefore was almost missed by the excavation crew." Jim gave me a look of appreciation.

"Any hiding spot that takes twenty centuries to find must qualify as pretty good," Sackett added.

Feiglin wanted to know exactly what happened during the April 2009 dig. Jim showed him pictures from the excavation with graphics demonstrating how the probes stopped too short at all three test sites. Even if Jim understood Peleg's hesitation in digging deep holes at every test site in Qumran, he could not understand why Hizmi denied an unobtrusive electronic survey. Jim told the group that the IAA initially showed significant interest in the research, but then, suddenly and without explanation, Hizmi stonewalled him.

Feiglin's sympathy was complete. He knew what it was like to be sidelined by those in power. As party chairman, Netanyahu tried multiple times to have Feiglin ousted from Likud. In 2002, Israel's High Court of Justice successfully blocked Feiglin from the slate of Knesset candidates. They invoked a last-minute rule which disqualified anyone with recent criminal convictions. Since Feiglin had been charged with sedition after organizing the Oslo protests, the move kept him out of the Knesset. In 2008, Feiglin won the twentieth spot in Likud's primaries. An ally of Netanyahu successfully petitioned party leaders to have Feiglin demoted sixteen spots, keeping him out of the Knesset once again. By 2013, Netanyahu could no longer deny Feiglin's rising popularity. Feiglin, rewarded with the number eleven spot on the party list, finally won a seat in the Knesset.

"What can I do to help you?" Feiglin offered. Tiredly propping up his head with one hand, he brainstormed, "I can use my position as Deputy Speaker of the Knesset to engage the Minister of Culture and the Minister of National Infrastructure. I believe they work with the archaeological agencies."

"Something like that might help," Jim said. Though Jim never turned away offers to intervene on his behalf, he knew that Asher had already petitioned both ministers. They had shown no inclination to get involved.

Sackett chimed in. "Jim, we are more than happy to help in any way we can," he said. "But one thing you need to think about is whether Moshe's intervention will help or hurt your cause." To that, everyone agreed.

"It's true," Feiglin said. "Anything I touch right now ignites the fury of the Arab world. If these objects are there, I wouldn't want to draw too much negative attention to them."

"Your assistance is worth that risk," Jim said. He turned his chair a few inches to face Feiglin directly and spoke honestly, "I have very few doors that are open to me right now."

Jim handed Feiglin a brochure for his metal detector. "All I want is to bring a high-quality metal detector to Qumran and scan all the locations. A scan will not harm the ruins in any way. After I finish, I'll hand over all the information to the archaeological authorities. They'll have the proof they need to justify a professional excavation."

"But we don't know if they even want to find this stuff," Muchnik said.

The comment struck a chord with Feiglin. "The real war is not between us and the Arabs," he said. "It's among ourselves. Some Israelis are bent on us becoming like all the other nations. They want to get rid of our Jewish identity."

"Unearthing our past unsettles *am ha'aretz*. They have a deep fear of meaning," the host added.

"If avoiding radioactive conflict is their explicit agenda," Jim said, "then the Temple Mount is a nuclear bomb, and the holy relics are the button."

"The Israeli dream and the Jewish dream are against each other," Feiglin continued. "It's a quiet revolution, but one that we can win. Since Israel's rebirth, the nation's existence has been threatened on three primary fronts: economic, security, and spiritual. Israel has overcome most of its economic challenges; our strong military has minimized our security challenges. That makes room for the last challenge, the spiritual one. Until that happens, the State of Israel is like a Jewish body without a Jewish head."

Jim shut his laptop in reverence to the heaviness of the conversation. "Mack and I are heading to Israel next month," he offered. "Would you want me to give you a tour of Qumran and show you the actual locations?"

"Yes, yes, of course," Feiglin responded. "I haven't been to Qumran in years and years." He gained energy from the mere mention of returning to Israel.

Scratching his stubby beard pensively, Feiglin asked, "On this trip, are you bringing that good metal detector?"

"It's already there," Jim said. "I keep it in storage at a house I always stay at in Arad."

"Why haven't you ever scanned the locations in secret?" Feiglin asked.

"Many people ask me that," Jim laughed. "The simple answer is because I don't want to be thrown out of the country and never let back in."

"True," Feiglin said. He paused momentarily, wiping the pizza sauce from his lips. "But they couldn't kick me out of the country." I squirmed in my chair, anxious to endorse the plan that I could see taking shape in Feiglin's mind. Mack sat erect, no longer concerned about being the giant in the room. Sackett could also tell what Feiglin was thinking and smirked provocatively.

"I'll tell you what," Feiglin began. "You come to Israel and meet me at Qumran with the metal detector. I'll do some scanning."

Jim gulped. "I would love that. I have to tell you that it's a crime to show up to an antiquities site, unauthorized, with a metal detector."

"Knesset immunity has to be good for something," Feiglin mumbled. Like Jim, he was a man loathe to second-guess his first intuition. As long as Feiglin felt he was defending the spiritual identity of Israel, the door separating legality from illegality rested on wobbly hinges.

Sackett clapped his hands in excitement. Normally aides use their positions to caution and temper their political candidates. To the contrary, Sacket looked congratulatory. "We should go ahead and dig while we're at it!" he said.

The lunch session concluded on a high note. Feiglin went upstairs to take a power nap and the others scooted off to the banquet site to finalize the evening's arrangements.

From Feiglin's street protests against Oslo to his regular visits to the Temple Mount, the legislator had proven over and over that he preferred action to mere talk. Feiglin had also shown that he wasn't scared of being questioned, stoned, or arrested at Judaism's sacred sites. I had never imagined the meeting ending with Feiglin's commitment to scan at Qumran himself. Once Feiglin had made the offer, however, it struck me for its inevitability. Feiglin's Israeli chutzpah ideally matched Jim's Okie perseverance.

MACK KIZER

Jim, Mack, and I sat in the food court at LaGuardia Airport, waiting for our separate return flights. Pregnant once again, I picked at my breakfast bagel, thinking about how almost a decade of my own life had been consumed with the *Copper Scroll Project*.

In lucid moments, with the benefit of hindsight, I had questioned if I would walk through the door of that Texas conference again or follow the advice of my colleague who warned me that "everyone has a story." What if I had thrown away the pamphlet with Jim's number and never thought any more about his grand claims? I would have been spared the insufferable timeline, the setbacks, the endless reading lists, and the closed doors. I would never have known the anxiety of chasing the carrot of an excavation which, despite forward movement, always slipped further away. What would life have looked like if I hadn't followed each bunny trail of new Dead Sea Scroll research and Qumran publications? What other journalistic inquiries might I have pursued? Where else might I have gone if I hadn't used my vacation days and travel budget for repeat trips to Israel?

I still got what Jim called "Pentecostal goosebumps" when I considered the promise of Qumran and the possibility that its treasures awaited discovery. What the Copper Scroll revealed about Israel's ancient past and how it latched on to her future was the ultimate study aid for my own faith. But more than anything, I gambled in 2009, standing among the kiosks in Fort Worth, that the long-haired Oklahoma man was good crazy, not bad crazy. This trip to New York reminded me why I stuck by my bet.

My thought train was interrupted by Jim's cell phone. It was a phone call from an equipment technician from Florida. The technician explained that he was the on-site engineering consultant for a treasure hunter reality show for History Channel. The plotline of the series inched forward with a series of increasingly bigger, better, and more expensive equipment. He explained that—as an archaeology enthusiast—he had been following Jim's website and progress. He wanted to explore the idea of working together on a documentary.

Jim received similar inquiries from storyhunters throughout the years with varying degrees of seriousness. He informed the gentleman that, unfortunately, without a scheduled excavation at Qumran, there was nothing to film. Without revealing his latest plan for a scan, Jim took the opportunity to get advice from the expert about the capabilities of his White's metal detector. As a technological consultant for the show, the man knew everything about the advances in tools of the trade, an ever-widening array of treasure hunting possibilities. If Feiglin was willing to take a giant political risk, Jim wanted to be sure he had the best equipment available. He had to minimize the chance of a scan giving a false negative or false positive result.

"Theoretically," Jim asked, "what is the best equipment available for scanning at a place like the Dead Sea for large deposits of precious metals buried deep underground?"

The technician didn't hesitate. He told Jim he needed to get the Lorenz Deepmax Z1 detector with a six-foot coil cube. Sold for seven thousand dollars, the detector has all the newest innovations in the field. Most importantly, the detector is sensitive to metals as deep as fifty feet underground and is unaffected by heavily mineralized soils like those around the Dead Sea. He also recommended a two-thousand-dollar software system to download and analyze the detector's output.

Jim felt attached to his White's metal detector, especially since the people at White's had been so supportive and openhanded. However, he needed something as powerful as the Lorenz to impress the decision makers in Israel. Also, the Lorenz was transportable since it could be inconspicuously broken down and stored in a duffle bag, an important detail considering that the upcoming scan was unauthorized.

Mack stared at Jim when he hung up the phone. He overheard the details of the call. "Jim, I sold some more property," he said. "We should get that detector."

Jim was hesitant. He wanted to be a good steward of his friend's generosity. Still, Jim hadn't done any fundraising since the excavation stalled in 2009. The project's funds were depleted. Mack reminded him the *Copper Scroll Project*'s path had whittled down to a small alleyway. If Jim had one shot to get things right, technology needed to be his best friend in the process. It was Jim's good fortune that he had a faithful patron who saw it that way. What the aristocratic Lord Carnarvon was to Howard Carter, the successful rancher Mack Kizer was to Jim. Only Mack's humility contrasted with Carnarvon's eccentricity.

LORENZ

When the Lorenz Deepmax Z1 was delivered to Lawton the following week, Jim found himself longing for his father. Dusting off Styrofoam packing peanuts, he recalled all the stories of the Wichita Mountains which had steeped in his brain since childhood. If his father was still alive, Jim knew he would have relished the process of testing the detector's capabilities, all the while dreaming of finding Spanish gold. What the iron door was to Jim's father, the *hill of Kokhlit* was to Jim, only more so. Jim's hopes extended further than a private helicopter to land in his front yard. Jim dreamed of a messianic age.

Jim and Chris drove to New Mexico to conduct metal detector tests on Mack's property. Turning off the two-lane highway, they drove under a large metal sign welded with the family name: Kizer. Cornfields merged with the horizon. Mack lived in a one-story home that he built himself. The living room walls were covered with hundreds of mounted arrowheads that Mack had dis covered on the family property over the years. The floor was overlaid with a cowhide rug. He still had the couch which his wife Shirleen laid on when she passed away. In the kitchen, a chair propped up the faulty door of his wood stove. A deer head and full set of antlers hung above Mack's recliner.

After a hearty lunch, the trio set to work. They put a mile of distance between the test area and the side of the farm house which Mack referred to as his dumpster. The dumpster included a corrugated metal shed, drilling rigs, an abandoned jeep, and a broken-down yellow truck which he had driven to his first meeting with Jim. Before the trip, Jim purchased a dozen silver bars, ten ounces each, from a bullion exchange in Oklahoma City. With the Lorenz detector's sensitivity settings dialed back, Jim buried the silver bars and scanned over them to assure a positive read. An icon for classifying metal shown on the flat-panel display exactly as they expected. However, when using the six-foot coil attachment intended for Qumran, the logger is built to download the data without showing the metal classification icons on the detector's display.

Mack used his backhoe to dig a ten-foot hole, and then placed an iron plate at the bottom. The detector correctly differentiated between metal types. Mack buried some steel reinforcing bar and had Jim scan over it to ensure it wouldn't give a false positive for non-ferrous metal. It did not. "That's a relief," Jim said. "I can't have a metal detector that accidentally picks up rebar from Qumran's modern walkways."

They tested the detector's battery life to ascertain the maximum square footage it could scan before requiring a download of the data. Jim had nightmares about pulling off the scan with Feiglin only to find out later that the battery had died, leaving no proof of the readings. After the trial runs in New Mexico, they felt confident that the project had the best equipment available to peer into Qumran's depths. The detector outperformed their already high expectations.

MORTAR SAMPLES

After experimenting with the Lorenz in New Mexico, Jim got an itch for more scientific evidence. The Qumrusalem maps, the *Treatise of the Temple Vessels*, and biblical clues had not proven to be the kind of pragmatic data that persuaded the archaeological authorities. And unfortunately, his prized trophy, the 296-page research report, was thoroughly unhelpful for making elevator pitches. Even if Jim got positive results from Qumran with Feiglin's scan, he wasn't sure how Hizmi would take the news of an unpermitted scan with a Knesset member. However, if Jim could provide other scientific data to Hizmi, it might help square the circle.

One thing had been bothering Jim since 2009: When Peleg excavated at the *hill of Kokhlit*, the Bedouin hit a lip in the rock that looked to Jim to be a man-made shelf. Peleg dismissed it as naturally occurring sediment. For five years, however, Jim couldn't shake the notion that the rock lip, which looked so out of place, was a seal to the cave entrance. He thought of II Maccabees 2 which claimed that after Jeremiah hid the treasures in a cave, he sealed up the entrance. Jim imagined Jeremiah, with masonry stones and mortar, plastering the entrance smooth to form a solid, water tight barrier to protect the cave's contents. When Mike, Jim's teammate who dressed as a faux monk, stuck his pipe cross into the sediment bordering the *hill of Kokhlit* and hit an unseen barrier, Jim felt all but certain.

Jim recalled a conversation he had once at Campbell's house in Arad after hearing the Masada director and his brother cover classic rock hits at the local soccer stadium. The Campbell brothers regaled Jim with stories of their conservation efforts at Masada. Campbell's brother worked with an international team in concocting original plaster recipes to conserve Masada's mortar joints, grouting, and undercoats. Besides the specific requirements for porousness and flexibility, the plaster's mud coloring had to match the weathered surface to maintain the site's authenticity. This gave Jim an idea.[1]

Jim asked a friend, Hosea, who lived in Israel and had a background in scientific research to visit the *hill of Kokhlit* and chip off a small sample from the lip in the rock. He mailed the vial to CTLGroup—a laboratory in Skokie, Illinois, which specialized in material science research. Dr. Sang Lee, a petrographic analyst, fully examined the composition of the sample material, looking for attributes that determined the sediment's point of origin. Certain features in the binding matrix indicated that the material was prepared. It had fillers not common to natural rock and limestone; the fillers appeared to be heat-altered. The lab technician sent Jim photomicrographs to demonstrate their findings. In a nine-page report, Lee concluded that the mixture of sand particles and rock fragments was most likely man-made mortar.

While Jim was getting a head start on his packing for Israel to meet Feiglin for the scan, Skeeznix reached out to Jim again. It had been five years since Jim last spoke to his Kiowa friend, but Skeeznix said that he felt his spirit stir about the *Copper Scroll Project*. He thought that it was time for a follow-up meeting at his sweat lodge.

"Your timing is impeccable," Jim told him. The next day he was once again tiptoeing around buffalo skulls on the outside of a Kiowa sweat lodge with a deerskin dome.

CHAPTER 21

THE SCAN

For his twelfth trip to Israel in June 2014, Jim brought along Laurie, Mack, Chris, and his youngest son Michael. I was too far along in my third trimester to get on an international flight but I stayed in close touch. Jim told very few people that he was in Israel. He couldn't risk the loquacious Asher Levy knowing about the scan with Feiglin. He didn't even meet with Gershon Solomon. However, as a favor to Feiglin, Jim did make time to meet with Rabbi Yehuda Glick, an American-born Israeli and important leader in the Temple Mount movement.

Rabbi Glick didn't know what was set to transpire at Qumran, but he heard from Feiglin, his close friend, that Jim possessed a cutting-edge metal detector. Glick asked if Jim had time to meet in person. Believing Mount Eilat in southern Israel possessed deposits of raw gold, Glick and a business partner were set to receive a two-year exclusive license from the Israeli government to survey the mountain range. They wondered if Jim's Lorenz detector would be useful in mapping the gold deposits.

They arranged to meet in the courtyard in front of the Hurva Synagogue in the Old City. Jim left the detector in Arad and brought along a pamphlet. He informed him of the metal detector's suitability for searching at significant depths, even in mineralized areas. The conversation naturally turned to its appropriate use for the *Copper Scroll Project*. Though Glick had picked up small nuggets of information about the quest from Feiglin, he had no idea, until meeting Jim in person, that his theory implied that all the Temple items were stored away underneath Qumran. Jim explained that even though Qumran was closed to excavation, with no sign of the hiatus lifting, he had one shot left: a concealed cave adjacent to the ruins.

The idea of secreting the Temple treasures into the desert and consolidating them in one place struck the rabbi for its practicality. A licensed tour guide in Jerusalem, Glick had a strong grasp on the rituals and implements of the former Temples. "If I were organizing the operation," he mused, "I would put them in a place that is extremely deep—a place that nobody would even think was there."

They were interrupted by a succession of Glick's acquaintances. An older Jewish woman, carrying bags of groceries on each arm, recited a Psalm that she said reminded her of the rabbi fighting for the Temple Mount. Standing to face her, he put his hands together, signaling his thankfulness for the blessing. While Glick greeted an owner of a nearby Judaica shop, several ultra-Orthodox men scurrying through the courtyard glanced over at Glick and grumbled. Chris overheard them, in Brooklyn-accented English, refer to the rabbi as the most dangerous man in Israel, a superlative originally bestowed on Glick by the Israeli police because of his Temple Mount activism.

"Are you nervous about the court proceedings today?" Jim asked, changing the subject as Glick returned and sat down on the courtyard steps. He was scheduled for a hearing at a Jerusalem district court that afternoon. Though the court had previously determined that it was unlawful for Glick to be banned from the Temple Mount, the Israeli police regularly prohibited his entry. His case was due for another hearing.

"I have been to court many times already," Glick said. "Once, I was on day twelve of a hunger strike before they permitted me to ascend the Mount again. I know that many people call me a right-wing fanatic. I don't deny that I am an extremist: an extremist for human rights."

"Do you think that the Supreme Court senses the injustice of denying Jews their religious freedom?" Chris asked, his voice softer than normal. He was on day three of a fast himself.

"Yes, they have said as much in the past," Glick asserted. "I'm sure you have read the book of Micah."

"Of course," Chris answered.

"According to Micah, the Temple Mount will be the source of God's wisdom to radiate out over all the nations," Glick said. His freckles deepened in the sun as he paraphrased scripture. "The Temple Mount does not have to be a point of conflict. It will one day be the ultimate source of peace. Jews, Muslims, and Christians will worship there together." He continued, "Zechariah also prophesizes that all the nations, even Muslims, will turn to the Jewish people for instruction when they finally realize that God is with us."

Walking away from the meeting, Jim thought how once again the Jewish drama was staged on their most sacred space—a place familiar to blood and battles, sanctified through generations of sacrifice and prayer.

"The Temple Mount awaits," Jim told Mack and Chris.

"I think *am ha'aretz* is ready," Chris added.

IT'S ON

Sackett spoke with Jim before the trip and tentatively scheduled a day when Feiglin could meet him at Qumran. On the day Sackett was expected to call and finalize plans, Jim never heard from him. Chris worried that Feiglin might be the next person in their journey who reneged on a proposal. He braced himself for a letdown. Jim maintained his hard-headed optimism. The headlines that morning announced the upcoming Knesset vote for a president to replace the 90-year-old Shimon Peres. He assumed Feiglin was busy lobbying his fellow Members of Knesset to vote for the candidate who articulated the hardest stance on Jerusalem and the Temple Mount.

Since it was Michael's first trip to Israel, Jim didn't waste their downtime hanging out in Arad. He toured his crew around the ruins of Caesarea Philippi. Set off the coast of the Mediterranean, between Tel Aviv and Haifa, the ancient harbor is a crown jewel in Herod the Great's architectural legacy.

While Jim quietly prayed on a dusty bench near the famous hippodrome, he got a phone call from Sackett. He had to pay close attention to track Sackett's voice over the sound of waves thumping against the rocky shore. Sackett confirmed Jim's suspicions that Feiglin had a busy day in the Knesset. He apologized for the delay and got right to the point. "Can you meet Moshe at Qumran tomorrow morning?" Sackett asked.

"You bet," Jim responded.

"Then it's on!" Sackett bellowed.

Laurie and Chris stood nearby, trying to read Jim's facial cues. He climbed down and danced a little jig where the Roman chariot racers once gathered.

Back at the Arad house kitchen table, which had served as the project's unofficial headquarters countless times, Jim had everyone make a list of his emergency contacts in the United States. He wanted to know the right people to call on the off chance that any of them were arrested. About then, Emmie and her son spontaneously dropped by after her waitress shift ended at *Muza's*. Jim and Chris made a habit of always letting Emmie know when they were in Arad even before they dined at *Muza's*. The kitchen was immediately filled with the aroma of her homemade burekas, phyllo dough pockets stuffed with potato and glazed with butter. Intuitively, no one uttered a word about the next day's operation. Jim slipped out of the room to take a phone call from Professor Weiss, whom he also kept ignorant of the coming scan. The others sat down to the platter of warm burekas with Emmie.

That night Jim could hardly sleep. His memory flooded with thoughts of the Dead Sea Scrolls. He never could fully explain his compulsion to study them ever since he had first become a believer. As a young fireman, he plotted dates and prophecies from the biblical books and the lost sectarian texts on his Messiah Timeline, and he felt his heart connecting to Israel's past. Over the last decade, as he journeyed to Israel and gained allies and made friends with Israelis across the political and religious spectrum, he felt himself connecting to Israel's present in a way he could have never imagined. Waiting out wars and witnessing extended periods of terror, seeing how Israeli archaeologists led double lives as tank commanders, he shared in the burden of the embattled state and fell in love with its citizens. The rebirth of Israel, from its miraculous victories in battle to its revival of the Hebrew language, was powerful evidence that God's hand was still at work in the world. It was the Copper Scroll, however, that tethered Jim to Israel's future. The people of Israel were God's "treasured possession," and it was for them that Jim sought to restore her lost treasures.

That night in the house that had become Jim's second home, the fireman had one goal, one living dream. He wanted to give Israel, and through Israel the world, a visible reminder of their invisible God. The Dead Sea Scrolls, discovered on the eve of Israel's rebirth, had reminded the Jewish people, whose hearts were still throbbing from the trauma of the Holocaust, of the highest gift she had secured for the world, the Bible. The Copper Scroll, a long-lost secret, held out hope that the Jewish people still had a final dowry to reclaim.

FORT KNOX

On the drive to Qumran the next morning, Jim said, "Right before we flew here, Laurie and I were watching a documentary on the Dead Sea Scrolls. I realized something strange. Over the course of the years, I have met every expert and archaeologist that they interviewed in the show."

"It's been a good ride, right Jim?" Chris replied. He was bright-eyed since he had taken melatonin and lavender oil the night before to overcome jetlag.

"It sure has." Jim sighed. "All I ever wanted was to fulfill God's will in my life. I hope I did my best. When I stand before *Hashem* at least he can say, 'Ok Jimmy D. You weren't great, but you still made it!'"

Though Jim had gone through many highs and lows throughout the last eight years, it was the long episodes of waiting—an exquisite form of purgatory—that took the biggest toll on him. Now sixty, his hair had gone from smoky gray to steel-white. His doctor told him he had to lay off coffee to rid himself of acid reflux. The crow's feet that once only appeared when he laughed were now permanently etched on his face. Once again, after a series of disappointments, a new hopeful prospect materialized. Jim tried to control his expectations. He was deeply aware that if the scan produced no positive results, he may well be at the end of his quest.

"You have been like a father to me," Chris said. He reached over and patted him on the shoulders. Both of their eyes filled with tears. Jim gripped the steering wheel tighter. The alarm on Jim's watch started beeping.

When they arrived at Qumran, Jim asked Laurie and Michael to wait in the parking lot. They had the emergency contact numbers in case anything happened. Two Bedouin wearing checkered scarves secured on their foreheads with rope stood nearby with a camel, soliciting the arriving tourists to pay for their picture atop the long-lashed desert beast.

Feiglin drove up to Qumran at almost the same moment. He brought with him his seventeen-year-old son, his driver, and the executive director of *Manhigut Yehudit*. Feiglin must have debriefed his companions on the commute because they were nervously excited. Sackett had to stay back in Jerusalem.

Standing in the shade, outside of the main gate, Jim asked Feiglin, "Are you sure you want to do this?"

"Yep," Feiglin replied with his trademark coolness.

"I guess it's better to ask for forgiveness than permission," Jim said.

Jim carried the metal detector equipment folded up in a compact, black carrying case. Despite the busloads of tourists, most everyone had moved inside, escaping the morning heat by visiting the museum, shopping for Dead Sea facial creams, or snacking in the cafeteria.

As soon as they paid the admission, Jim pointed to the treasury—the square building commonly thought of as the watchtower or Jim's *House of Hakkoz*. According to Jim's research, the highest density of caches was buried right outside of the tower's slanting walls. He believed the treasury had the greatest chance of a positive scan. The risk was that the treasury was in full view of the visitor's center and Qumran's employees.

Jim set the case down in the dirt and began taking out the equipment. In plain view of Qumran's armed security guard, Jim fitted Feiglin with the shoulder bag that held the five-pound battery pack. Feiglin's job was to stand in back of the coil and operate the control box, the simplest job but also the most accountable. Chris and Mack adjusted the detector's six-foot coil to grab hold of its corners and keep it at a constant height above the ground. Dragging the detector would cause a false signal. Feiglin's driver positioned himself to film the operation.

Jim checked for the security guard over his shoulder. Chris signaled the start of the scan. To obtain the best reading, they had to coordinate their pace on a straight path, carrying the scanner coil between them. Like the leader of a marching band, Jim kept cadence of their unity of movement and made sure they maintained a cubed shape.

After several minutes, the security guard sauntered over to the watchtower and inquired about the purpose of their actions. Jim stayed quiet. Shading his brow, Jim eyed the exit in case they needed to make a quick getaway. Feiglin threw up his palms, gesticulating his innocence. He told the guard that he had brought scientific researchers to Qumran for a quick test. The guard ran his eyes over the Lorenz Deepmax Z1, then Jim, Mack, Chris, and back to Feiglin. The guard's facial expression changed at the exact moment that he connected Feiglin's mug to the Israeli politician in the newspapers. What happened next no one could interpret. The guard dismissed himself and walked behind Qumran's office building. He turned his back to the group and began dancing and singing. The spontaneity of his solitary performance confused the group, but they had to take advantage of the diversion. It seemed he was intentionally trying to keep them out of eyeshot.

After the watchtower, they scanned the large adjacent courtyard, still in full view of the visitor's center. The perimeter of the *broken protective wall,* the *great cistern,* and the *peristyle* were three adjacent burial locations highlighted frequently in Jim's Copper Scroll research. Since the courtyard covers a large surface area, the crew had a clear run. The rubble remains of the courtyard stand only a few inches high. Outside of the protective wall, they hovered the coil over Peleg's test probe from the 2009 excavation. With a glance, Jim and Chris telecommunicated their memory of Peleg's disappointing scan over the probe with the IAA's metal detector. The three-foot-deep hole had since been refilled with dirt.

The electronic survey was going quick. Seeing that his son was jumpy with excitement, Feiglin proposed to Jim, "Let's do an extra one." While tourists gathered on a nearby observation deck, Jim led them to the dining hall on the opposite end of Qumran. Because de Vaux had found stacks of broken dishes in the pantry that adjoined the long enclosure, he first identified the room—the largest at Qumran—as the dining hall where the Essenes shared communal meals. Yet de Vaux's later critics felt the quantity of dishes was disproportionate to the number of inhabitants at Qumran. Jim explained to Feiglin how the Copper Scroll reconciled both theories. According to his translation of the Copper Scroll, the room was both the communal dining hall and a soup kitchen, where the Essenes fed the widows and the poor of nearby Jericho. His understanding of the Copper Scroll's ninth line in the eleventh column described the room as *the building of lending to Jericho's sons.*

After they scanned the floors and around the narrow entrance of the room, Feiglin peeled off the shoulder bag with the control box. Sweat marked the outlines of the straps. The driver stopped recording. Though everything had gone smoothly thus far, Feiglin suggested that they secure the Lorenz detector. Someone from the ADCA could still show up any second and confiscate the equipment. Jim asked Chris and Mack to dash back to the car with the scanner and memory stick. Before Mack packed up the equipment, he whispered, "But what about the cave? Jim, we gotta do the cave."

The *hill of Kokhlit* was heavy on Jim's mind as well. Still, he was hesitant to push the Knesset member. It would involve Feiglin walking all the way through Qumran and up the hill. The sun was directly overhead and beating down. Scanning the potential cave area would also be complex and time consuming because of the jagged rock formations and sloping surface. Going to the *hill of Kokhlit* would run contrary to the hit-and-run mentality of the scan.

Feiglin was not quite ready, however, to leave Qumran and miss out on a teachable moment for his son. "Could you show us around a little bit?" Feiglin asked.

As part of a personalized Qumran tour, Jim showed them several Copper Scroll locations which were too confined to scan with the large coil. They would require a smaller attachment. Feiglin asked questions about the Dead Sea Scrolls and the Essenes. Jim emphasized their piety and outlier status—elbowing the executive director as he likened the ancient sectarians to *Manhigut Yehudit*. As they moved over to the scriptorium, Jim pointed in the direction of the *hill of Kokhlit*. He explained how the rock formation was the Copper Scroll's only location placed outside of the Qumran complex, but it potentially held the most important items.

Feiglin asked pointedly, "Why didn't we scan over there?"

"Well, I didn't want to trouble you anymore," Jim answered.

"Let's go," Feiglin motioned.

Mack made it back from the parking lot, but as soon as he overheard Feiglin inquiring about the cave, he trotted back out to the car. Mack's long legs quickened from excitement. He returned with the equipment in hand within minutes. Jim and Feiglin's entourage ambled up to the rock heap together. Along the way, they passed the security guard whose dancing had transitioned to pacing. He still refused to look over at them.

As they paused for a quick water break, Jim showed them the trench which remained from the 2009 excavation and the spot where he first noticed a sinkhole. He described other caves in the area which also had gauntlet shapes, tapered in at their opening. From the top of the heap, he illustrated the last writer for the Copper Scroll's strategy in making a perfectly straight and ascending burial pattern which pointed right to the cave entrance.

The ensemble felt content to be out of plain sight while they readied the equipment. Walking in the same back and forth pattern on an incline was difficult. They carefully avoided tripping over rocks so the coils would not require repositioning. The detector hummed and the large bar graph on the flat-panel display indicated signal strength as the data downloaded. Once each pass was complete, Jim stepped several feet to the side and pointed his arm in the direction of the next straightest path. Their foreheads reddened while sweat dripped from their noses. After they finished scanning the *hill of Kokhlit*, Feiglin turned to his son and announced, "Now, I am Indiana Jones!"

When they got back to the parking lot, no law enforcement or journalists were waiting. Tourists wandered the ruins, unaware that they were technically witnesses to a clandestine operation. The security guard was nowhere to be found.

Jim assured Feiglin that he would be in touch as soon as possible. The logger had been storing the data from each location. They could only know if the scans were positive once Jim got offsite to process the information with the specialized software. He cautioned Feiglin, "Even if we don't get positive results from these four areas, it doesn't mean that the other locations in Qumran shouldn't be scanned. I don't mean to overlook anything." Despite the truth in the statement, even Jim knew that his research would drop like a jellyfish if all four scans came up negative.

Feiglin headed back to Jerusalem for Knesset meetings. Jim wanted some safe distance from Qumran in case the IAA's Theft Prevention Unit showed up. However, he was too anxious to drive all the way back to Arad. The closest place they could sit and regroup was the Ein Gedi Nature Reserve. It took thirty minutes to drive there. Laurie's legs shook nervously the entire drive. Sitting at a picnic table shaded by date palms, Chris downloaded the data from the memory stick onto a small computer. The aroma of salt and myrrh stirred in the air with each cooling wind. Jim caught his sober-lined reflection in the computer display.

Nearby stood the ruins of Ein Gedi's fifth-century synagogue. The synagogue floors host one of Israel's most stunning mosaic carpets. Among designs of peacocks and flowers, a curious Hebrew and Aramaic inscription reads: *Warnings to those who commit sins causing dissension in the community, passing malicious information to the gentiles, or revealing the secrets of the town.* Though the inscription is commonly believed to be referring to the town's recipe for balsam oil perfumes, the warning felt particularly relevant to Jim's circumstances.

As the computer downloaded the files, Jim felt like he was waking from a long dream. Compass points from the last eight years flooded his memory: barbequing with Vendyl, proofing the *Messiah Timeline*, discovering a Vogel crystal, praying with state senators, debating by the lakeside during Sukkots, and singing with the head of Masada. Could it be that after all this time, and all its related tangents, his objective to restore Israel's spiritual treasures was finally going to manifest? Or would his dreams stay out of reach, like his father's plans for a private helicopter to land in their front yard? Was naivety hereditary? Did it skip a generation?

When the images popped up on the computer, it took Jim a moment to realize what he was looking at. Some of the images were two-dimensional and some were three-dimensional. Each display was color coded to indicate what category of metal, if any, the detector located. The Lorenz metal detector discriminates between ferrous and non-ferrous metals. Ferrous metals have iron in them. They are represented in charts by green and yellow. Non-ferrous metals are copper, brass, silver and gold. Thin non-ferrous objects are coded blue and large non-ferrous metals are orange and red. Purple means nothing was found.

The first three-dimensional image of the watchtower displayed several large blue bumps, indicating thin non-ferrous metals. "Gold and silver vessels or coin deposits would count as thin metal," Jim stated calmly. As the entire image from the watchtower scrolled on the screen, a large red and orange column began to emerge standing out like a beacon. Laurie and Chris cheered. Jim stared at the computer, unblinking. He adjusted the screen to check for a glare from the palm-filtered light. The reality refused to sink in. The image was showing him large quantities of precious metal objects stashed outside the building that he believed to be Qumran's treasury, exactly where he had predicted. Instead of accepting the momentous evidence, Jim ran through the details of the scan: the pace, turning radius, coil positions. He kept wondering, *what if we did something wrong and caused false images to appear?*

Jim pulled up the next file from the courtyard. The scan detected a stash of nonferrous metal in the middle of the courtyard where Jim had predicted a large cache of silver to be buried. In the northwest corner of the courtyard, the image revealed a blanket of blue cubes, indicating a cache of thin non-ferrous metals. The two-dimensional map also had a singular blob of red. Since Jim was too stunned to act elated, Mack clarified, "Red means gold, right Jim?" Jim glanced back at his metal classification map in the software manual.

"Gold or some other precious metal," Jim answered. "Red also means big, but I don't know how big."

Jim clicked open the file from the dining hall. Except for one green and yellow spot that Jim suspected was the detector picking up a modern signpost, the images from the dining hall gave no indication of any concealed metal. The maps looked like the practice scans that Jim did in Flynn's empty backyard. As he looked at the purple charts, Jim couldn't help feeling the first tinge of disappointment. Then he noticed a faint wave of blue at the corner of the dining hall.

Jim purposefully saved the file from the cave for last. Chris mumbled an audible prayer. Jim gnawed the knuckles of one hand while he used the other to click on the keypad to open the images from the *hill of Kokhlit*. Everyone gulped. The two-dimensional image showed big globs of blue, orange, and red. The three-dimensional chart showed three huge red columns practically jutting out from the computer screen. They were positioned exactly where Jim expected an underground cavity.

"I'll be darned!" Jim exclaimed, slapping his palms down on the table. "The cave looks like a scan of Fort Knox!" The discovery of the Copper Scroll's treasures finally felt within reach.

Jim called Feiglin's cellphone. "Moshe, we have the preliminary findings. At all the sites we got a positive reading," Jim announced. "Something is buried underground there that is gold, silver, or bronze. And according to the metal detector, it's big!"

Five seconds of silence passed on the other end of the phone.

"Moshe, are you there?" Jim asked.

"What should we do now?" Moshe finally replied.

This question momentarily bewildered Jim. Jim felt that the news of this finding would put the world on notice. Whatever the future held, the question was no longer *if* anything was buried under Qumran. The question was now *what* was buried under Qumran. Jim felt the enormity of his calling, all that he had given to answer the first question, and all that he might have to give in the future to answer the second. There was no turning back.

"Moshe," Jim replied. "We can't put smoke back in that bottle."

POSTSCRIPT

Two weeks after the scan of Qumran, sad news came from Israel. Yuval Peleg died in a tragic excavation accident. Peleg had been tasked with a routine survey of a cave in the West Bank. The cave was discovered by construction workers building a new road in the area. While Peleg was inside the cave, he was caught in a rock landslide. Paramedics tried to resuscitate his half-buried body, but his wounds were fatal. Peleg was pronounced dead on the scene. At age 46, he left behind a wife and two children. Shockingly, a few short weeks after Peleg's accident, Shuka Dorfman also died. Only 64 and still Director General of the IAA, Dorfman succumbed to a long battle with cancer.

In Jim's memory, Peleg and Dorfman were the first archaeological authorities to take a chance on a firefighter with a crazy idea. Though both men went silent after the 2009 excavation, and offered Jim no closure, he was eternally thankful for their early efforts and openness. Without them, Jim doubted that he would have ever gotten a foot in the door. They also never joined the fault-hunting bibliobloggers in publicly ridiculing Jim, neither personally, nor his theory. Jim had maintained hope that Peleg would be willing to revisit the cave if Jim could somehow show him the evidence from the Lorenz scan and the mortar analysis. Jim had also hoped that Dorfman would eventually intervene with Hizmi on his behalf, if for no other reason than his unwillingness to deny Juanita a favor. Alas, neither Peleg nor Dorfman were given that chance.

TERRORISM

Throughout 2014, particularly the five months after the scan of Qumran, Jewish visits to the Temple Mount continued to rise, creating no small amount of Palestinian agitation. During the Jewish High Holidays, Hamas and other terrorist groups prepared for the encroachment of Jewish visitors by improvising barricades inside Al-Aqsa Mosque and stocking up on small explosives. The Temple Mount was a powder keg. In a fiery speech, President Abbas proclaimed that the Jews had no right to enter the Temple Mount and desecrate it. To protect the site from sacrilege, he ordered an onslaught of Palestinians to seize the site and repel the "herds of cattle" by all means.

A fit of terror overtook the streets of Jerusalem. Rogue Palestinian motorists used their accelerators as weapons, mowing down Israeli soldiers and pedestrians on sidewalks. A rash of terrorists pulled knives on unarmed Jews at bus stops and city streets. In the middle of the Knife Intifada, the Temple Mount movement suffered a direct and personal hit. Rabbi Yehuda Glick, leaving an annual conference addressing Jewish rights on the Temple Mount, was confronted by a Palestinian terrorist on a motorcycle. The terrorist dryly warned Glick, in perfect Hebrew, "I'm sorry. You are an enemy of Al-Aqsa." He pulled out a pistol and shot Glick in the neck, chest, stomach, and hand. Glick was ambulanced to the closest hospital where he received emergency surgery and over a dozen pints of blood. He miraculously survived.

Feiglin, just steps away, was an eyewitness to the attempted assassination of his friend. Shaken but not weakened, he and other Temple Mount devotees planned a visit to the Temple Mount the next day to demonstrate their support for Glick. The Israeli police, fearing a violent escalation, closed the area to Jews and Muslims. President Abbas declared the closure an act of war.

Although Netanyahu deployed emergency measures to quell the spasmodic violence taking over the capital, he promised that Israel retained its long-term policies in a meeting with the UN Secretary-General Ban Ki-moon. The status quo held firm: The Western Wall was for Jewish worship, and the Temple Mount was for Muslim worship. In a letter to Netanyahu, Feiglin responded to what he understood as the Prime Minister's flawed commitment to the status quo. He wrote, "Israel has been deceiving itself into thinking that it can manage the height of the flames on the Temple Mount without restoring its control there."[1] Terrorists did not succeed in silencing the Temple Mount movement; they amplified it.

Even still, Feiglin's political reality caught up to his oversized ambitions and he paid for his reputation as a Temple Mount gadfly. In December 2014, the Israeli Knesset's inability to pass a budget triggered early elections. Feiglin launched an aggressive campaign to secure one of the top ten spots in the Likud party leadership. Instead, Feiglin dropped from number 11 on the Likud party slate to number 36, a crushing blow that pushed him completely out of the Knesset. The Temple Mount movement suffered a weighty setback by this sudden loss of a political insider, and so did the *Copper Scroll Project*.

OPERATION SCROLL

Jim, Chris, and I returned to Israel to meet with Oren Gutfeld in May of 2015. As a bombshell to everyone but his closest confidants, Gutfeld abandoned the tenure track at Hebrew University to pursue an alternative career in archaeology. He was no longer interested in pure academia. He saw a bright future in the business side of archaeology, a niche he knew few others were occupying.

In his twenty years of experience, Gutfeld understood the lucrative potential of aiding foreign universities with the logistic and administrative portions of digs. He had already done so with Randall Price at Qumran for eight seasons. Gutfeld established Israel Archaeological Services (IAS) as a consulting business for foreign expeditions. IAS's tagline is "You dig—we'll do the rest!" Gutfeld built a team of graduate students, surveyors, photographers, dig supervisors, and conservators. They acquired equipment, secured lodging or built base camps, navigated bureaucracy, conducted field surveys, and arranged for the processing of finds.

As an independent agent, no longer constrained by a university, Jim hoped Gutfeld was finally free to work with him. Jim wanted to hire Gutfeld to excavate the *hill of Kokhlit*. Gutfeld was the only one Jim knew who might be willing to finish the excavation that Peleg started. Before Jim left for Israel, Mack informed him that he was prepared to pay Gutfeld's price.

Gutfeld, more than anyone, believed surveying the Judean Desert was always worth the effort. "Much has been overlooked," he said. Though getting a permit to dig in Qumran proper remained an impossibility, for anyone, the *hill of Kokhlit* was the only location in Jim's research that stood a chance to be tested. At the time of our meeting, Gutfeld had the maximum number of permits that he could acquire at a time. He needed to wait until the next calendar year before applying for an additional permit.

Following his gut, Jim did not tell Gutfeld about the scan results with Feiglin. He didn't want to incriminate a man with a license to lose. Also, Gutfeld took the Copper Scroll seriously enough that Jim didn't think he needed to reveal the extra intelligence.

Gutfeld divulged that he had an upcoming excavation in the Judean Desert, searching for additional Dead Sea Scroll caves that were previously undetected because of seismic activity which caused their collapse. New technology made their location easier. It was part of a new initiative entitled "Operation Scroll," under the directive of the IAA's new Director General, Dorfman's successor. Incidentally, one of Gutfeld's upcoming excavations was adjacent to Vendyl's *Cave of the Column.*

While Jim waited for Gutfeld to confirm a date for the excavation, news came from Israel that Operation Scroll lived up to its charge. Gutfeld located the twelfth Dead Sea Scroll cave—the first scroll cave discovery since 1956. No new scrolls were found, but he unearthed a piece of blank parchment rolled up in an undamaged jug. Half of a century prior, Bedouin cleared the cave of the valuable scrolls—as evidenced by pickax heads. Scroll wrappings and storage jars remained. Pictures of Gutfeld, wearing a headlamp inside the cave, appeared on major news sites across the world. Amid the frenzied press coverage, he sent word to Jim that an excavation at the *hill of Kokhlit* would be pushed back indefinitely. His year was officially booked.

Israel Hasson—the new director of the IAA—announced in a press release, "The important discovery of another scroll cave attests to the fact that a lot of work remains to be done in the Judean Desert, and finds of huge importance are still waiting to be discovered." He added, "The State of Israel needs to mobilize and allocate the necessary resources in order to launch a historic operation, together with the public, to carry out a systematic excavation of all the caves of the Judean Desert."

UNESCO

In October 2016, the United Nations Educational, Scientific and Cultural Organization (UNESCO) executive board ratified a resolution which attempted to erase 3,000 years of Jewish religious history in Jerusalem. In addition to designating the World Heritage Sites, UNESCO is charged with safeguarding cultural and religious sensitivities—except when it applies to Jews, apparently.

The UNESCO resolution made the Temple Mount an exclusively Islamic prerogative. By only referring to the Temple Mount by its Arabic name *Al-Haram al-Sharif*, the resolution's language severed ties between Judaism and the Temple Mount. Even the Western Wall was Islamicized in the resolution to Al-Buraq Plaza, the place where Muhammad tethered his horse. The Arabic name was only twice followed by the Western Wall's Hebrew name, but it was placed in quotation marks—a detail that Israelis took as direct belittling of Judaism's linkage to the site. The resolution made no mention of the Jewish Temples that stood at the site for a thousand years, nor the next two thousand years of continuous Jewish attachment to Jerusalem. Only once did the drafters soften their bias by making a generalized reference to the importance of the Old City and its walls "for the three monotheistic religions."

Israelis refused to cower and lick their wounds after the international blow. Jerusalem still remains the center point of the Jewish faith; the holy places are not the exclusive domain of Islam. Two days after the ratification of the UNESCO resolution, 50,000 Jews gathered at the Western Wall to receive the blessing recited annually during Sukkot. A record number of Israelis—3,000 in three weeks—ascended the Temple Mount, including IDF soldiers in uniform.

The resolution was more than a public insult. It raised the stakes in the battle over the Temple Mount. The international community went too far. Internalizing their isolation, the new tone of the Israeli government shifted from cautious to defensive. Netanyahu denied UNESCO's authority to manipulate human history: "These distortions of history are only reserved for the Jews. Does anyone claim that the pyramids in Giza have no connection to the Egyptians? That the Acropolis in Athens has no connection to the Greeks? That the Coliseum in Rome has no connection to the Italians? It is ridiculous to try and sever the connection between the Temple Mount and the Jewish people."

In the flurry of diplomatic bustle that preceded the UNESCO resolution, Israel's Foreign Ministry distributed pamphlets to its ambassadors in foreign governments. To demonstrate Judaism's historic affiliation with Jerusalem and the Temple Mount, the pamphlet contained pictures of archaeological findings. A close-up picture of the Arch of Titus—once a full color monument, but long faded white—graced the brochure's cover. Since the nation's revival, Israel has incorporated the monument's menorah into the national emblem.

How much longer, Jim wondered, *would Israel's historic reference point be the image of her oppressors parading her relics into exile?* He awaited the day when a counter image would take its place: Israelis, free in their own nation, with Jerusalem as their restored capital, marching up from the Valley of Achor—Hosea's door of hope and Isaiah's resting place—their hands gripping the long-lost treasures of their holy Temple: dusty, weathered, but never forgotten. Jim felt certain that a fresh chapter in the Jews' very long history was being recorded. The Copper Scroll was just the prologue.

SHELLEY NEESE

Shelley Neese is the Vice President of *The Jerusalem Connection Internatio-nal* (TJCI), a nonprofit organization based out of Washington DC. TJCI's mission is to inform, educate, and activate support for Israel and the Jewish people.

Shelley lived and studied in Israel from 2000-2004, where she learned conversa-tional Hebrew and received her M.A. in Middle Eastern Studies from Ben Gurion University of the Negev. The high point of her studies—and first crack at investigative journalism—was her master's thesis exam-ining the secret, multilateral negotiations ending the 2002 siege of the Church of the Nativity in Bethlehem.

After graduation, Shelley moved to Boston where she served as the assis-tant to the Consul General at the Consulate of Israel to New England. She was the first Christian to hold such a position. In addition, she worked as a consul-tant for the Middle East program at Conflict Management Group, a nonprofit organization connected to Harvard Law School that taught negotiation strat-egy to Israeli and Palestinian leaders.

As a freelance columnist for several publications, her articles have appeared in *The Jerusalem Post*, *Arutz Sheva*, and *FrontPage Magazine*. Her first article on Jim Barfield and the Copper Scroll, "Cracking the Code," was featured as the cover article in the Jerusalem Post Metro Edition in August 2009. Over the last decade, Shelley has chronicled every central event in the *Copper Scroll Project*.

Shelley currently resides in Washington DC with her four children and husband, a Family Physician in the U.S. Air Force.

NOTES

CHAPTER 1 - PROMISE

[1] Throughout the book, I use the New International Version (NIV) Bible translation.

[2] The first scroll that Sukenik opened was the *Thanksgiving Psalms*. For Eleazar Sukenik's diary entry, see Weston Fields, *The Dead Sea Scrolls: A Full History* (Leiden: Brill, 2009), 45.

[3] Esther never mentions the name of God, in any variation, which gives credence to the theory that the Dead Sea Scrolls were part of a genizah, a temporary storage unit for any unserviceable Hebrew texts with the name of God. The Dead Sea Scroll caves had 36 copies of the Psalms, 29 copies of Deuteronomy, and 17 copies of Exodus.

CHAPTER 2 - CRAZY

[1] Judith Anne Brown, *John Marco Allegro, the Maverick of the Dead Sea Scrolls* (Grand Rapids, MI: Wm. B. Eerdmans, 2005), xii.

[2] Ibid., 63.

[3] John Marco Allegro, *The Treasure of the Copper Scroll: The Opening and Decipherment of the Most Mysterious of the Dead Sea Scrolls, a Unique Inventory of Buried Treasure* (London: Routledge & Kegan Paul, 1960), 23.

[4] Brown, *John Marco Allegro*, 68.

[5] Fields, *The Dead Sea Scrolls*, 272.

[6] Stanley Rowland Jr., "Dead Sea Scrolls Tell of Treasure: 'Key' to Vast Riches Written on Copper is Deciphered," *New York Times*, June 1, 1956.

[7] Jim Barfield has since come up with an intriguing theory about the Greek ciphers. He matched the numeric and phonetically equivalent Greek letters

to their Hebrew counterparts. Doing so rendered the words: sixth age, hand, priest, drink, spirit, grace, and wilderness. The words struck him as the same prophetic terms given in Isaiah 43 where God promises to send waters of mercy in the wilderness.

[8] Copper Scroll expert Bargil Pixner eyed with curious suspicion the Greek ciphers, which he believed matched the initials of leading Jews in Josephus' history of the Jewish-Roman war, *The Wars of the Jews*. See Bargil Pixner, "Unraveling the Copper Scroll Code: A Study on the Topography of 3Q15," *Revue de Qumran* 11 (1983).

[9] Scholars have no guarantee that the Hebrew abbreviation in the Copper Scroll is a weight measurement. It could also be interpreted as a cash value. For a full calculation based on several readings, see Émile Puech, *The Copper Scroll Revisited* (Leiden: Brill, 2015), 10–11.

[10] "They serve at a sanctuary that is a copy and shadow of what is in heaven. This is why Moses was warned when he was about to build the Tabernacle: 'See to it that you make everything according to the pattern shown you on the mountain.'" (Hebrews 8:5)

[11] "The Lord had made the Egyptians favorably disposed toward the people, and they gave them what they asked for; so, they plundered the Egyptians." (Exodus 12:36)

[12] I Kings 8:9 indicates that the Ten Commandments were the only object placed in the Ark of the Covenant. Rabbinic and Christian writings held that the Ark also housed the rod of Aaron, a jar of manna, and the original smashed set of tablets.

[13] "Greater in riches and wisdom than all the other kings of the earth." (I Kings 10:23)

[14] "When all the work King Solomon had done for the temple of the Lord was finished, he brought in the things his father David had dedicated—the silver and gold and the furnishings—and he placed them in the treasuries of the Lord's temple." (I Kings 7:51)

[15] "The king made silver as common in Jerusalem as stones, and cedar as plentiful as sycamore-fig trees in the foothills." (I Kings 10:27)

[16] "In all, there were 5,400 articles of gold and of silver. Sheshbazzar brought all these along with the exiles when they came up from Babylon to Jerusalem." (Ezra 1:11)

[17] Flavius Josephus, *The Works of Josephus, Complete and Unabridged*, New Updated Edition, Translated by William Whiston (Peabody: Hendrickson Publishers, 1987), 747.

The account reads:

But now at this time it was that one of the priests, the son of Thebuthus, whose name was Jesus, upon his having security given him, by the oath of Caesar, that he should be preserved, upon condition that he should deliver to him certain of the precious things that had been deposited in the temple came out of it, and delivered him from the wall of the holy house two candlesticks, like to those that lay in the holy house, with tables, and cisterns, and vials, all made of solid gold, and very heavy. He also delivered to him the veils and the garments, with the precious stones, and a great number of other precious vessels that belonged to their sacred worship. The treasurer of the temple also, whose name was Phineas, was seized on, and showed Titus the coats and girdles of the priests, with a great quantity of purple and scarlet, which were there deposited for the uses of the veil, as also a great deal of cinnamon and cassia, with a large quantity of other sweet spices, which used to be mixed together, and offered as incense to God every day. A great many other treasures were also delivered to him, with sacred ornaments of the temple not a few; which things thus delivered to Titus obtained of him for this man the same pardon that he had allowed to such as deserted of their own accord.

[18] See Kyle McCarter's provisional translation prepared for the Dead Sea Scroll Commentary Project of the Princeton Theological Seminary. In Hershel Shanks, *The Copper Scroll and the Search for the Temple Treasure* (Washington, DC: Biblical Archaeology Society, 2007), 98–101.

[19] Pixner, "Unraveling the Copper Scroll Code."

[20] Al Wolters, "Paleography and Literary Structure as Guides to Reading the Copper Scroll," in *Copper Scroll Studies*, eds. George Brooke and Philip Davies, Journal for the Study of the Pseudepigrapha Supplement Series 40 (Sheffield: Sheffield Academic Press, 2002), 331.

[21] Al Wolters, *The Copper Scroll: Overview, Text, and Translation* (Sheffield: Sheffield Academic Press, 1996), 55.

[22] "Moses could not enter the tent of meeting because the cloud had settled on it, and the glory of the LORD filled the Tabernacle." (Exodus 40:35)

[23] K.G. Kuhn, "Les Rouleaux de Cuivre de Qumran," *Revue Biblique* 61 (1954), 197. Also in Shanks, The Copper Scroll, 13.

CHAPTER 3 - SOURCE

[1] The parchment scrolls have gone through other rigorous examinations. Though these tests are not an option for copper, they have provided an ever-growing number of insights for the rest of the scroll corpus. DNA samples can determine the type of animal which provided the skin for various parchments; chemical testing on a scroll can localize the water source used to prepare the carbon ink. Infrared photography has brought forth inked letters once imperceptible to the human eye. Computer imaging programs have revolutionized the once tedious job of piecing together tattered fragments.

[2] Because Jim Barfield was taught by Vendyl Jones about the history and background of the Copper Scroll, Jim credits Vendyl with more than he is due. Before Vendyl, Józef Milik recognized the parallels between the Copper Scroll, II Maccabees, and the *Treatise of the Temple Vessels*. Also, a Norwegian scholar, S. Mowinckel, independently and simultaneously, came to the same conclusion as Milik about the Copper Scroll's connection to the Temple folklore. Mowinckel published his conclusions in an article for a newspaper in Norway.

[3] II Maccabees 2:6–8, *New American Bible*.

[4] Ibid.

[5] 587 BCE is the historical date for the destruction of the First Temple. The date is derived from merging biblical and secular sources—Greek, Babylonian and Persian records. Rabbinic dating synchronizes prophecies and puts the First Temple's collapse at 423 BCE—a huge chronological discrepancy referred to as "the missing years." Jim Barfield uses chronology dating from his own research.

[6] While Jeremiah sat in confinement, his cousin Hanamel came to visit him in the year of Jubilee. Hanamel solicited Jeremiah, unmarried and childless, to redeem a piece of family property—a field a few miles northeast of the Jerusalem Temple, in the land of Benjamin. Despite the fact the land had already been captured by the roving Babylonian army, Jeremiah was told in a dream to buy the land for seventeen shekels. Once he had the title deed,

Jeremiah gave specific instructions to Baruch to bury the clay jar until the day when Israel had propriety over their fields and valleys again.

"Take these documents, both the sealed and unsealed copies of the deed of purchase and put them in a clay jar so they will last a long time. For this is what the Lord Almighty, the God of Israel, says: 'Houses, fields and vineyards will again be bought in this land.'" (Jeremiah 32: 14–15)

[7] The English translation of the *Treatise of the Temple Vessels* that I use throughout the book is the work of Vendyl Jones. For the authoritative English translation see, Richard Bauckman, James Davila, and Alex Panayotov, *Old Testament Pseudepigrapha* (Grand Rapids, MI: Wm. B. Eerdmans, 2013), 393–409.

[8] James Davila, "Scriptural Exegesis in the Treatise of the Temple Vessels, A Legendary Account of the Hiding of the Temple Vessels," in *With Letters of Light*, eds. Daphna V. Arbel and Andre A. Orlov (Berlin & New York: De Gruyter, 2011), 46.

[9] Nechoshet in Hebrew can mean copper or bronze. The word occurs frequently in biblical Hebrew as a reference to metal ore. See the definition in W.E. Vine, Merrill F. Unger, and William White Jr., *Vine's Complete Expository Dictionary of Old and New Testament Words* (Nashville: Thomas Nelson, 1996).

[10] Milik and Starcky associated the *Treatise* tiles with a collection of 66 marble tiles containing the text of Ezekiel, known as the Ezekiel Plates. The assumption was based on their similar appearance, material, and provenance. The Ezekiel Plates have been housed in the Yad Izhak Ben-Zvi Institute in Israel since 1953. In 2014, I visited the Yad Izhak Ben-Zvi Institute. I was informed by the curator, Dr. Nirit Shalev Khalifa, that it is now known that the Ezekiel Plates and *Treatise* tiles are not from the same collection. The only surviving evidence of the Treatise marble tiles is the picture from Starcky. New research shows the Ezekiel Plates are a fairly modern creation. But the *Treatise* tiles have never been dated.

CHAPTER 4 - DISCOVERY

[1] Mark Seal, "Masquerader of the lost Ark," *Texas Monthly*, August 1992, 140.

[2] *Time*, "The Nation: The People," vol. 89/24 (June 16, 1967), 7–18.

[3] Conventional translations of the Copper Scroll do not list anointing oil. Vendyl never shared his translation.

[4] Daniel C. Browning Jr., "The Strange Search for the Ashes of the Red Heifer," *Biblical Archaeologist* 59, no. 2 (June 1996), 85.

[5] García Martínez, F., *The Dead Sea Scrolls Translated: The Qumran texts in English*, 2nd ed. (Grand Rapids, MI: Wm. B. Eerdmans, 1996).

[6] Barbara Thiering argues that Martínez had good reason for translating the first line of the Copper Scroll: *In the ruin which is in the valley, pass under the steps leading to the east*. Although she believes he was correct to go with the common noun "ruin" in the first line, he was wrong to translate the next word as the verb "pass" when it should have been the proper name for "Valley of Achor." Though Jim Barfield was unfamiliar with Thiering's argument, he used the same judgment in his translation. See Barbara Thiering, "The Copper Scroll: King Herod's Bank Account," in *Copper Scroll Studies*, eds. George Brooke and Philip Davies, Journal for the Study of the Pseudepigrapha Supplement Series 40 (Sheffield: Sheffield Academic Press, 2002), 276.

[7] Martínez, *The Dead Sea Scrolls Translated*, 461–463.

[8] Yitzhak Magen and Yuval Peleg, "The Qumran Excavations, 1993–2004, Preliminary Report," *Judea and Samaria Publications* 6 (2007), 40.

[9] Martínez, *The Dead Sea Scrolls Translated*, 461–463.

[10] Ibid.

[11] Jodi Magness, *The Archaeology of Qumran and the Dead Sea Scrolls* (Grand Rapids, MI: Wm. B. Eerdmans, 2002), 25.

[12] Thiering presented a scenario where the Essenes offered King Herod the deserted buildings of Qumran as a place to store his bank account. See Thiering, "King Herod's Bank Account," 276.

[13] Pixner, "Unraveling the Copper Scroll Code."

[14] See Ben Zion Luria, Megillat han-Nahoshel mem-Midbar Yehudah [The Copper Scroll from the Judean Desert], *Publications of the Israel Bible Research Society* XIV (1963).
Luria identified the authors of the Copper Scroll as followers of the second-century guerilla leader Simon bar Kokhba. With their salvaged Temple treasure, Luria believed, the renegades took refuge in the caves of the Judean Desert after fleeing the renewed Roman assault in Jerusalem.

Also see Richard A. Freund, *Secrets of the Cave of Letters: Rediscovering a Dead Sea Mystery* (New York: Humanity Books, 2004).

Professor Richard Freund, from the University of Hartford, extends Luria's theory. He associates the Cave of Letters with the Copper Scroll's Cave of the Column. Freund argues that a basket of bronze vessels, discovered by Yigal Yadin in his excavation of the Cave of Letters, are in fact from the Jerusalem Temple, secreted there by refugees during the Bar Kokhba Revolt and recorded on the Copper Scroll.

[15] In 1981, Yehuda Meir Getz, the rabbi of the Western Wall, discovered a rock-hewn eastward tunnel under the Temple Mount. Secretly, the rabbi worked with Rafi Eitan, a counter-terrorism advisor in three governments. Their goal was to locate the Holy of Holies and reclaim the Temple artifacts. When their covert chiseling was discovered by Muslims on the Temple Mount, the situation escalated and threatened a religious war. The Israeli government defused the crisis by sealing the tunnel opening with concrete.

CHAPTER 5 - LAND

[1] "And from among the priests: The descendants of Hobaiah, Hakkoz and Barzillai (a man who had married a daughter of Barzillai the Gileadite and was called by that name). These searched for their family records, but they could not find them and so were excluded from the priesthood as unclean." (Ezra 2:61–62)

[2] Nehemiah 3:4 notes that the head of the Hakkoz family was "Meremoth son of Uriah, son of Hakkoz." Ezra 8:33 explains, "On the fourth day, in the house of our God, we weighed out the silver and gold and the sacred articles into the hands of Meremoth son of Uriah [son of Hakkoz], the priest."

[3] Historical texts indicate that the Essenes had concentrations of followers sprinkled throughout Israel. Some scholars believe the *Damascus Document* applied to zealots living in towns across Israel. Two copies of it were discovered in the Old Cairo genizah. The *Community Rule*, on the other hand, regulated the community life of a monastic settlement, like what is thought to have existed at Qumran.

[4] In the area de Vaux labeled the "pantry," he found neatly stacked piles of bowls and plates. The room de Vaux labeled the "scriptorium" contained inkwells, a stylus, lamps, and long benches. De Vaux interpreted a large

rectangular room, closest to the pantry, as the "refectory," a communal dining room estimated to hold up to 120 people. De Vaux's labeling of rooms show how his experience as a Catholic priest framed his point of reference. Qumran was like a monastery.

[5] The coins found throughout the site ranged in dates from 136 BCE to 68 CE. De Vaux used the coins for his stratigraphic analysis, concluding that the date ranges with the most coin representation pointed to the most active phases of the site's occupation.

[6] In the gospel of Matthew, Temple tax collectors accusingly asked Peter if his master paid the Temple tax. Jesus responded by having Peter collect a Tyrian shekel from a fish's mouth for their taxes. See Matthew 17:24.

[7] De Vaux based his interpretation off of II Chronicles 26:10: "He [Uzziah] also built towers in the wilderness and dug many cisterns, because he had much livestock in the foothills and in the plain."

[8] It is remarkable that the Essenes had the prowess to build complicated cisterns and pools for harnessing rainwater, and tunnels efficient at directing the water flow to provide the annual water needs for as many as 200 people.

[9] Martínez, *The Dead Sea Scrolls Translated*, 461–463.

[10] Nahman Avigad, "Two Hebrew Inscriptions on Wine-Jars," *Israel Exploration Journal* 22, no. 1 (1972), 1–9.

[11] See Bauckman, Davila, and Panayotov, *Old Testament Pseudepigrapha*, 400. Davila notes that in the *Treatise of the Temple Vessels*, the author uses the place name *Ein Kokhel* which could be the same place name as the Copper Scroll's *Kokhlit*. The marble tile's *Ein Kokhel* describes a spring near a sloping mountain with a barricaded gate hiding the Temple treasures.

[12] Pixner, "Unraveling the Copper Scroll Code."

[13] According to the Quran, using the foundation stone as his takeoff point, Muhammad and the angel Gabriel ascended the seven heavens to receive instructions on prayer from Abraham, Moses, Jesus, and eventually Allah.

CHAPTER 6 - GATEKEEPERS

[1] Jim's critics attack his use of a Strong's Concordance as anachronistic since the Copper Scroll is given a first-century dating and the Strong's Concordance applies to biblical Hebrew. Jim's standard response is that despite objections to his translation method, among the conventional Copper

Scroll translations, the text still points to Qumran. For the most developed criticism of Jim's translation, see Adam Smith, "119 Ministries and the Copper Scroll Project-Part 2," *Bearded Disciple*, February 27, 2015, https://beardeddisciple.wordpress.com/2015/02/27/119-ministries-and-the-copper-scroll-project-part-2/

[2] Allegro, *Treasure of the Copper Scroll*, 31.

[3] Vendyl's "Gilgal" ruins were the remains of evaporation ponds constructed in the 1930s.

Chapter 7 - Connection

[1] Nir Hasson, "Great Excavations: Israel's Antiquities Authority head won't cave in just yet," *Haaretz*, June 15, 2012.

[2] The most essential law is the 1970 UNESCO Convention on the Means of Prohibiting and Preventing the Illicit Import, Export, and Transfer of Ownership of Cultural Property.

[3] Dylan Bergeson, "The Biblical Pseudo-Archaeologists Pillaging the West Bank," *The Atlantic*, February 28, 2013.

[4] For a detailed eye witness account from the perspective of the interrogator, see Matti Friedman, *The Aleppo Codex* (Chapel Hill, N.C.: Algonquin Books of Chapel Hill, 2012), 164–167.

[5] In their lengthy report, Magen and Peleg present the theory that during the Iron Age, Qumran was little more than huts with stone foundations. They claim that the large cistern was too sophisticated to be from the Iron Age and the walls were from the Hasmonean period. See Magen and Peleg, "The Qumran Excavations, 1993–2004, Preliminary Report."

Chapter 9 - Predators

[1] The City of David is an active excavation outside the Old City walls, unique in that it is not conducted under the auspices of the IAA. Instead, the Ir David Foundation underwrites and directs the dig. Although the City of David is popular among tourists, the excavation has caused controversy because its borders encroach on Silwan Village, a historic Palestinian neighborhood. Other Palestinian areas are also threatened by the dig's expansion.

CHAPTER 10 - HOPE

[1] One of the most popular commentaries among the Dead Sea Scrolls construes the prophecies of Hosea as being fulfilled in the times contemporary to the authors.

CHAPTER 11 - TEASER

[1] The Dome of the Rock's octagonal arcade includes Arabic inscriptions that date to 692 CE and are meant to demonstrate Islam's primacy over Christianity. Though the inscriptions recognize the exalted status of Jesus as prophet, they explicitly deny his divinity or the Christian concept of a triune God.

[2] Isidore Singer and Cyrus Adler, *The Jewish Encyclopedia: A Descriptive Record of the History, Religion, Literature, and Customs of the Jewish People from the Earliest Times to the Present Day*, 2, 1901, Reprint (London: Forgotten Books, 2013), 105.

CHAPTER 12 - HUNT

[1] Magen and Peleg, "The Qumran Excavations, 1993–2004, Preliminary Report."

[2] Ofri Ilani, "Dead Sea Scrolls Scholar Defends Son Arrested for Impersonating Rival," *Haaretz*, March 12, 2009.

[3] Roland de Vaux, *Archaeology and the Dead Sea Scrolls* (London: The British Academy, 1973).

[4] Pauline Donceel-Voûte, "Les ruines de Qumran réinterprétées," *Archeologia* 298 (1994), 24–35.

[5] Catherine M. Murphy, *Wealth in the Dead Sea Scrolls and in the Qumran Community* (Leiden: Brill, 2001).

[6] Norman Golb, *Who Wrote the Dead Sea Scrolls? The Search for the Secret of Qumran* (New York: Scribner, 1995).

[7] The *Temple Scroll* is the longest of all the Dead Sea Scrolls. Written in a Hebrew text type close to the Copper Scroll, the *Temple Scroll*, a redacted Torah, describes a future Temple with three concentric square courts. The author clarifies that the ideal Temple is meant to be built before the end of days. Strangely, the dimensions and tribal segmentation correspond with the Tabernacle and wilderness camp, a scaled-up version. The rest of the

Temple Scroll gives an extensive law code, reformed calendar, and strict regulations for the sacrificial system. The *Temple Scroll* is written in the first person, a direct message from God to Moses.

[8] Nir Hasson, "Overlooked Relics May Help Unearth Dead Sea Scrolls' Authors," *Haaretz*, November 28, 2011.

[9] Devorah Dimant, *History, Ideology, and Interpretation in the Dead Sea Scrolls* (Heidelberg, Germany: Mohr Siebeck, 2014).

[10] Joe E. Zias, James D. Tabor and Stephanie Harter-Lailheugue, "Toilets at Qumran, the Essenes, and the Scrolls: New anthropological data and old theories," *Revue de Qumran* 22. no. 88 (2006), 631–640.

[11] Kyle McCarter's provisional translation. In Shanks, *The Copper Scroll*, 98–101.

CHAPTER 13 - HAZING

[1] Shelley Neese, "Cracking the Code," *The Jerusalem Post*, August 19, 2009.

[2] Eric H. Cline, "Fabulous Finds or Fantastic Forgeries? The Distortion of Archaeology by the Media and Pseudoarchaeologists and What We Can Do About It," in *Archaeology, Bible, Politics, and the Media: Proceedings of the Duke University Conference, April 23–24, 2009*, Duke Judaic Studies Series 4 (Winona Lake, Ind. Eisenbrauns, 2012).

[3] Robert R. Cargill, "Pseudo-Science and Sensationalist Archaeology: An Exposé of Jimmy Barfield and the Copper Scroll Project," *Bible and Interpretation*, August 1, 2009, http://www.bibleinterp.com/articles/cargill208261.shtml

[4] Ibid.

[5] Robert R. Cargill, "The Copper Scroll Project Gives an Exclusive TV Interview," *Excavator: The official blog of Robert Cargill*, November 13, 2009, https://robertcargill.com/2009/11/13/the-copper-scroll-project-gives-an-exclusive-tv-interview/

[6] Robert R. Cargill, "Double checking the 'research' of Jim Barfield," *Excavator: The official blog of Robert Cargill*, January 20, 2010, http://robertcargill.com/2010/01/20/double-checking-the-research-of-jim-barfield/

[7] Robert R. Cargill, "On the Insignificance and the Abuse of the Copper Scroll," *Bible and Interpretation*, July 2009, http://www.bibleinterp.com/opeds/copper.shtml

[8] In 2017, a local Oklahoma paper, *Enid News & Eagle*, ran a story on the *Copper Scroll Project*. They reached out to Robert Cargill to update his protests to Jim Barfield and account for the silence. Cargill softened his criticism and made less personal attacks on Jim. Instead, he limited his objections to Jim's methodology and translation. See James Neal, "Emmanuel Hosts Man Who Believes He's Found Site of Ancient Jewish Relics," *Enid News and Eagle*, July 13, 2017.

[9] Robert R. Cargill, "The Copper Scroll Project Gives an Exclusive TV Interview," *Excavator: The official blog of Robert Cargill*, November 13, 2009, http://robertcargill.com/2009/11/13/the-copper-scroll-project-gives-an-exclusive-tv-interview/

CHAPTER 14 - PANTHEON

[1] Believed to be where the resurrection of the dead first begins, burial plots in Kidron Valley have been prime real estate going back to the reign of King Josiah.

"He took the Asherah pole from the temple of the LORD to the Kidron Valley outside Jerusalem and burned it there. He ground it to powder and scattered the dust over the graves of the common people." (II Kings 23:6)

[2] Allegro, *Treasure of the Copper Scroll*, 33–55.

[3] Ibid.

[4] Brown, *John Marco Allegro*, 131.

[5] The Kidron Valley was professionally surveyed in 1945 by archaeologist Nahman Avigad. That, in addition to time constraints, might be why Allegro did not excavate Absalom's Pillar.

[6] Select scholars infer that the parched valley bordering Hyrcania's isolated hill was the biblical Valley of Achor.

[7] The General was likely avoiding a repeat of an incident fifty years earlier when Jerusalem notables stood trial for being complicit in a European-backed secret expedition, known as the Parker expedition. An English aristocrat, Montague Parker, led a covert operation underneath the Al-Aqsa Mosque in search of Solomon's treasures. He based his mission off two primary sources: the counsel of a clairvoyant and an eccentric interpretation of Ezekiel. When the local Muslims discovered the violation, they rioted. Parker had to flee the country for his life.

[8] Fields, *The Dead Sea Scrolls*, 271.

[9] Ibid., 273.

[10] Oren Gutfeld, "Hyrcania's Mysterious Tunnels: Searching for the Treasures of the Copper Scroll," *Biblical Archaeology Review*, September/October 2006.

[11] The Al-Aqsa Intifada, also called the Second Intifada, was a violent Palestinian uprising, launched in 2000. Over five years, suicide bombers killed 830 Israelis and wounded 4,000 more. 3,000 Palestinians were killed by IDF operations. The construction of a separation barrier through the West Bank drastically reduced the number of suicide bombers.

CHAPTER 15 - SECRETS

[1] Jewish tradition reflects the vow of silence on the Ark. Every year on the Ninth of Av in the Jewish calendar, Jews mourn and fast to mark the destruction of the First and Second Temples. In Orthodox Jewish homes, often one small part of the wall or floor is left unfinished as a symbol of the loss of the Temple. Since the Ark was the object that imparted the lion's share of holiness onto the Temple, it seems odd that Judaism lacks a day of lamentation for the Ark.

[2] The text is preserved in a sixth-century apocryphal reading in Syriac, a Middle Eastern literary language close to Aramaic. For the English translation, see Robert Henry Charles, *The Apocalypse of Baruch* (New York: The Macmillan Company, 1918), 38.

[3] Robert Kraft and Ann Elizabeth Purintu, "Paraleipomena Jeremiou: An English Translation" in *Seminar Papers of the Society of Biblical Literature* 2 (1971), 327–346.

[4] For the published English translation see, Bauckman, Davila, and Panayotov, *Old Testament Pseudepigrapha*, 393–409.

[5] The cistern is made from brittle limestone. It's also possible that it cracked under the weight of an influx of water.

[6] Michael O. Wise, "David J. Wilmot and the Copper Scroll," in *Copper Scroll Studies*, eds. George Brooke and Philip Davies, Journal for the Study of the Pseudepigrapha Supplement Series, 40 (Sheffield: Sheffield Academic Press, 2002), 304.

[7] The remains of the Pool of Siloam from the Second Temple period were accidentally uncovered in 2004 by city authorities installing a sewer system. It has since been excavated and is part of the popular archaeological park, City of David. The Pool of Siloam from the First Temple period has never been located although it is likely underneath or nearby the Second Temple period site.

[8] Magness, *The Archaeology of Qumran*, 128–129.

[9] Thiering, "King Herod's Bank Account," 284.

[10] Murphy, *Wealth in the Dead Sea Scrolls*, 356.

[11] Jodi Magness, *The Archaeology of the Holy Land: From the Destruction of Solomon's Temple to the Muslim Conquest* (New York: Cambridge University Press, 2012), 116-121.

[12] Daniel 11: 33–35

[13] The inclusion in the scroll corpus of many original Psalms of praise for Jerusalem show the Yahad only imagined their internal exile to be short-term. The *Halakhic Letter* expresses the sect's longing for the Holy City: "For Jerusalem is the camp of holiness, and it is the place which God chose from all the tribes of Israel, for Jerusalem is the chief of the camps of Israel."

[14] From Jim's study of the Dead Sea Scrolls and scriptures, he believed that the priests at Qumran were the Melchizedek priesthood named in Genesis, Psalms and Hebrews, better known as the "school of the prophets." Jim believed the community kept the law of Moses pure and corrected the Levitical priesthood and even the kings in Jerusalem.

CHAPTER 16 - FALSE STARTS

[1] Nina Burleigh, *Unholy Business*, (New York: Harper Collins, 2008), 28.

CHAPTER 17 - SANHEDRIN

[1] Marvin Ellis, "Ashes of Red Heifer Site Believed Located," *Tyler Courier Times Telegraph*, October 12, 1989.

CHAPTER 19- RACE

[1] Nir Hasson, "Temple Mount Faithful: From the fringes to the mainstream," *Haaretz*, October 4, 2012.

[2] For an in-depth study of key milestones in the Temple Mount movement, see Motti Inbari, "Religious Zionism and the Temple Mount Dilemma—Key Trends," *Israel Studies* 12, no. 2 (Summer 2007), 29–47.

[3] Kobi Nachshoni, "Poll: Israel's Jews Abandoning Temple," *YNetnews.com*, July 16, 2013.

[4] Moshe Feiglin, "The Cease-fire," *Israel National News*, November 26, 2012.

[5] Ricki Hollander, "UNESCO and the Denial of Jewish History," *The Algemeiner*, July 19, 2016.

[6] Dore Gold, "Abbas' Temple Denial," *Israel Hayom*, March 2, 2012.

[7] An official guidebook, entitled *A Brief Guide to Al-Haram al-Sharif*, published in 1925 by the Supreme Muslim Council, states that the existence of Solomon's Temple on the Temple Mount was "beyond dispute." Page four of the guidebook reads, "This, too, is the spot, according to universal belief, on which David 'built there an altar unto the Lord.'"

[8] Oded Golan, an avid Israeli antiquities collector, was accused of buying genuine artifacts on the black market and counterfeiting intriguing inscriptions to increase their value. After a seven-year forgery trial, Oded Golan was acquitted. Most scholars still believe the prominent pieces from Golan's collection were forgeries, albeit masterful. Golan's court case aside, expert paleographers André Lemaire, Robert Deutsch, and Ada Yardeni insist on the authenticity of the pomegranate inscription. See Hershel Shanks, "Ivory Pomegranate: Under the Microscope at the Israel Museum," *Biblical Archaeology Review* (March/April 2016).

[9] Simon Sebag Montefiore, *Jerusalem: The Biography*, (New York: Knopf, 2011), xxvi.

CHAPTER 20 – BREAKTHROUGH

[1] Craig Rogers, a mutual friend of Jim and Mike, also suggested the idea of mortar analysis after first seeing the potential cave.

POSTSCRIPT

[1] Moshe Feiglin, "Moshe Feiglin Warns PM Netanyahu: Dangerous Escalation of Hamas Violence on Temple Mount," *Manhigut Yehudit*, August 24, 2014.

BIBLIOGRAPHY

Ahren, Raphael. "Israel will build in Jerusalem, No Matter the Criticism, Vows Senior Minister." *Times of Israel*, December 25, 2012. https://www.timesofisrael.com/israel-will-keep-building-in-jerusalem-no-matter-how-bitter-the-criticism-vows-senior-minister/

Allegro, John Marco. *The Treasure of the Copper Scroll: The Opening and Decipherment of the Most Mysterious of the Dead Sea Scrolls, a Unique Inventory of Buried Treasure*. London: Routledge & Kegan Paul, 1960.

Arbel, Daphna V., and Andre A. Orlov, eds. *With Letters of Light*. Berlin & New York: De Gruyter, 2011.

Avigad, Nahman. "Two Hebrew Inscriptions on Wine-Jars." *Israel Exploration Journal* 22, no. 1 (1972): 1–9.

Baillet, Maurice, Józef T. Milik, and Roland de Vaux, eds. "Les 'Petites Grottes' de Qumrân." *Discoveries in the Judean Desert of Jordan*, no. 3. Oxford: Clarendon Press, 1962.

Bauckman, Richard, James Davila, and Alex Panayotov, eds. *Old Testament Pseudepigrapha*. Grand Rapids, MI: Wm. B. Eerdmans, 2013.

Bergeson, Dylan. "The Biblical Pseudo-Archeologists Pillaging the West Bank." *The Atlantic*, February 28, 2013.

Brooke, George, and Philip Davies, eds. *Copper Scroll Studies*, Journal for the Study of the Pseudepigrapha Supplement Series 40. Sheffield: Sheffield Academic Press, 2002.

Brown, Judith Anne. *John Marco Allegro: The Maverick of the Dead Sea Scrolls*. Grand Rapids, MI: Wm. B. Eerdmans, 2005.

Browning Jr., Daniel C. "The Strange Search for the Ashes of the Red Heifer." *Biblical Archaeologist* 59, no. 2 (June 1996): 74–89.

Burleigh, Nina. *Unholy Business*. New York: Harper Collins, 2008.

Cargill, Robert R. "Pseudo-Science and Sensationalist Archaeology: An Exposé of Jimmy Barfield and the Copper Scroll Project." *Bible and Interpretation*, August 1, 2009. http://www.bibleinterp.com/articles/cargill2_08261.shtml

Cargill, Robert R. "The Copper Scroll Project Gives an Exclusive TV Interview." *Excavator: The official blog of Robert Cargill*, November 13, 2009. http://robertcargill.com/2009/11/13/the-copper-scroll-project-gives-an-exclusive-tv-interview/

Cargill, Robert R. "Double checking the 'research' of Jim Barfield." *Excavator: The official blog of Robert Cargill*, January 20, 2010. http://robertcargill.com/2010/01/20/double-checking-the-research-of-jim-barfield/

Cargill, Robert R. "On the Insignificance and the Abuse of the Copper Scroll." *Bible and Interpretation*, July 2009. http://www.bibleinterp.com/opeds/copper.shtml

Charles, Robert Henry. *The Apocalypse of Baruch*. New York: The Macmillan Company, 1918.

Cline, Eric H. "Fabulous Finds or Fantastic Forgeries? The Distortion of Archaeology by the Media and Pseudoarchaeologists and What We Can Do About It." In *Archaeology, Bible, Politics, and the Media: Proceedings of the Duke University Conference, April 23–24, 2009*, edited by Eric Meyers and Carol Meyers. Duke Judaic Studies Series 4. Winona Lake, Ind.: Eisenbrauns, 2012.

De Vaux, Roland. *Archeology and the Dead Sea Scrolls*. London: The British Academy, 1973.

Dimant, Devorah. *History, Ideology, and Interpretation in the Dead Sea Scrolls*. Heidelberg, Germany: Mohr Siebeck, 2014.

Donceel-Voûte, Pauline. "Les ruines de Qumran réinterprétées." *Archeologia* 298 (1994): 24–35.

Feather, Robert. *The Mystery of the Copper Scroll of Qumran: The Essene Record of the Treasure of Akhenaten*. London: Duncan Baird Publishers, 2006.

Feiglin, Moshe. "Moshe Feiglin Warns PM Netanyahu: Dangerous Escalation of Hamas Violence on Temple Mount." *Manhigut Yehudit*, August 24, 2014. http://www.jewishisrael.org/mk-moshe-feiglin-warns-pm-netanyahu-dangerous-escalation-hamas-violence-temple-mount/

Feiglin, Moshe. "The Ceasefire." *Israel National News*, November 26, 2012. http://www.israelnationalnews.com/Articles/Article.aspx/12498

Feiglin, Moshe. "Text of Moshe Feiglin's Likud Resignation Speech." *The Jewish Press*, January 5, 2015. http://www.jewishpress.com/news/breaking-news/text-of-moshe-feiglins-likud-resignation-speech/2015/01/05/0/

Fields, Weston. *The Dead Sea Scrolls: A Full History*. Leiden: Brill, 2009.

Freund, Richard A. *Secrets of the Cave of Letters: Rediscovering a Dead Sea Mystery*. New York: Humanity Books, 2004.

Friedman, Matti. *The Aleppo Codex.* Chapel Hill, N.C.: Algonquin Books, 2012.

Golb, Norman. *Who Wrote the Dead Sea Scrolls?* The Search for the Secret of Qumran. New York: Scribner, 1995.

Gold, Dore. "Abbas' Temple Denial." *Israel Hayom*, March 2, 2012. http://www.israelhayom.com/opinions/abbas-temple-denial/

Gross, Netty C. "Old Scrolls, New Controversy." *The Jerusalem Post*, September 16, 2009.

Gutfeld, Oren. "Hyrcania's Mysterious Tunnels: Searching for the Treasures of the Copper Scroll." *Biblical Archaeology Review* (September/October 2006).

Hasson, Nir. "Temple Mount Faithful: From the Fringes to the Mainstream." *Haaretz*, October 4, 2012. https://www.haaretz.com/israel-news/temple-mount-faithful-from-the-fringes-to-the-mainstream-1.468234

Hasson, Nir. "Great Excavations: Israel's Antiquities Authority Head Won't Cave in Just Yet." Haaretz, June 15, 2012. https://www.haaretz.com/israel-news/great-excavations-israel-s-antiquities-authority-head-won-t-cave-in-just-yet.premium-1.436585

Hirschfeld, Yizhar. *Qumran in Context: Reassessing the Archaeological Evidence*. Peabody: Hendrickson Publishers, 2004.

Hollander, Ricki. "UNESCO and the Denial of Jewish History." *The Algemeiner*, July 19, 2016. https://www.algemeiner.com/2016/07/19/unesco-and-the-denial-of-jewish-history/

Ilani, Ofri. "Dead Sea Scrolls Scholar Defends Son Arrested for Imperson-ating Rival." *Haaretz*, March 12, 2009. https://www.haaretz.com/dead-sea-scrolls-scholar-defends-son-arrested-for-impersonating-rival-1.271923

Jones, Vendyl. *Door of Hope: My Search for the Treasures of the Copper Scroll*. Springdale, Arkansas: Lightcatcher Books, 2005.

Josephus, Flavius. *The Works of Josephus*. Complete and Unabridged, New Updated Edition. Translated by William Whiston. Peabody: Hendrickson Publishers, 1987.

Kuhn, K.G. "Les Rouleaux de Cuivre de Qumran." *Revue Biblique* 61 (1954).

Lefkovits, Judah K. *The Copper Scroll* (3Q15): A Reevaluation. Leiden: Brill, 2000.

Lev, David. "Muslim rioters attack MK Feiglin on Temple Mount." *Israel National News*, March 20, 2014. http://www.israelnationalnews.com/News/News.aspx/178704

Luria, Ben Zion. "Megillat han-Nahoshel mem-Midbar Yehudah" [The Cop-per Scroll from the Judean Desert]. *Publications of the Israel Bible Research Society* XIV (1963).

Magen, Yitzhak, and Yuval Peleg. "The Qumran Excavations, 1993–2004, Preliminary Report." *Judea and Samaria Publications* 6 (2007).

Magness, Jodi. *The Archeology of Qumran and the Dead Sea Scrolls*. Grand Rapids, MI: Wm. B. Eerdmans, 2002.

Magness, Jodi. *The Archeology of the Holy Land: From the Destruction of Solomon's Temple to the Muslim Conquest*. New York: Cambridge University Press, 2012.

Martínez, García F. *The Dead Sea Scrolls Translated: The Qumran texts in English*, 2nd ed. Grand Rapids, MI: Wm. B. Eerdmans, 1996.

McCarter Jr., P.Kyle. "The Mystery of the Copper Scroll." In *Understand-ing the Dead Sea Scrolls*, edited by Hershel Shanks. New York: Random House, 1992.

Meyers, Eric, and Carol Meyers, eds. "Archaeology, Bible, Politics, and the Media: Proceedings of the Duke University Conference, April 23–24, 2009." *Duke Judaic Studies* Series 4. Warsaw, IN: Eisenbrauns, 2012.

Milik, Józef. "Notes D'épigraphie et de Topographie Palestiniennes," *Revue Biblique* 66 (1959).

Montefiore, Simon Sebag. *Jerusalem: The Biography*. New York: Knopf, 2011.

Murphy, Catherine M. *Wealth in the Dead Sea Scrolls and in the Qumran Community*. Leiden: Brill, 2001.

Nachshoni, Kobi. "Poll: Israel's Jews abandoning Temple." *YNetnews.com*, July 16, 2013. https://www.ynetnews.com/articles/0,7340,L-4404982,00.html

Neal, James. "Emmanuel Hosts Man Who Believes He's Found Site of Ancient Jewish Relics." *Enid News & Eagle*, July 13, 2017.

Neese, Shelley. "Cracking the Code," *The Jerusalem Post*, August 19, 2009.

Pixner, Bargil. "Unraveling the Copper Scroll Code: A Study on the Topography of 3Q15." *Revue de Qumran* 11 (1983).

Puech, Émile. *The Copper Scroll Revisited*. Leiden: Brill, 2015.

Rosenberg, Joel. *The Copper Scroll*. Wheaton, IL: Tyndale House Publishers, 2006.

Rowland Jr., Stanley. "Dead Sea Scrolls Tell of Treasure: 'Key' to Vast Riches Written on Copper is Deciphered." *New York Times*, June 1, 1956.

Rubinstein, Danny. "Tunneling into Hyrcania." *Haaretz*, April 23, 2007.

Seal, Mark. "Masquerader of the lost Ark." *Texas Monthly*, August 1992.

Schiffman, Lawrence H. *Reclaiming the Dead Sea Scrolls: The History of Judaism, the Background of Christianity, the Lost Library of Qumran*. New York: Doubleday, 1995.

Schiffman, Lawrence H. "The architectural vocabulary of the Copper Scroll and the Temple Scroll." In *Copper Scroll Studies*, Journal for the Study of the Pseudepigrapha Supplement Series 40, edited by George Brooke and Philip Davies, 180–197. Sheffield: Sheffield Academic Press, 2002.

Shanks, Hershel. *The Copper Scroll and the Search for the Temple Treasure*. Washington, DC: Biblical Archeology Society, 2007.

Shanks, Hershel. "Ivory Pomegranate: Under the Microscope at the Israel Museum." *Biblical Archaeology Review* (March/April 2016).

Singer, Isidore, and Cyrus Adler. *The Jewish Encyclopedia: A Descriptive Record of the History, Religion, Literature, and Customs of the Jewish People from the Earliest Times to the Present Day* 2. 1901. Reprint, London: Forgotten Books, 2013.

Taylor, Joan. "Buried Manuscripts and Empty Tombs: The Qumran Genizah Theory Revisited." In *'Go Out and Study the Land' (Judges 18:2): Archaeological, Historical and Textual Studies in Honor of Hanan Eshel* edited by Aren M. Maeir, Jodi Magness, and Lawrence H. Schiffman, 269–315. Leiden: Brill, 2011.

Thiering, Barbara. "The Copper Scroll: King Herod's Bank Account." In *Copper Scroll Studies*, Journal for the Study of the Pseudepigrapha Supplement Series 40, edited by George Brooke and Philip Davies, 276–287. Sheffield: Sheffield Academic Press, 2002.

Vine, W.E., Merrill F. Unger, and William White Jr. *Vine's Complete Expository Dictionary of Old and New Testament Words*. Nashville: Thomas Nelson, 1996.

Wise, Michael O. "David J. Wilmot and the Copper Scroll." In *Copper Scroll Studies*, Journal for the Study of the Pseudepigrapha Supplement Series 40, edited by George Brooke and Philip Davies, 291–310. Sheffield: Sheffield Academic Press, 2002.

Wolters, Al. *The Copper Scroll: Overview, Text, and Translation*. Sheffield: Sheffield Academic Press, 1996.

REFERENCED TRANSLATIONS FOR THE COPPER SCROLL

Allegro, John Marco. *The Treasure of the Copper Scroll: The Opening and Decipherment of the Most Mysterious of the Dead Sea Scrolls, a Unique Inventory of Buried Treasure*. London: Routledge & Kegan Paul, 1960, 33–55.

Martínez, García F. *The Dead Sea Scrolls Translated: The Qumran texts in English*, 2nd ed. Grand Rapids, MI: Wm. B. Eerdmans, 1996, 461–463.

McCarter Jr., P.Kyle. "The Mystery of the Copper Scroll." In *Understanding the Dead Sea Scrolls*, edited by Hershel Shanks. New York: Random House, 1992, 98–101.

Wolters, Al. "Paleography and Literary Structure as Guides to Reading the Copper Scroll." In *Copper Scroll Studies*, Journal for the Study of the Pseudepigrapha Supplement Series 40, edited by George Brooke and Philip Davies. Sheffield: Sheffield Academic Press, 2002.

Morgan James
Speakers Group

www.TheMorganJamesSpeakersGroup.com

We connect Morgan James published
authors with live and online events
and audiences who will benefit
from their expertise.

Morgan James makes all of our titles available
through the Library for All Charity Organization.

www.LibraryForAll.org

CPSIA information can be obtained
at www.ICGtesting.com
Printed in the USA
BVHW07s1952060718
520834BV00003B/12/P

9 781683 509158